I0024842

A History of the Scottish Conservative and Unionist Parties

A History of the Scottish Conservative and Unionist Parties

David Torrance

EDINBURGH
University Press

Edinburgh University Press is one of the leading university presses in the UK. We publish academic books and journals in our selected subject areas across the humanities and social sciences, combining cutting-edge scholarship with high editorial and production values to produce academic works of lasting importance. For more information visit our website: edinburghuniversitypress.com

© David Torrance, 2024

Edinburgh University Press Ltd
The Tun – Holyrood Road
12 (2f) Jackson's Entry
Edinburgh EH8 8PJ

Typeset in 10.5/13pt Sabon by
Cheshire Typesetting Ltd, Cuddington, Cheshire

A CIP record for this book is available from the British Library

ISBN 978 1 3995 0642 7 (hardback)
ISBN 978 1 3995 0643 4 (paperback)
ISBN 978 1 3995 0644 1 (webready PDF)
ISBN 978 1 3995 0645 8 (epub)

The right of David Torrance to be identified as author of this work has been asserted in accordance with the Copyright, Designs and Patents Act 1988 and the Copyright and Related Rights Regulations 2003 (SI No. 2498).

Contents

Introduction

'There is no satisfactory general account of the Conservative Party in Scotland', observed James Kellas in 1994, and 'a great deal of work remains to be done ... to provide a proper academic analysis of the Scottish Conservative Party.'[1] The introduction to the first in this series of monographs, *A History of the Scottish Liberals and Liberal Democrats*, also noted the scant literature in relation to that party despite its electoral dominance until the early 20th century. Although this is less true of the Scottish Unionists (later – and indeed earlier – the Scottish Conservatives), Kellas's criticism remains valid. This, therefore, is an attempt to provide the first – and one hopes satisfactory – general account of the Scottish Conservative and Unionist Party.[2]

As with the Scottish Liberals, the fact that Scottish Conservatives once dominated politics for lengthy periods strikes modern eyes as novel. Indeed, the electoral weakness of the party for much of the 19th century most likely explains its academic neglect until the early 1980s. The only exceptions were Basil Crapster's snapshot of Scottish Conservatism in 1876 and Derek Urwin's study of party organisation until 1912.[3] In 1982, John T. Ward published a useful study of Scottish party organisation in the century after 1882.[4]

Political scientists and historians finally started taking an interest in the mid-1980s. In particular, Iain Hutchison provided detailed flesh on the bones of previous work with studies of Scottish party politics between 1832 and 1979.[5] In one book chapter, the inter-war Scottish Unionists were revealed as moderate protagonists of their own success.[6] More recently, Gary D. Hutchison has made a detailed study of the period between the first and second Reform Acts (1832–68),[7] while Catriona Burness examined the old Scottish Conservative Party and its relationship with Scottish Liberal Unionism between 1886 and 1912.[8] William L. Miller's valuable study, *The End of British Politics*, meanwhile, made a systematic and convincing attempt to account for Scottish Unionism's post-Second World War success,[9] while he was also the first to examine the early Thatcher years through a 'mandate' lens.[10] Some studies of the UK Conservative Party have virtually ignored Scotland,[11] while others have rightly treated it as an integral part of what was, after all, a unionist organisation. Impressive examples of the latter approach are three volumes from the party's official historian, John Ramsden,[12] while Stuart Ball's magnum opus, *Portrait of a Party*, provides a lucid analysis of the principles and temperament of (English and Scottish) Conservatism between the wars.[13]

The performance of the Scottish Conservatives after 1959, however, ensured that academic scrutiny focused on the party's long-term decline. To Hutchison, this fell into two broad and 'slightly overlapping' categories, one stressing 'policy defaults', the other 'changing cultural and social processes'. To those he added party organisation.[14]

Following the party's poor showing at the general election of 1987, there was a glut of declinism. A. D. R. Dickson linked falling Conservative support to distinct aspects of Scottish culture (including the decline of Orangeism), society and socio-economics.[15] Stephen Kendrick and David McCrone focused on the last of that trio, arguing that the establishment of Scotland as a separate unit of economic management (by, ironically, the Conservatives) – as well as its subsequent decline – had been a significant factor.[16] James Mitchell instead focused on the constitution, drawing a link between the party's stance on devolution and its electoral success.[17] There were more declinist studies during and immediately after John Major's premiership (1990–97).[18] James Kellas agreed with Mitchell by concluding that the party was no longer seen as supporting Scotland's 'national aspirations',[19] while Lynn Bennie et al. considered a number of factors that had combined to form a disadvantageous perception of the Scottish Conservatives as an 'English' party.[20]

Revisionists also got to work. Kellas doubted the importance of Protestantism given its urban concentration and general weakness after the Second World War.[21] Using extensive survey data, David Seawright cast doubt on three by then standard explanations of Scottish Conservative decline: the loss of the party's Protestant base, its opposition to devolution and being too right wing. He instead pointed to organisational changes in 1965 and the shift from 'Unionist' to 'Conservative' when it came to nomenclature.[22] In statistical analysis conducted with John Curtice, Seawright identified the party's 'short-term economic record at election times' as another contributing factor.[23] Seawright's work helped fuel another consensus that the reforms of 1965 had been detrimental to the party. Mike Dyer, however, saw both as a response to increasing unpopularity rather than its cause. Dyer also questioned what he called the 'left-nationalist' thesis exemplified by Kendrick and McCrone, not least because electoral decline had pre-dated a Thatcherite tilt towards free markets and away from state economic intervention.

Dyer instead located Scottish Conservative decline within broader UK phenomena, what he called 'a waning of the cultural conditions which produced the centre-right coalition which dominated Scottish politics' between 1931 and 1964 'and its fragmentation into Conservatism, Liberalism and Scottish Nationalism'.[24] Malcolm Petrie concurred, further exploring this fragmentation in two richly detailed monographs,[25] while Taym Saleh viewed this through a regional lens, arguing that in North-East Scotland between 1965 and 1979 Conservatives had relied too much on its 'centrist anti-socialist mantle' and superior organisation forged between the wars.[26]

All this might be seen as a belated response to E. H. H. Green's conclusion that ideology (as was the case 'for all political parties') was actually 'central to the history of the Conservative party',[27] a key departure from the consensus that a 'conscious rejection' of ideology by Conservatives had arguably been 'one of the reasons for their long-term success'.[28] For Robin Harris, the 'Conservative Party exists, has always existed and can only exist to gain and exercise power',[29] something it had achieved through a 'quite remarkable facility for adaptation and ... readiness to subordinate all other considerations to that one objective'.[30]

A failure of pragmatism when it came to the 'Scottish Question' has too easily been accepted as a key aspect of Conservative decline in Scotland. Whig-like analysis simply assumed it *must* have been a factor given the growing desire for devolution in the late 1980s, yet as Seawright has highlighted, Edward Heath's support for a devolved Scottish Assembly did little to revive the party's fortunes in 1970 or 1974, while in 1979 and 1992, when Scottish Conservatives went to the polls rejecting any sort of legislative devolution, its share of the vote actually increased. As Ewen Cameron has observed, the 'orthodoxy of Mrs Thatcher as the matriarch of devolution' emerged after her downfall in 1990 and 'we are in need of a more nuanced account'.[31]

Two such studies were published on the thirtieth anniversary of Mrs Thatcher's first election victory (perhaps Cameron did not consider them nuanced enough): this author's attempt to dismantle pervasive aspects of Thatcherite political mythology and a more systematic historical analysis by David Stewart.[32] More recently, this author also edited two collections analysing the modern Scottish Conservative Party – one declinist, the other moderately revivalist[33] – while Alan Convery compared how the Welsh and Scottish Conservatives adapted to devolution after 1999, arguing that a coherent 'philosophy of devolution' was a necessary basis for electoral credibility.[34] This analysis was vindicated, at least in Scotland, shortly after Convery's book was published in 2016.

What of Conservatism and Unionism? Dyer stressed that the distinction between the two was important in a Scottish context, 'for while the former was a thoroughbred the latter was decidedly mongrel'.[35] Ideological analysis of the Scottish party, however, has proved a minority pursuit. Only Colin Kidd and Jonathan Wales have charted Scottish Conservative thought of the 19th and 20th centuries in any depth.[36] This author also looked at the lively and influential ideas of the inter-war Scottish Unionist MP Noel Skelton in a short biographical study.[37]

According to Kellas:

> There has never been much that is distinctive about Scottish Conservative policy. The partial autonomy of the party organisa-tion has produced no challenge to the programme or party leader-ship in Britain as a whole … The Scottish Unionists are British Conservatives, consider the British Conservative Party leaders as their leaders, and accept British Conservative Party policy, even on Scotland, as their own. Here is a source of their weakness, for a policy for Scotland must be initiated in Scotland, and the party which appears to have none loses votes.[38]

Although true of the party for periods during the 20th century, this fails to capture the distinctiveness of Scottish Conservative and Unionist policy in times of electoral success and failure. This was especially true between the wars when the likes of Skelton and Walter Elliot contributed much to both Scottish and UK Conservative thinking. The latter remarked that Conservatism was based on 'an observation of life and not *a priori* reasoning',[39] while John Buchan said it was 'above all things a spirit not an abstract doctrine'.[40] Addressing students at Edinburgh University, Buchan even placed his unionism above his Toryism and Conservatism:

> First we are unionists, we believe the Union makes strength, that co-operation is the seed of success. Secondly we are Tories, with a critical and questioning attitude of mind which refuses to take things on hearsay. Lastly, we are Conservatives; we wish to preserve the continuity of history, we are the creators of the past, and if we are to build anything enduring it must be erected on the foundation laid by those who have gone before us.[41]

To Michael Keating, Conservative unionism tended to be 'traditionalist, based on Burkean notions of respect for the wisdom of ages',[42] and indeed in 1986 Malcolm Rifkind asserted that Scottish Conservatives were 'in politics to maintain all that is best in Scotland's way of life' as 'radicals [wanted] to remove all that is bad'.[43] A few years earlier Lord Home, a Scottish party grandee capable of a broader view, considered the essence of Conservatism to be 'trusteeship and evolution':

> [I]ts practice is to conserve the best of the past and to shape events so that the future is an improvement on that which has gone before ... [a] theme of Conservative philosophy has always insisted on the preservation of the liberties of the individual within the law: the maximum freedom with the minimum intervention by the State. But that apart, Scotland's Conservatives have always been suspicious of the elevation of principle into doctrine. By instinct and preference, they have taken the middle ground of politics − not in any sense sitting on the fence, but always seeking the substance in policies which will bring the greatest good to the greatest number.[44]

This was an insightful observation which supported the notion, bolstered by the historians and political scientists cited above, that during key periods of Scottish Conservative success − chiefly the 1890s, 1920s, 1950s and 1970s − the party had adopted a utilitarian stance more progressive than that of its English equivalent. To J. T. Ward, Conservatives in Scotland were 'not urged to "contract out" of politics, but to keep it in perspective'.[45]

Lord Home added that if there was one 'belief' Scottish Conservatives raised 'to the status of a principle it is that the Party is National': 'Decentralisation and devolution – yes; but they must always be consistent with the unity of the Kingdom. For that the Party is a Trustee.'[46] The 'National' in this dictum was a complex palimpsest of the 1688 (English and Scottish) constitutional settlement, a limited monarchy regulated by an elected and sovereign Parliament, and three Unions: the 1603 'personal union' of the English and Scottish Crowns; the 1707 Union of the kingdoms and parliaments of Scotland and England (which had created 'Great Britain'); and, finally, the 1801 Union of the kingdoms and parliaments of Great Britain and Ireland (which had formed the 'United Kingdom').

Although the writer Sir Walter Scott – later claimed by both Tories and Nationalists – recognised the 1707 Union as 'a treaty between two nations, forming a state whose best guarantor was the Tory Party',[47] for more than a century much the most important union was that between Great Britain and Ireland. The 1912 rebranding as the 'Scottish Unionist Party' thus represented 'the ultimate act of communion with Ulster Unionists' in the context of a perceived threat to the 1801 Union from the Third (Irish) Home Rule Bill. But even when the Anglo-Irish Treaty of 1921–2 produced the United Kingdom of Great Britain and *Northern* Ireland (complete with asymmetric devolution), Scottish Unionism was undimmed, for there remained other unions to defend.[48]

According to Graham Walker, Scottish Unionism fused the appeals of Empire, religion, Ulster and a definition of Scottishness derived to a large extent from Presbyterian mythology.[49] This definition of Scottishness and its constitutional expression was far from dogmatic. As Colin Kidd has argued, a 'historiography polarized around positions of unionism and nationalism' has served to obscure the 'hybridity of the middle ground in Scottish political culture' long commanded by Scottish Conservatives and Unionists.[50] James Mitchell (1993) used Rokkan and Urwin's distinction between the 'unitary' and 'union state' to demonstrate the party's ability to refashion its 'territorial code' to present that union as one 'in which Scottish distinctiveness was fully catered for'.[51] To Convery, this was the 'fundamental tension' at the heart of Scottish Unionist ideology: 'how far (and how) Scottish distinctiveness can be accommodated whilst still retaining a commitment to the Union'.

Scottish Conservative answers to this question ranged through the invention of 'administrative devolution' (1885), its subsequent extension (1930s and 1950s), support for a Scottish Assembly (1967–76), opposition to any form of legislative devolution (1979–97), grudging acceptance of the Scottish Parliament (1999–2012) and, finally, proposals for greater 'fiscal autonomy' (2013–14).[52] As Miller observed:

> From the Scottish Office reforms in the late 1930s to [Lord] Balfour in the mid-1950s, the Conservatives bolstered Scottish national consciousness, used Scottish nationalism as a weapon against socialism, and built up the Scottish Office. And over the same period, their electoral performance in Scotland was significantly better than they could normally expect.[53]

To quote H. J. Hanham, Scottish nationalism had 'always tended to speak with different voices',[54] and its loudest voice for long periods was neither Liberal nor Labour but Conservative, another necessary (but not necessarily) sufficient component of its electoral success.[55] There was nothing un-conservative about this. Robert Blake viewed the Conservative Party 'as the party of English nationalism' or 'patriotism'. This card, while in many ways 'a defensive reaction to threats and dangers from outside', was usually a winner when played.[56]

The same was true in Scotland, where Mitchell and Keating viewed Unionism itself as 'a form of nationalism, in the sense that it is the ideology which favours the territorial integrity of the state',[57] a feature that became 'more obvious when it is faced with challenges from within (from Scottish nationalism) and without (from European integration)'.[58] These twin pressures made contemporary Unionism both electorally successful and fragmented, helping Scottish Conservatives attract new supporters for the first time in decades but also splintering between pragmatic and 'muscular' approaches.[59] As Ramsden noted, Conservatives had long appealed to something over and above party politics, symbolised by Disraeli's dictum that the Conservative Party was 'a national party' or it was 'nothing'.[60]

'I love deadlines,' quipped Douglas Adams. 'I love the whooshing noise they make as they go by.' There was, I am afraid to say, a significant amount of whooshing before Edinburgh University Press finally received this typescript, for which I must congratulate Tom Dark on his patience. As usual, a book of this sort would not have been possible without the help of others. Valued colleagues in the House of Commons Library, where I have the pleasure of making a living, helped locate often obscure books, pamphlets and academic articles. Particular thanks must go to Greg Howard and Paul Little. Douglas Pattullo, a friend of nearly two decades, is indirectly responsible for many of the details and insights herein, while I have also gained much from speaking to Scottish Conservative strategists (who preferred to remain anonymous) as well as, for previous projects, several protagonists listed in the bibliography. Finally, I must thank those whose financial support made the research and writing possible: Lord Sanderson, the Marquess of Lothian, Lord Forsyth, Lord Mackay of Clashfern and Sir Michael Hirst. I am particularly grateful to Alan Massie, whose contribution proved essential for completion of the project. None, I should hasten to add, attempted to interfere with my judgments or assessments, for which responsibility is mine alone.

Dr David Torrance
Peckham, South London
December 2022

NOTES

1. J. Kellas (1994), 'The Party in Scotland', in A. Seldon and S. Ball (eds), *Conservative Century: The Conservative Party since 1900*, Oxford: Oxford University Press, 671.
2. Gerald Warner's *The Scottish Tory Party: A History* (London: Weidenfeld & Nicolson, 1988) must be viewed as more a political act than a balanced historical account. Margaret Thatcher, the then Prime Minister, contributed a glowing foreword.
3. See B. L. Crapster (1957), 'Scotland and the Conservative Party in 1876', *Journal of Modern History* 29:4, 355–60 and D. W. Urwin (1965), 'The development of Conservative Party organisation in Scotland until 1912', *Scottish Historical Review* 44(2):138, 89–111.

4. J. T. Ward (1982), *The First Century: A History of Scottish Tory Organisation 1882–1982*, Edinburgh: SCUA. Professor John Towers Ward was the first Professor of Modern History at the University of Strathclyde.

5. See I. G. C. Hutchison (1986), *A Political History of Scotland, 1832–1924: Parties, Elections and Issues*, Edinburgh: John Donald, *Scottish Politics in the Twentieth Century* (Basingstoke: Palgrave, 2001) and *Industry, Reform and Empire: Scotland, 1790–1880* (Edinburgh: Edinburgh University Press, 2020).

6. I. G. C. Hutchison (1998), 'Unionism between the two World Wars', in C. M. M. Macdonald (ed.), *Unionist Scotland 1800–1997*, Edinburgh: John Donald, 73–99.

7. G. D. Hutchison (2017), 'The Origins of the Scottish Conservative Party, 1832–1868', PhD thesis, University of Edinburgh.

8. C. Burness (2003), *'Strange Associations': The Irish Question and the Making of Scottish Unionism, 1886–1918*, East Linton: Tuckwell Press.

9. W. L. Miller (1981), *The End of British Politics? Scots and English Political Behaviour in the Seventies*, Oxford: Clarendon Press.

10. W. Miller, J. Brand and G. Jordan (1981), 'Government without a mandate: The Conservative Party in Scotland', *Political Quarterly* 52:2, 203–13.

11. See, for example, R. Harris (2011), *The Conservatives: A History*, London: Bantam Press.

12. See J. Ramsden (1978), *The Age of Balfour and Baldwin 1902–1940, The Age of Churchill and Eden 1940–1957* (1995) and *The Winds of Change: Macmillan to Heath, 1957–1975* (1996), all London: Longman.

13. S. Ball (2013), *Portrait of a Party: The Conservative Party in Britain 1918–1945*, Oxford: Oxford University Press.

14. I. G. C. Hutchison (2007), 'The Scottish Young Conservatives: A local case study – Central Ayrshire Constituency, 1950–c.1979', in A. Murdoch (ed.), *The Scottish Nation: Identity and History – Essays in Honour of William Ferguson*, Edinburgh: John Donald, 120.

15. A. D. R. Dickson (1988), 'The peculiarities of the Scottish: National culture and political action', *Political Quarterly* 59:3, 358–68.

16. S. Kendrick and D. McCrone (1989), 'Political studies in a cold climate: The Conservative decline in Scotland', *Political Studies* 37:4, 589–603.

17. J. Mitchell (1990), *Conservatives and the Union: A Study of Conservative Party Attitudes to Scotland*, Edinburgh: Edinburgh University Press.

18. Michael Fry planned a book entitled 'Tories in Trouble' for Polygon in the late 1980s, but it was not published.
19. J. G. Kellas (1994), 672.
20. L. Bennie, J. Brand and J. Mitchell (1997), *How Scotland Votes: Scottish Parties and Elections*, Manchester: Manchester University Press.
21. J. G. Kellas (1994), 677–8.
22. D. Seawright (1999), *An Important Matter of Principle: The Decline of the Scottish Conservative and Unionist Party*, Aldershot: Ashgate.
23. D. Seawright and J. Curtice (1995), 'The decline of the Scottish Conservative and Unionist Party 1950–92: Religion, ideology or economics?', *Contemporary British History* 9:2, 339.
24. M. Dyer (2001), 'The evolution of the Centre-Right and the state of Scottish Conservatism', *Political Studies* 49:1, 30.
25. See M. Petrie (2018), *Popular Politics and Political Culture: Urban Scotland, 1918–1939* and *Politics and the People: Scotland, 1945–1979* (2022), both Edinburgh: Edinburgh University Press.
26. T. Saleh (2017), 'The decline of the Scottish Conservatives in North-East Scotland, 1965–79: A regional perspective', *Parliamentary History* 36:2, 218–42.
27. E. H. H. Green (2002), *Ideologies of Conservatism: Conservative Political Ideas in the Twentieth Century*, Oxford: Oxford University Press, 14.
28. J. Ramsden (1978), x.
29. R. Harris (2011), 4.
30. J. Ramsden (1998), *An Appetite for Power: The History of the Conservative Party*, London: HarperCollins, 495.
31. E. A. Cameron (2016), 'Unionism and nationalism: The historical context of Scottish politics', in D. McTavish (ed.), *Politics in Scotland*, London: Routledge, 15.
32. See D. Torrance (2009), *'We in Scotland': Thatcherism in a Cold Climate*, Edinburgh: Birlinn and D. Stewart (2009), *The Path to Devolution and Change: A Political History of Scotland Under Margaret Thatcher*, London: I. B. Tauris. See also D. Torrance (2008), *George Younger: A Life Well Lived*, Edinburgh: Birlinn.
33. D. Torrance (ed.) (2012), *Whatever Happened to Tory Scotland?* and *Ruth Davidson's Conservatives: The Scottish Tory Party, 2011–19* (2020), both Edinburgh: Edinburgh University Press.
34. A. Convery (2016), *The Territorial Conservative Party: Devolution and Party Change in Scotland and Wales*, Manchester: Manchester University Press.
35. M. Dyer (2001), 38.
36. See C. Kidd (2008), *Union and Unionisms: Political Thought in*

Scotland, 1500–2000, Cambridge: Cambridge University Press and J. Wales (2021), *Scottish Unionist Ideology 1886–1965: Political Thought, Ecclesiology and Historiography*, Baden-Baden: Nomos.
37. D. Torrance (2011), *Noel Skelton and the Property-Owning Democracy*, London: Biteback.
38. J. G. Kellas (1968), *Modern Scotland: The Nation since 1870*, London: Pall Mall Press, 192.
39. W. Elliot (1927), *Toryism and the Twentieth Century*, London: Philip Allan, 4.
40. A. Bryant (1929), *The Spirit of Conservatism*, London: Methuen, vii.
41. G. McKechnie (2013), *George Malcolm Thomson: The Best-Hated Man – Intellectuals and the Condition of Scotland Between the Wars*, Glendaruel: Argyll, 170.
42. M. Keating (2010), 'The strange death of Unionist Scotland', *Government and Opposition* 45:3, 368.
43. M. Rifkind (1986), *Leading Scotland*, Edinburgh: Scottish Conservative Party, 1.
44. J. T. Ward (1982), *The First Century: A History of Scottish Tory Organisation 1882–1982*, Edinburgh: SCUA, 3–4.
45. J. T. Ward (1982), 5.
46. J. T. Ward (1982), 4.
47. G. Warner (1988), 123.
48. See J. Evershed (2020), 'Scottish Conservatism and Northern Ireland: Mapping an ambivalent relationship', in D. Torrance (2020), *Ruth Davidson's Conservatives: The Scottish Tory Party, 2011–19*, Edinburgh: Edinburgh University Press.
49. See G. Walker (1996), 'Varieties of Scottish Protestant identity', in T. M. Devine and R. Finlay (eds), *Scotland in the 20th Century*, Edinburgh: Edinburgh University Press, 250–68.
50. C. Kidd (2008), 263–4.
51. D. Seawright (1996), 'The Scottish Unionist Party: What's in a name?', *Scottish Affairs* 14, 100.
52. See A. Convery (2020), 'The Scottish Conservative Party', in M. Keating (ed.), *The Oxford Handbook of Scottish Politics*, Oxford: Oxford University Press, 237–54.
53. W. L. Miller (1981), 26.
54. H. J. Hanham (1969), *Scottish Nationalism*, London: Faber & Faber, 12.
55. See D. Torrance (2020), *'Standing Up for Scotland': Nationalist Unionism and Scottish Party Politics, 1884–2014*, Edinburgh: Edinburgh University Press.
56. R. Blake (1997), *The Conservative Party from Peel to Major*, London: Heinemann, 409–10.

57. J. Mitchell (1998), 'Contemporary Unionism', in C. M. M. Macdonald (ed.), *Unionist Scotland 1800–1997*, Edinburgh: John Donald, 117.
58. M. Keating (2009), *The Independence of Scotland: Self-government and the Shifting Politics of Union*, Oxford: Oxford University Press, 38.
59. See D. Torrance (2020), *Ruth Davidson's Conservatives*.
60. J. Ramsden (1998), *An Appetite for Power: The History of the Conservative Party*, London: HarperCollins, 4.

1

'A Distant and Whiggish Country':
1832–1882

A standard joke during the 19th century was that all Scotland's Conservative MPs could travel from Edinburgh to London in a single compartment of the southbound train.[1] It happened to be true: the party won only seven seats in the nine general elections held between 1832 and 1868, and at contests in 1857, 1859 and 1865, Scottish Conservatives did not return a single Member of Parliament. This meant that in the eyes of Westminster-based Tories, Scotland appeared as a 'distant and Whiggish country'.[2] They did politics differently there.

Conservative success prior to the Scottish Reform Act of 1832 had relied upon corrupt and often unthinking 'management' of Scotland's limited political representation by Henry Dundas (Viscount Melville), a leader whose 'voluminous correspondence ... it is possible to read and re-read ... and not once light upon anything that resembles an idea let alone an ideal'.[3] Under the new system, Scottish election results diverged from those in England. Conservatives were routed in both, but while the party won a quarter of contests in England, they managed just under a fifth in Scotland. In the first election conducted under the new franchise, Conservatives returned just eight out of Scotland's 53 MPs.[4] 'The regeneration of Scotland is now secured!' declared the Whig lawyer Lord Cockburn, adding: 'The Tory party, as such, as such, is extinguished.'[5] In elections for Scotland's 16 representative peers, however, the Conservatives achieved a clean sweep. Indeed, no non-Tory peer would be returned until 1850.[6]

Voters in Scotland proved to have long memories, the decisive shift to the Liberals after 1832 owing 'much to revulsion against the generations of corrupt political management by the Tories both nationally and in the Scottish cities'.[7] The term 'Tory' became deeply pejorative.[8] When the Duke of Buccleuch ('the epitome of Tory reaction' and the party's nominal leader in Scotland) appeared in Edinburgh in July 1832, the windows of his carriage were broken by missiles and a journeyman baker held 'out a rope in the presence of the Duke, calling out, "I'll give anybody 5s (25p) to hang the Juck"'. The candidate for Fife in that election was also warned against entering several towns in the county given his opposition to the Reform Bill. Thereafter, Conservative Party agents deliberately sought candidates without a record of resistance to reform.[9]

Another consequence of this altered political terrain was that Scottish Conservatives had 'no need to develop any constituency party organisation, however rudimentary':

> After the Reform Act, the party in Scotland found it much harder to establish a grassroots structure, as there was no pre-history, and socio-economic bases were virtually non-existent. It was essentially a party of feudal landowners, with few other interests attached to it, whereas in England, prominent Tories such as Peel, Canning and Huskisson had risen from business backgrounds.[10]

Burgh constituencies were overwhelmingly Liberal and so Conservative strength, such as it was, was concentrated in the counties and owed more to 'manipulation than the mobilisation of popular sentiment'.[11] In 1835 the Duke of Buccleuch was advised by a former MP that the principal goal of the Scottish party ought to be choosing commercial agents who could attend to electoral registration. If challenged, voters were required to demonstrate their right to vote in special Registration Courts. Doing so was not straightforward, and parties took to acting on voters' behalf.

Scottish Conservatives proved particularly skilful in this respect: decisions were made by local sheriffs, and local sheriffs tended to be Tory. This meant Tories could be kept *on* the electoral roll and Liberals *off*. And given it was wealthier than the Liberals, the Conservative Party could also afford to bribe or entertain voters, something known as 'treating'.[12] Legislation also provided opportunities to create 'fictitious' or 'faggot' voters by contriving 19-year £50 leases or splitting up tracts of land into £10 leases of 57 years' duration.[13] When the

Scottish Conservatives won one by-election by such means, Lord Cockburn blamed a 'confederacy of Lairds to domineer over their dependents. It is the victory of the owners of the soil achieved by the forced services of their helots and serfs.'[14]

By the late 1830s, most 'ultra' Conservatives had morphed into 'country Tories', who predominated in the Scottish party.[15] By the close of that decade, the failure of the Edinburgh-based Conservative Association of Scotland together with the success of Sir Robert Peel's 1837 visit saw Glasgow, Scotland's largest city, replace Edinburgh as its political centre. Peel, Leader of the Conservative opposition at Westminster, had spent childhood holidays in Scotland and was friendly with Sir Walter Scott, imbibed the economics of Adam Smith and 'admired the simple, hard-working piety which he supposed to be dominant in the Scottish Character'. His rectorial address at Glasgow University in January 1837 was widely circulated – such contests were regarded as important indicators of middle-class opinion – while two days later Conservative supporters paid 25 shillings a head to attend a great banquet:

> No building in the city was big enough for the purpose. A tempo-rary hall of wood and tarpaulin was put up in twenty-six days. The tables were grouped round a set piece of solid rock, which sym-bolised the British Constitution, inscribed with the words, 'King, Lords, Commons'. Three thousand four hundred guests attended. Peel spoke for two hours. The balance of his message was [that the] Conservative Party was the enemy of corruption and abuse, but also of perpetual meddling with the institutions of the country. In particular he defended the rights of the House of Lords and the established Churches of Scotland and England. After him speech followed enthusiastic speech. The dinner began at five in the evening and continued until half past one in the morning, nineteen toasts having been drunk between ovations.[16]

Arising from Peel's visit was the Glasgow Operatives' Conservative Society, whose motto was 'Fear God; honour the King; and meddle not with those who are given to change.'[17]

At the same time, local Conservative organisations in Scotland, which emerged after 1832, tended to be 'more autonomous, flexible and deeply rooted in broader society than might be assumed'.[18] But Scottish Conservatives nevertheless continued to be haunted by their past association with the Dundas system of political management and opposition to the 1832 reforms, which meant 'meagre' footholds of support were maintained 'through the existence of an ingrained attitude of deference'.[19] No great Scottish Conservative leaders emerged, and those who served in that capacity had the difficult task of explaining their distant and Whiggish country to the (more successful) party based in London.

Having accepted a 'dependent role' in politics, observed D. W. Urwin, Scotland 'refused to be dictated to on the question of religion'. Unable to conceive of a situation where church trumped state, Sir Robert Peel could not understand the resentment generated by lay patrons (such as Tory landowners) appointing ministers in Church of Scotland parishes. In 1841, the Glasgow Operatives' Conservative Society supported the Duke of Argyll's Bill to legalise a congregational veto, but as this interfered with property rights it did not become government policy.[20] When Peel told a deputation of 'non-intrusionists' that the Bill yielded too much, Scottish Conservatives realised the general election of that year would not improve their fortunes.[21]

Similarly recognising it was likely to produce 'the most fatal divisions in the Conservative ranks of Scotland',[22] the Anglo-Scottish Home Secretary Sir James Graham rejected the General Assembly's declaration that all Acts of Parliament passed without the Kirk's consent, or any court judgments (and there were many), would be 'null and void'. This led directly to the 'Disruption' of 1843 and the formation of the 'Free' Church of Scotland, a schism which provided a further boost to Scottish Liberalism by constituting yet another 'voting block hostile to the Conservatives in Scotland'.[23] The subsequent refusal of Scottish Conservative landowners, including the Duke of Buccleuch, to grant land to Free Church congregations 'created the beginnings of social divisions that were later to amount to a political cleavage along denominational lines'.[24]

The Glasgow Conservative Operatives' Association was soon dissolved and later, when the Conservative candidate was defeated at a by-election in Kirkcudbrightshire, the local newspaper gloated that it served him right for supporting a government which had increased the grant to Maynooth College in Ireland, a seminary for Catholic priests. Whereas in England, Conservatives had exploited this in opposition to the Liberals, in Scotland, opposition to Maynooth was the preserve of Protestant denominations allied to the Scottish Liberals.[25] It demonstrated that religion, as Hutchison put it, remained the 'central and binding factor' for urban Scottish Conservatism.[26] Another schism – this time UK-wide – over the conversion of Sir Robert Peel (Prime Minister since 1841) to repealing the Corn Laws in 1846 brought further disruption for the Scottish Conservatives, who, like their English colleagues, split into Peelite (or 'Liberal Conservative') and Protectionist factions. Neither proved able to develop a distinctly Scottish platform, although Gordon Millar has questioned 'the blanket view that this split led only to the direct acquisition by the Liberals of former Conservative supporters'.[27] Conservatives had won 22 Scottish seats at the 1841 general election (including a rare urban victory in the Falkirk burghs), which fell only slightly in 1847 to 20 (12 free trade Peelites and 8 Protectionists), although what Hutchison called 'a sort of informal non-aggression pact' had minimised the split, as it would again in 1852.[28] The Earl of Eglinton, the leading Scottish Protectionist, acknowledged as much prior to the 1847 election:

> The general feeling among the Conservative party here is that it will be very unwise to oppose any of the moderate adherents of Sir Robert Peel, who would be likely to join our party hereafter, not only because the effect of doing so would be then bringing in the Whig, but because it is quite clear that we are not strong enough to do much good without some assistance.[29]

Gary Hutchison has argued that far from neglecting Scottish business, Sir Robert Peel's 1841–6 government included four Scottish ministers and carried three significant Scottish Bills in 1845 alone.[30] Conservative Lord Advocates became the new party 'managers', the convention being that any appointee (as Scotland's senior law officer) sit for a Scottish constituency. Given the continuing decline of Scottish Conservative MPs after 1847, this caused the party some anxiety. When Lord Advocate John Inglis stood for Orkney in 1852, he was narrowly defeated, as he was again at a by-election in County Antrim. On being appointed again in 1858, Inglis could only find refuge in the English borough of Stamford.[31]

During his 1858–9 administration, the Conservative Prime Minister the Earl of Derby considered ending 'Parliament House rule' by making the Lord High Commissioner to the General

Assembly of the Church of Scotland 'a rival Official Agent, the minister for Scotland in the House of Lords, [and] a member of the Cabinet'.[32] The plan came to nothing, although it might have done something to combat the impression that the Scottish party, as Gary Hutchison has put it, 'was less distinctively "Scottish" at Westminster than in Scotland itself, being (to an extent) subsumed within the broader UK parliamentary party'.[33]

If the diminished Scottish party possessed a leader after 1847, it was the 13th Earl of Eglinton. He made a concerted effort to promote Conservative interests north of the border and, shortly after expressing his hopes for a reconciliation between Peelites and Protectionists in 1852, founded the National Association for the Vindication of Scottish Rights (NAVSR). Looking beyond his organisation of a medieval tournament in Ayrshire in 1839, Alex Tyrell has described Eglinton as a political figure of substance who shaped the Scottish Conservative approach to what became known as 'administrative devolution', i.e. the creation of a dedicated government minister and department for Scotland, as first suggested by Sir Robert Peel in the 1820s. The NAVSR was shaped by several factors, chiefly perceived Liberal neglect of Scotland (as well as undue attention to Ireland) and a desire to give expression to a long-standing 'invented tradition' of Scottish national identity. The choreography of King George IV's 1822 visit to Scotland – masterminded by Sir Walter Scott – and the later 'Balmorality' of Queen Victoria mainstreamed what had hitherto been fringe concerns.[34] More broadly, Graeme Morton has identified what he called a 'unionist nationalism' in 1850s civic Scotland,[35] a defence of Scotland's distinctiveness within the Union that appealed to many Scottish Conservatives.[36]

Eglinton died in 1861, after which the Conservatives in Scotland lacked an acknowledged leader. The Liberal Prime Minister Lord Palmerston (1855–8, 1859–65), meanwhile, proved attractive to Scottish Peelites or free traders, something that exacerbated Conservative decline. By the general election of 1865, Scottish Tories secured only 11 out of 53 Scottish seats and 14.6 per cent of the vote.[37] Even Benjamin Disraeli's enlargement of the franchise to include urban workers via the Second Reform Act did the Scottish party no favours. At the 1868 election it won just 17.5 per cent of the vote and seven seats (of which there were now 60, including two for the four ancient universities).[38] The 'popular belief', wrote D. W. Urwin, 'was that it [an extended franchise] had been given by the Liberals':

> Toryism was consistently identified with certain historical contentions incompatible with the Scottish creed of independence. As a creed it was dead and discredited.[39]

'The state of Scotland alone is most serious,' wrote Benjamin Disraeli, then Chancellor, to the Earl of Derby. 'All influence appears to have slipped away from its proprietors.' Even the novelist Anthony Trollope observed in his novel *Phineas Finn* (1869) that 'there are not half a dozen Conservatives returned by all the counties in Scotland'. Shortly after the 1868 election, the Scottish Conservatives lost another of its leaders, W. E. Aytoun, who 'was laid out with bouquets of Tory-Jacobite white roses on his breast'. 'Scottish Toryism had lost its bard,' wrote Gerald Warner.[40]

Despite the election result, the creation of thousands of new voters sowed the seeds of future success. The Scottish National Constitutional Association (SNCA) had been founded in 1867. Consisting mainly of individual subscribers, any local association could join and send representatives to a General Council which met twice a year. Organisationally, it was divided into Eastern and Western sections based in Edinburgh and Glasgow respectively and controlled by a single committee. But according to Mike Dyer, it 'was never popular, most of its activities centred on a committee of Edinburgh lawyers, and was by-passed by local constituency associations, who preferred to conduct their external relations directly with London'.[41]

Although Disraeli had famously told his secretary in 1866 that the 'Scotch shall have no more favours from me until they return more Tory members to the House of Commons',[42] he took a close personal interest in reviving Scottish Conservatism. His Scottish whip, Sir Graham Montgomery, gave Disraeli a frank assessment of Tory prospects in January 1867:

> In Scotland the Presbyterian dissenters are a very numerous & powerful body. Their enmity to the Established church is bitter and undying. They look upon conservatives as greater friends to and stronger supporters of the Established Church than the liberals & hence their support of the latter at the elections. One other thing that tells against conservative opinion spreading amongst us is that

most of the newspapers are on the liberal side & so are the best conducted & clearest written papers and too many conservatives I am sorry to say take the leading Whig paper the 'Scotsman' in preference to their own leading Journal.[43]

Perhaps as a result of this gloomy take, Disraeli had to be cajoled into visiting Scotland during the autumn of 1867. Having given in, he addressed a large Conservative banquet and audience of 'working men' at Edinburgh's Music Hall. The banquet speech (at Edinburgh's Corn Exchange) included valuable observations for a party which had yet to find broad acceptance among Scottish voters:

> In a progressive country change is constant; and the question is not whether you should resist change which is inevitable, but whether that change should be carried out in deference to the manners, customs, the laws, and the traditions of a people, or whether it should be carried out in deference to abstract principles, and arbitrary and general doctrines.[44]

Given that Disraeli was about to succeed the Earl of Derby as Prime Minister, his speech was of great public interest. Conscious of this, he took care to tell Scottish Conservatives that their party was:

> not formed of a combination of oligarchs and philosophers who practise on the sectarian prejudices of a portion of the people. It is formed of all classes from the highest to the most homely, and it upholds a series of institutions that are in theory, and ought to be in practice, an embodiment of the national requirements and the security of the national rights.[45]

This foreshadowed the 'patriotic imperialism' that would 'finally crack the near-monopoly that the Liberals had enjoyed in Scotland',[46] although Hutchison has pointed out that imperialism was barely discussed among Scottish Conservatives during the 1870s.[47] Whatever the case, Disraeli's 1867 visit was a triumph, demonstrating that anti-Tory hostility in Scotland was not complete. Having 'fancied ... that north of the border I was not loved', wrote the Chancellor to Sir John Skelton, the Disraelis 'actually danced a jig (or was it a hornpipe?) in our bedroom'.[48]

Two years later, Scottish Conservatives managed to win a by-election for the new Glasgow and Aberdeen Universities constituency with E. S. Gordon, who had served as Lord Advocate (and would again in 1874–6). That year (1869) also saw the formation of the Glasgow Working Men's Conservative Association (GWMCA), which Disraeli addressed during a visit to Glasgow to be installed as Lord Rector of the city's ancient university. To the GWMCA he ruminated on Scotland's political allegiances:

> It was once, and I hope is still, a land of liberty, of patriotism, and of religion. I think the time has come when it really should leave off mumbling the dry bones of political economy and munching the remainder biscuit of an effete Liberalism.[49]

The unexpected victory of Colonel Campbell in the November 1873 Renfrewshire by-election – he was the area's first Conservative MP since 1832 – was taken as conclusive evidence of the 'increasing usefulness of this association and its like'.[50] As Catriona Burness has argued, the general election of 1874 marked 'a turning-point in Conservative fortunes' in Scotland's largest city,[51] although the Conservatives contested only 43 of Scotland's 58 constituencies, caught unawares (as were Liberals) by W. E. Gladstone's sudden recommendation to the Queen to dissolve Parliament in January of that year. But Scottish Conservatives won 11 additional MPs (producing a total of 18) and increased its share of the vote to a respectable 31.6 per cent. One new MP was Alexander Whitelaw, whose great-grandson William would sit for Penrith and the Border and serve as Margaret Thatcher's Deputy Prime Minister.

During the 1874–80 Conservative government, Disraeli and other Conservative leaders paid closer attention to Scotland, doubtless keen to consolidate its electoral gains. Not only was Scotland included in the government's programme of social legislation, which included public health measures and housing for working men, it attempted to heal past divisions by abolishing the long-disputed right of lay patrons to nominate clergy in the Church of Scotland.[52] Although welcomed by the Church of Scotland, this backfired in that it pushed the Free Church towards supporting disestablishment, angry that its sacrifices in the 1840s had gone unrecognised. As I. G. C. Hutchison has observed: 'The Conservatives thus instigated the major crisis of later nineteenth-century Scottish politics which challenged the survival of the very church they were seeking to make secure.'[53]

Another grievance concerned game-hunting laws. While Scottish farmers were forbidden from killing 'ground' game (hares, rabbits and deer) despite the damage they did to crops, English tenant farmers faced no such restriction.[54] County Scottish Conservatives spent the 1860s and 1870s 'exploiting Liberal indifference' over this and Hypothec.[55] Organisationally, the poor election results of 1868 and 1874 also led to some improvements. Formal associations were created in counties such as Perthshire, Stirlingshire, Wigtownshire and Kirkcudbrightshire, for the purpose of recruiting tenant farmers to the Conservative cause, while re-registration drives were undertaken in counties such as Dumfries and Roxburgh. The number of Conservative candidates contesting elections gradually increased.[56]

Keen to build on these improvements, in 1876 Disraeli tasked a committee of Scottish landowners and English MPs with surveying the prospects for Scottish Conservatism.[57] The journalist Alexander Mackie thus provided a vivid picture of the party's position in Scotland:

> We found our agents in every case the leading men of their districts, and they were delighted on hearing that London was about to interest itself in the condition of Scotland. We found in every part the greatest loyalty to the Party and willingness to work even without pay if only good generalship, or even life, at headquarters was manifested, but these headquarters must not be Edinburgh ... I cannot close without [saying] how desirable it is that the landowners of Scotland should be more genial with their tenantry, and mix more amongst them 'at both kirk and market'. Probably a meeting of Scottish landowners once a year in London for the consideration of Scotland's wants and the Conservative Party's interests would be attended with permanent benefits.[58]

Another report by the solicitor and Perth Conservative agent Horace Skeete observed that:

> The present Government have therefore a good opportunity of making friends in Scotland. There exists however at present, to some extent, a feeling of dissatisfaction. The general public are unable to understand why the Government with a powerful majority in both houses should introduce Scottish bills, thereby admitting their necessity, and fail to pass them ... If satisfactory measures on these subjects were passed by the Government the position of their supporters at the next general election would be greatly strengthened. To command success organization is no doubt essential, but it

is equally essential that the Conservative candidates should be able to point to the fact that Scottish business has been better attended to by the present Government than it was by the Liberals – on this very much depends.

Skeete added that the:

> Conservatives of Scotland have been so long excluded from power that very many of them seem to have lost hope. They appear to look upon the present Conservative Government as the result of accidental circumstances which may not occur again ... The Conservatives of Scotland from their family traditions and social position would without difficulty exercise almost irresistible political influence, if they could be induced to use ordinary means of making themselves popular. They have lost much of their political power solely through their supineness. If any means could be adopted for at once stirring them up from Headquarters much good might arise.[59]

Based on these reports, Crapster summarised the state of Scottish Conservatism in 1876 thus:

> Organization and techniques in this period of the infancy of the mass party were still fluid. Agents were reasonably hardworking and generally optimistic, but they shared the not uncommon feeling of the man on the spot that the chieftains at headquarters ignored local needs. The rank and file were pretty thoroughly discouraged by the apparently irresistible victories of Scottish liberalism and by the feeling that both parties took Scotland for granted. This demoralization probably accentuated the difficulty in finding suitable candidates. Dissatisfaction with the way things were handled at Westminster had not, however, reached the proportions of a serious nationalist revolt for 'home rule' in either government or party.

Scottish Conservatives, however, 'still supported the central leadership loyally and looked to it for guidance'. Indeed, added Crapster, 'theirs was less a Scottish Conservative party than the Scottish branch of the party, aware of local interests but hesitant to embarrass a Conservative government'.[60] The London leadership appears to have taken note. During the next three years Westminster legislated to reform Scotland's sheriff courts, prevent pollution of its rivers, and improve its prisons, roads and bridges. In 1878 the Home Secretary even revived the old idea of creating an under-secretary for Scottish affairs in his department, although this was later dropped.

The pejorative reference to Edinburgh in Mackie's report illustrated the relative strength of the party's Glasgow-based Western division and a growing distrust of lawyers, many of whom had been interviewed for the 1876 report.[61] Socially, however, Edinburgh became an important political centre. The Scottish Conservative Club was founded there in 1877 with 800 members, while in June 1879 a conference of agents, association chairmen and other activists took place in the Scottish capital. Attended by more than 120 leading Scottish Conservatives, who discussed burgh and county organisation, registration, election expenses and the media, Central Office in London had also despatched an organising agent, who had toured more than 40 burghs and several counties with the secretary of the SNCA.[62]

But as Gerald Warner observed, even such diligent activity could not counter Gladstone's 'oratorical crusade' during his Midlothian Campaign of 1879–80. Furthermore, the Liberal leader's choice of that constituency, where the incumbent MP was the SNCA president Lord Dalkeith, 'was a carefully planned challenge to the Buccleuch interest, the principal power-base of Scottish Toryism'.[63] The Conservatives in Scotland won only six seats (albeit on almost 30 per cent of the vote) amid another Scottish (and indeed British) Liberal landslide. In Midlothian, the Grand Old Man beat Dalkeith by 211 votes. Following this defeat, Conservatives in Glasgow – where the Orange Order had grown influential enough to impose one of its own candidates on the party[64] – were so demoralised they considered disbanding.

Two years later, one Glaswegian activist produced an acerbic sketch of political life in Scotland's largest city, its premise being the sudden realisation of 'ardent Conservatives or gentlemen of leisurely positions in life' that the interests of their party were 'being neglected':

> They arrange a meeting of those in the district known to share their political opinions. The hour of conference arrives, and about a dozen persons of apologetic mien appear at the trysted place. A chairman is appointed. That gentleman makes a speech. The first half is devoted to impressing his friends with a due sense of how melancholy their prospects are. Radicalism, he says, is in the air. The working men are Radical ... Then the speaker goes on to lament the progress of destructive legislation ... Freedom of contract has been abolished; the value of property is undermined; in short revolution is approaching. As Conservatives, the Chairman

continues, it is their duty to do what they can to stem the flood that is sweeping away the landmarks of their social and political systems. They must do their best, but they have an up-hill battle to fight.

The speaker resumes his chair amidst the feeble noise of a few hesitatingly tramping feet. His snuffbox is passed around; and he will be glad to hear suggestions. Someone thinks that to form themselves into an Association is the proper step to begin with.

A motion to that effect is unanimously adopted; then there is another pause. By and by it is perceived that an Association requires office-bearers, and it is proposed that the excellent chairman should be made President. The Chairman feels highly flattered at the honour; and as no one else seemed inclined to have it, he will be glad to do all he can to discharge the duties of the position. Vice-presidents and a secretary are appointed, and as 'Committee' is a word of imposing, business-like aspect, the whole of those present are formed into a body of that name. Then 'refreshments' are called for. During the evening the spirits of the meeting become perceptibly higher. To be a member of a political organisation, it is thought, is, after all, a thing of considerable account; to hold office in it is really almost as good as being an Elder of the Church or a Deacon in the Trades.[65]

To D. W. Urwin, the Scottish Conservative attitude during the early 1880s was 'not only one of pessimism and supineness, but also one of arrogance'. Members, he added, 'took it for granted that they were socially and intellectually superior to everyone else'.[66]

NOTES

1. See W. Earl Hodgson (1883–4), 'Why Conservatism fails in Scotland', *National Review* ii, 236.
2. N. Gash (1948), 'F. R. Bonham: Conservative "political Secretary", 1832–47', *English Historical Review* 63:249, 513.
3. W. Ferguson (1968), *Scotland: 1689 to the Present*, London: Oliver & Boyd, 237. For a revisionist account of 'the Dundas despotism', see M. Fry (2004), *The Dundas Despotism*, Edinburgh: John Donald. For the pre-1832 Scottish Conservatives, see J. T. Ward (1986), 'The origins of Scottish Toryism', *Contemporary Review* 249:1446, 35–40, and R. M. Sunter (1986), *Patronage and Politics in Scotland, 1707–1832*, Edinburgh: John Donald.
4. Other sources say ten, but party allegiance was less easy to discern in the 1830s.
5. G. Warner (1988), *The Scottish Tory Party: A History*, London: Weidenfeld & Nicolson, 122.

6. G. Warner (1988), 124. Scotland's 16 representative peers are an often-overlooked product of the 1707 Union settlement. See Sir J. Fergusson, Bt (1960), *The Sixteen Peers of Scotland: An Account of the Elections of the Representative Peers of Scotland 1707–1959*, Oxford: Clarendon Press.
7. S. and O. Checkland (1984), *Industry and Ethos: Scotland, 1832–1914*, London: Edward Arnold, 83.
8. As Gerald Warner has explained, the word 'Tory' was a corruption of the Irish Gaelic *tóiridhe*, meaning 'pursuer' or 'brigand'.
9. I. G. C. Hutchison (2020), *Industry, Reform and Empire: Scotland, 1790–1880*, Edinburgh: Edinburgh University Press, 241.
10. I. G. C. Hutchison (2020), 227.
11. M. Dyer (2001), 'The evolution of the Centre-Right and the state of Scottish Conservativism', *Political Studies* 49, 39.
12. G. D. Hutchison, 'The electioneering methods of the Victorian Conservative Party and how they shaped Scotland's political culture', LSE blog, 30 July 2020.
13. See G. D. Hutchison (2020) '"A distant and Whiggish country": The Conservative Party and Scottish elections, 1832–1847', *Historical Research* 93:260, 333–52.
14. A. Marr (1992), *The Battle for Scotland*, London: Penguin, 109. When the Scottish Conservative Association was formed in 1835 the *Scotsman* predicted its main purpose would be 'bribery, influence and intimidation' (I. G. C. Hutchison, 1986, *A Political History of Scotland, 1832–1924: Parties, Elections and Issues*, Edinburgh: John Donald, 8).
15. G. D. Hutchison (2017), 'The Origins of the Scottish Conservative Party, 1832–1868', PhD thesis, University of Edinburgh, 272.
16. D. Hurd (2007), *Robert Peel: A Biography*, London: Weidenfeld & Nicolson, 200–1. Peel was later active in alleviating the suffering of Paisley during a localised economic crisis (see D. Hurd, 261–9).
17. J. T. Ward (1976), 'Some aspects of working-class Conservatism in the nineteenth century', in J. Butt and J. T. Ward (eds), *Scottish Themes, Essays in Honour of Professor S. G. E. Lythe*, Edinburgh: Edinburgh University Press, 148.
18. See G. D. Hutchison (2019), '"Party Principles" in Scottish political culture: Roxburghshire, 1832–1847', *Scottish Historical Review* XCVIII:248, 390–409.
19. D. W. Urwin (1965), 'The development of Conservative Party organisation in Scotland until 1912', *Scottish Historical Review* 44(2):138, 93.
20. J. T. Ward (1976), 149 & 156.
21. I. G. C. Hutchison (2020), 247.
22. I. G. C. Hutchison (1986), 21.

23. I. G. C. Hutchison (1986), 84.
24. C. Burness (1983), 'Conservatism and Liberal Unionism in Glasgow, 1874–1912', PhD thesis, University of Dundee, 31.
25. I. G. C. Hutchison (2020), 293.
26. I. G. C. Hutchison (1986), 120.
27. G. F. Millar (2001), 'The Conservative split in the Scottish counties, 1846–1857', *Scottish Historical Review* 80(2): 221–50. See also C. Burness (1983), who has argued that the elections of 1847, 1852 and 1859 suggested 'room in Scotland for a halfway house between Liberalism and Conservatism before the raising of the Irish question' (32).
28. I. G. C. Hutchison (2020), 250.
29. G. F. Millar (2001), 224.
30. G. D. Hutchison (2017), 'The Origins of the Scottish Conservative Party, 1832–1868', 189.
31. See G. D. Hutchison (2019), 'An "Illegal union of lawyers, and writers, and political Baronets": The Conservative Party and Scottish governance, 1832–1868', in J. Gregory and D. J. R. Grey (eds), *Union and Disunion in the Nineteenth Century*, London: Routledge, 127–47.
32. G. D. Hutchison (2019).
33. G. D. Hutchison (2017) 'The Origins of the Scottish Conservative Party, 1832–1868', 341.
34. See A. Tyrell (2010), 'The Earl of Eglinton, Scottish Conservatism, and the National Association for the Vindication of Scottish Rights', *The Historical Journal* 53:1, 87–107.
35. G. Morton (1999), *Unionist Nationalism: Governing Urban Scotland, 1830–1860*, East Linton: Tuckwell Press.
36. Although, as Gerald Warner has observed, early 18th-century Scottish Conservatives had been the 'only party consistently and unanimously opposed to the Union' (G. Warner, 1988, 12).
37. In the concurrent election for Scotland's 16 representative peers, the result was more gratifying: 13 Conservatives, one Liberal Conservative (Lord Airlie) and two Liberals were elected.
38. The 1868 Act gave Scotland an electorate of 230,606.
39. D. W. Urwin (1965), 91.
40. G. Warner (1988), 154.
41. M. Dyer (1996), *Men of Property and Intelligence: The Scottish Electoral System prior to 1884*, Aberdeen: Scottish Cultural Press, 122.
42. R. Blake (1966), *Disraeli*, London: Eyre and Spottiswoode, 556. 'Of all parts of Scotland the most odious are the Universities,' added Disraeli. 'They have always been our bitterest and most insulting foes.'

43. H. J. Hanham (1959), *Elections and Party Management: Politics in the Time of Disraeli and Gladstone*, Brighton: Harvester Press, 161.
44. R. Blake (1997), *The Conservative Party from Peel to Major*, London: Heinemann, 411.
45. G. Warner (1988), 155.
46. J. Ramsden (1998), *An Appetite for Power: The History of the Conservative Party*, London: HarperCollins, 108.
47. I. G. C. Hutchison (1986), 119.
48. R. Blake (1966), 481–3.
49. G. Warner (1988), 159.
50. C. Burness (1983), 41.
51. C. Burness (1983), 29.
52. Most ministers of the Church of Scotland remained staunchly Tory; 1,221 out of 1,228 voted Conservative in 1868. See M. Lynch (1991), *Scotland: A New History*, London: Pimlico, 415.
53. I. G. C. Hutchison (1986), 116–17.
54. I. G. C. Hutchison (2020), 287–8.
55. I. G. C. Hutchison (1986), 110. Hypothec was an arcane system of land ownership.
56. M. Dyer (1996), 123.
57. B. L. Crapster (1957), 'Scotland and the Conservative Party in 1876', *Journal of Modern History* 29:4, 355.
58. B. L. Crapster (1957), 358.
59. B. L. Crapster (1957), 359.
60. B. L. Crapster (1957), 359.
61. D. W. Urwin (1965), 106.
62. G. Warner (1988), 163.
63. G. Warner (1988), 163.
64. I. G. C. Hutchison (1986), 120–2.
65. D. W. Urwin (1965), 107–8.
66. D. W. Urwin (1965), 108.

2

'The True National Party of Scotland': 1882–1911

On 24 November 1882, the National Union of Conservative Associations for Scotland (NUCAS) was formed. Its first president was James Campbell, the MP for Glasgow and Aberdeen Universities, and its chairman Frederick Pitman. By 1885 the NUCAS had grown from 58 local groups to 83 affiliates, which swelled further when it 'took over' the 57 affiliates of the rival Scottish National Constitutional Association (formed in 1867), making it 'the general Central Organisation of the Conservative Party in Scotland'.[1]

NUCAS was the brainchild of aristocratic Tories such as the Duke of Buccleuch, Donald Cameron of Lochiel and the 7th Earl of Hopetoun, the sorts of figures who had controlled local Scottish Conservative associations since 1832. This professionalisation of 'national' party organisation formed part of a wider trend, a unified Scottish Liberal Association having been formed the previous year.[2] The executive work of the NUCAS was originally performed by four secretaries 'selected with special reference to their connection with different districts of the country'. In addition, there was a full-time political secretary based in Edinburgh and a 'branch office' in Glasgow. The Central Council, meanwhile, was decided by 'a system of direct election by conference, and of limited co-option',[3] its meetings fluctuating between Edinburgh and Glasgow.

In 1884 Lewis Shedden began working at the Glasgow Conservative Association based on Renfield Street. Though not then 'the complete political machine' it would later become,[4] it was important as the party increased its presence and representation in Scotland's largest city. The *Franchise Act 1884* and the *Redistribution of Seats Act 1885* later increased Scotland's electorate to 56 per cent of the adult male population and its number of constituencies from 58 to 70, which made the case for professional and effective party activity all the more essential. In 1883 Reginald MacLeod, son-in-law of Sir Stafford Northcote, Conservative leader in the House of Commons, was appointed Central Office agent in Edinburgh. Although distrusted by London, he not only proved an adept fundraiser but helped build Scottish Conservative morale 'sufficiently to enable it to take full advantage of the [forthcoming] split in the Liberal party'.[5]

This shift to 'national' rather than 'local' organisation also reflected broader cultural shifts. In 1884 Conservatives and Liberals joined forces to demand a minister and department to manage Scottish business in London, having grown weary of legislative neglect and the cost of promoting private legislation. This promotion of 'administrative devolution' bore the traces of the Earl of Eglinton's agitation in the 1850s in that it was both practical *and* 'romantic', in that such reforms were promoted as acknowledging Scotland's distinct nationhood and traditions.[6] Lord Bute even told the Liberal Lord Rosebery there were many 'Tories like myself who would hail a more autonomous arrangement with deep pleasure. We would prefer the rule of our own countrymen, even if it were rather Radical, to the existing state of things.'[7]

This bilateralism continued when Gladstone's government fell, and Lord Salisbury formed a new administration which was pledged to carry the Secretary for Scotland Bill. During its consideration, the Prime Minister expressed his belief that:

> on the whole, it is better to localize as far as possible, rather than centralize, a business of this kind; and that those vast administrative mechanisms which we are building up are not without their inconvenience, and even not without their danger; and I should be, therefore, prepared to see them divided into smaller Departments.[8]

Privately, Salisbury was more cynical, describing the 'expectations of the people of Scotland' as 'approaching the Archangelic'. Offering the new position to his friend the Duke of Richmond, the Prime Minister said the government wanted 'a big man to float it – especially as there is so much sentiment about it'. If he were to offer the position to a less significant

Conservative grandee, the 'Scotch people would declare we were despising Scotland – & treating her as if she was a West Indian Colony. It really is a matter where the effulgence of two Dukedoms and the best salmon river in Scotland will go a long way.'[9] Despite considering the office 'quite unnecessary', Richmond agreed,[10] prompting Salisbury's memorable observation that the 'whole object' was to 'redress the wounded dignities of the Scotch people – or a section of them – who think that enough is not made of Scotland'.[11]

Finding new ways (short of legislative devolution) to redress those wounded dignities would hereafter preoccupy Conservatives in Scotland, while Salisbury's role in establishing the Scottish Office would be cited a century later as proof that the party had long been alive to Scotland's often quixotic expectations. The general election of November–December 1885, meanwhile, saw the Conservatives outnumbered by the combined force of Gladstone's Liberals and Charles Stewart Parnell's Irish Parliamentary Party, so in the end the first Scottish Secretary lasted only six months, resigning on 28 January 1886 along with the rest of Salisbury's ministry.

At that election the Conservatives won a meagre eight (out of 70) seats in Scotland, one burgh and seven counties. A contemporary article by 'A Conservative' blamed the media, 'for we Scotsmen do like to be told we are wiser and more moral and better in every way than any other people, and Mr. Gladstone has in this line fooled us to the top of our bent', although he also highlighted the fact that while the Scottish Liberal vote had increased by a third, that of the Scottish Conservatives had doubled.[12] The *Scotsman* had mocked Conservatives ahead of polling day, for:

> They are always sure they are going to win. They are confident that the bright days of Conservatism in Scotland have not only dawned, but have got almost to noontide splendour. No past experience modifies this tone.[13]

All this was soon to change. The Radical Liberals' push for disestablishment of the Church of Scotland had already given Scottish Conservatives a cause with which to detach churchmen from the Scottish Liberals, while the looming Home Rule split 'completed and widened the fissures of 1885'.[14] It also pushed the hitherto Liberal *Glasgow Herald* and *Scotsman* newspapers towards the Conservatives,[15] thus removing one of the major disadvantages faced by the party since 1832. With the July 1886 general election framed in terms of Irish Home Ruler versus Unionist rather than Liberal versus Conservative, 'Unionists' collectively won 28 seats (12 of which were Conservative). This marked the beginning of an initially informal alliance which was to transform the Scottish Conservatives 'from an impotent minor into a political party with a greater mass following'.[16]

Back in government, Lord Salisbury turned to his nephew Arthur James Balfour to fill the fledgling Scottish Office, despite the fact he sat for an English constituency. As Secretary for Scotland, the languid but intellectual Balfour assumed control of law and order, which associated Conservatives with the pragmatic extension of administrative devolution, a strategy which would reach its full expression six decades later. In 1887 Balfour was succeeded by the 9th Marquis of Lothian. A Catholic landowner, he lamented that the 'people of Scotland' were not 'as Conservative as I should like to see them'. But from 'one point of view':

> I do think the people of Scotland are strongly and thoroughly Conservative. They are so proud of their ancient history and institutions which affect themselves and everything connected with their daily life, that they would be reluctant to make any change which would tend to cut them off from the system of County Government which has gone before, and from their historic and local associations.[17]

Hanham, however, considered Scottish Conservatives of this period to be as dependent upon 'English' leadership as the Scottish Liberals:

> The nominal leader of the Lowland Conservatives, the Duke of Buccleuch, was old and discredited, and the nominal leader of the Highland Conservatives, the Duke of Richmond, Lennox and Gordon, was both an Englishman and incapable of leading anybody ... Indeed, in so far as the Scottish Conservatives had an effective political leader, it was Lord Salisbury, who had no wish to meddle in Scottish affairs, but had a special position in Scotland as brother-in-law of the Earl of Galloway, uncle of the Balfours, and friend of Campbell of Blythswood.[18]

While the Liberal Unionists had quickly created a separate organisation,[19] the 'official Conservative policy from the outset was one of non-interference and even of active support for them'. Local Conservative and Liberal Unionist parties collaborated in arranging meetings, negotiating candidates 'and in the detailed activity of local party life'.[20] That said, the peculiarities of Scottish politics still required Liberal Unionists to emphasise their Liberalism as well as their Unionism. As Lord Wolmer noted, 'it does not do for a Lib[eral] U[nioni]st. to go on a Conserv[ative] platform – In England nobody minds.'[21]

Another consequence of the Liberal split was the appointment of a small NUCAS committee, which met in Glasgow in 1888 to supervise the western constituencies.[22] By 1889 Conservatives and Liberal Unionists had merged to form a single organisation in Glasgow St Rollox, with the former admitting 'freely that their successes in Scotland had been due to the activity and support' of the latter.[23] In 1886 Scottish Conservatives also instigated the first 'Campaign Guide', later a UK-wide publication, its contents initially drafted by members of the Scottish Bar.[24] After 1886 Orangemen – who were influential in working-class areas – also became more active on behalf of 'Unionism'.[25] Although they and Glasgow's Tories had feted him during a 1884 visit, Randolph Churchill found 'the aristocratic and urban leaders of Toryism unpleasant and uninterested'.[26]

Although by 1892 the NUCAS had grown in strength – the central association of all but one county was now affiliated – the general election in July of that year saw 'Unionists' win just 19 MPs in Scotland and the Liberals re-enter government at Westminster (Maltman Barry, a friend of Karl Marx and former socialist, had failed to win Banffshire).[27] Agitation for reform of NUCAS's Central Council was already underway, particularly a situation which meant that, 'since a quarter of its members were elected by each annual conference, there was usually a preponderance of individuals from the area where that particular conference happened to be held'.[28] In 1890 Captain Middleton, the English party's senior agent, had also agreed to appoint an 'Agent for Scotland' to provide a hitherto non-existent link between the Scottish and UK parties.[29]

The 1893 NUCAS conference in Perth saw direct elections to the Central Council replaced with a new system of 'double election' from constituency to division, and from division to the central body. Six divisional committees were also created. Glasgow had already emerged as the 'capital of Scottish

Conservatism' and by 1895 the Western District Council was issuing its own propaganda material in addition to that of 'national' interest. This, however, paved the way for what Urwin called the 'consolidation of a sentiment of localism': 'Local regions or areas were completely uninterested in detailed occurrences in other parts of the country, and party officials preferred to be protons rather than electrons.'[30]

Party finance also emerged as a perennial issue for the party in Scotland. Previously, income had largely come from 'lords and lairds', and even after the formation of NUCAS in 1882 (something made permanent in 1893) this remained true in 1895, prompting the Central Council to pass a resolution noting its 'grave concern that the normal income is so far short of the ordinary expenditure necessary':

> But for the great generosity of a limited number of individual members in various parts of Scotland much very important work must have been left undone. At the beginning of the year the organising work of the Central Council was seriously crippled for want of money. The donations (about £1,000 in 1895) enabled that work to be resumed, but much previous work had been unavoidably lost ... There are many constituencies which cannot be expected to raise an adequate sum for local necessities; while at the same time it is for the manifest advantage, and to the direct interest, of other and wealthier constituencies that these poorer places should be well organised and heartily contested.[31]

Despite these challenges, E. H. H. Green reckoned NUCAS to be more radical than its English counterpart. In October 1894, it passed motions urging the House of Lords to initiate measures 'for the social well-being of the people', create old-age pensions, extend Employers' Liability to all forms of employment, arbitrate in industrial disputes and find ways of extending owner-occupation among the working classes.[32]

There was no such progressiveness when it came to Gladstone's second (and unsuccessful) attempt to legislate for Home Rule. 'Scotsmen are not more enamoured of Home Rule,' wrote William Wallace in the *Scottish Review*, 'since the veil that enshrouded it has been lifted, and the mechanism of the figure has been dissected':

> They know now that it means absolute betrayal of their kinsmen and co-religionists in Ulster, without pretence of protection or

compensation; they know that it means Scotland paying the piper to a grotesquely unfair extent, in order that Irishmen may dance; and they know that it means the swamping of their own 72 members in the House of Commons by a hand of 80 quasi foreigners, without responsibility, and holding in commission a dictatorial power.[33]

An anonymous 'Scottish Conservative' later judged that 'Scotsmen may in many cases be Radical in opinion, but they are all Conservative in nature':

Only those who know them best can realize what a strength of sentiment, of prejudice, and even of self-conceit had to be surmounted before the real convictions of many cut themselves free from bonds forged by the glamour of a great figure [Gladstone], and an inherited horror of a traduced party name [Liberal].

With Unionist candidates having secured 31 seats at the general election of 1895, the author believed they were poised to become 'the true national party of Scotland', partly because of the Liberal pursuit of disestablishment and Home Rule but 'very largely also to better political organisation, and to increased knowledge of Conservative principles among the electors'. Scotsmen impatient with 'neglect of their interests', he added, could now look with expectation to a government whose 'Scottish Secretary is a well-known Scotsman with a practical knowledge of the conditions of Scottish life'.[34]

This was the 6th Lord Balfour of Burleigh, considered too 'insignificant' to fill the Scottish Office in 1885 but now in charge of its affairs in the first officially 'Unionist' government. One of Scotland's 16 'representative peers' in the House of Lords, Balfour was a pillar of the Scottish presbyterian establishment,[35] and therefore a consistent opponent of disestablishment. At the general election of 1900, Unionists achieved a majority of Scottish seats (but not votes) for the first time since 1832, although 36 of those MPs were Liberal Unionists from the West of Scotland who took care to present themselves as a group distinct from the still-unpopular Scottish Conservatives.

The 'National' Union was increasingly divided between Western Unionism, 'with its strong populist tradition, based on Orange and Protestant sentiment, and Eastern, 'more Conservative in nature, with a lawyer tradition'.[36] In his memoirs, Lord Macmillan recalled the Parliament House of the late 1890s, when a young advocate was expected to declare his allegiance to either of the main parties:

> On the Conservative side a vigorous coterie, genially known as the 'Hellish Six', sought to enlist recruits as workers on the party's behalf and assigned various tasks to its adherents. My own sympathies being with the Conservatives I was asked to take a share in the work which chiefly consisted in addressing meetings throughout the country and writing leaders for the provincial Conservative Press ... All this afforded excellent, though unremunerated, practice in speaking, writing, and organisation.[37]

In 1902 A. J. Balfour – a former Scottish Secretary – succeeded his uncle, Lord Salisbury, as Prime Minister. Unionists had come to support tariff reform, taxes on imported goods with 'Imperial preference' for the British Empire, a policy which opened up new lines of division and weakened both Unionist parties in Scotland. Even within the Scottish Conservatives, there was considerable factionalism between 'whole hoggers' like Andrew Bonar Law and 'free fooders' such as the Scottish Secretary, Lord Balfour of Burleigh, who did not want to disrupt the consensus on free trade.[38] As a result, Balfour of Burleigh was unceremoniously sacked by the Prime Minister in September 1903. His successors at the Scottish Office, Andrew Graham Murray and the 1st Marquis of Linlithgow, were undistinguished, the former impatient for promotion to the Scottish bench and the latter afflicted with poor health.[39] These were hardly the leaders necessary to build support for Scottish Conservatism at the beginning of a new century.[40]

The 1906 general election reduced the Unionists to a rump of just 10 Scottish MPs, something the NUCAS Central Council attributed to a 'long period of party success' having 'induced a sense of security and complacency which stifled local activity'.[41] Two years later, Unionists (Scottish Conservatives and Liberal Unionists) took the plunge and merged. Their new candidate, Captain Duncan Campbell, explained that:

> the ideals of the old Conservative Party and the Liberal Unionist party were practically the same, for did they not realise that the Unionist Party of today largely embraced the Liberal principles of many years ago prior to the great mistakes the Liberals made in 1885? Did they not realise that the Liberal Unionists were simply what they might call the more progressive members of the great Unionist Party?[42]

The lack of a recognised leader for the Scottish Conservatives, meanwhile, came to be seen as a problem, there being no equivalent of the Liberals' 'Scottish Whip'. The party's 'Scottish Agent' (Guy Spier had been appointed in election year) lacked authority, his own office and even any staff. By 1909 a Scottish Conservative deputation was in London demanding a reconstruction of the Agent's duties, although it admitted lacking agreement from the Glasgow-based party, something which indicated that the party there 'had already achieved a position of considerable independence'.[43] Although the Unionists modestly improved their share of the vote at the two elections held in 1910, they still returned just 9 and 10 Members respectively. It remained a rump.

Finally, in 1911 there was established 'a position which could be claimed as representative of Scottish Conservatism'. This was, aping the more successful Liberals, the 'Scottish Whip', a position in the gift of the UK Conservative Party leader. The first was Sir George Younger, a past president of NUCAS and Unionist MP for Ayr since 1906. But while in England party reforms separated the Chief Whip's parliamentary duties from management of the party, in Scotland both tasks became the responsibility of the newly created office of Scottish Whip.

As the Scottish Conservative and Liberal Unionist parties edged towards a formal merger – hitherto strongly resisted by the latter despite harmonious relations at a local level – it was decided to invite the Scottish Whip to all meetings of the Central Council's executive (although Sir George was not made a full member). That the 'fusion' negotiations followed three successive election defeats found the Scottish Conservatives grumpy and divided. During 1912 the Central Council complained that most of its income still came from funds 'specially and privately collected', while attributing at least some of the blame for the party's misfortunes to constituency associations:

> It is sometimes found that local officials do not sufficiently avail themselves of the assistance which the National Union is prepared to give towards improving organisation ... The Central Council regards this with some regret, as it is obvious that in many constituencies in Scotland the local resources and opportunities are inadequate to provide the necessary machinery for effective propaganda which can only be supplied through the medium of a central institution.[44]

This was the backdrop to the creation of a 'new' political party – the Scottish Unionist – which, after an underwhelming start, was to dominate inter-war Scotland and banish unhappy memories of past electoral failures.

NOTES

1. J. T. Ward (1982), *The First Century: A History of Scottish Tory Organisation 1882–1982*, Edinburgh: SCUA, 11.
2. See D. Torrance (2022), *A History of the Scottish Liberals and Liberal Democrats*, Edinburgh: Edinburgh University Press, 20.
3. D. W. Urwin (1965), 'The Development of the Conservative Party Organisation in Scotland until 1912', *Scottish Historical Review* 14:138, 97.
4. Scottish Conservative & Unionist Association papers, Acc 10424/10, Edinburgh: National Library of Scotland.
5. H. J. Hanham (1959), *Elections and Party Management: Politics in the Time of Disraeli and Gladstone*, Brighton: Harvester Press, 159–60.
6. See D. Torrance (2020), *'Standing up for Scotland': Nationalist unionism and Scottish party politics, 1884–2014*, Edinburgh: Edinburgh University Press, 3.
7. H. J. Hanham (1969), *Scottish Nationalism*, London: Faber & Faber, 83–5.
8. HL Deb 9 July 1885 Vol. 299 c101.
9. Lord Salisbury to the Duke of Richmond, 7 August 1885, Goodwood MS 871.
10. H. J. Hanham (1965), 'The Creation of the Scottish Office 1881–87', *Juridical Review* 10, 229.
11. Lord Salisbury to the Duke of Richmond, 13 August 1885, Goodwood MS 871.
12. *The Scottish Review*, January 1886.
13. C. Burness (2003), *'Strange Associations': The Irish Question and the Making of Scottish Unionism, 1886–1918*, East Linton: Tuckwell Press, 17.
14. C. Burness (2002), 'The Making of Scottish Unionism, 886–1914', in S. Ball and I. Holliday (eds), *Mass Conservatism: The Conservatives and the Public since the 1880s*, London: Frank Cass, 22.
15. This shift rendered the Tory-supporting *Scottish News* surplus to requirements, and it folded in 1888. In 1880s Scotland there were 10 Liberal and three Conservative daily newspapers.
16. D. W. Urwin (1965), 94.
17. D. Torrance (2006), *The Scottish Secretaries*, Edinburgh: Birlinn, 36. Ninety years later Lothian's great-great-nephew Michael

Ancram, later the 13th Marquis of Lothian, was appointed
Minister of State at the Scottish Office.
18. H. J. Hanham (1959), 158.
19. Ian Cawood's *The Liberal Unionist Party: A History* (2012,
London: I. B. Tauris) has very little on Scotland.
20. D. W. Urwin (1965), 95–6.
21. C. Burness (2003), 3.
22. D. W. Urwin (1965), 100.
23. D. W. Urwin (1965), 96.
24. By 1910 the *Campaign Guide* had become a joint Anglo-Scottish
effort, with only one chapter on Scottish affairs.
25. D. W. Urwin (1965), 101.
26. A. Marr (1992), *The Battle for Scotland*, London: Penguin, 110.
27. J. T. Ward (1970), 'Tory-socialist: a preliminary note on Michael
Maltman Barry, 1842–1909', *Scottish Labour History Society
Journal* 2, 25–37.
28. D. W. Urwin (1965), 98.
29. The previous Agent, Reginald Macleod, had had no such connection with London, and had been effectively based in Edinburgh.
30. D. W. Urwin (1965), 100.
31. Quoted in D. W. Urwin (1965), 103.
32. E. H. H. Green (1995), *The Crisis of Conservatism: The politics, economics and ideology of the British Conservative party,
1880–1914*, London: Routledge, 130. A 'Unionism and the
Highlands' publication was even translated into Gaelic.
33. *The Scottish Review*, April 1894.
34. *The Scottish Review*, October 1895. Reminiscing in 1896, a
former *Scotsman* editor believed Scots to be 'conservative in their
customs, in their institutions, in the Radicalism of their politics'
(C. A. Cooper, 1896, *An Editor's Retrospect: Fifty Years of
Newspaper Work*, London: Macmillan, 166).
35. In 1911 Balfour of Burleigh published *An Historical Account of
the Rise and Development of Presbyterianism in Scotland*.
36. C. Stevens (1990), 'Scottish Conservatives – A Failure of Organization?', in A. Brown and R. Parry (eds), *The Scottish Government
Yearbook 1990*, Edinburgh: Edinburgh University Press, 78.
37. Lord Macmillan (1952), *A Man of Law's Tale: The Reminiscences
of Lord Macmillan*, London: Macmillan, 42.
38. E. A. Cameron (2010), *Impaled Upon a Thistle: Scotland since
1880*, Edinburgh: Edinburgh University Press, 84–5.
39. See D. Torrance (2006), 51–8.
40. The Scottish Conservatives did not lack lawyers. In 1912 seven of
its 11 vice-presidents and 101 of the 146 associate members based
in Edinburgh belonged to the legal profession.

41. D. W. Urwin (1965), 109.
42. C. M. M. Macdonald (1998), 'Locality, Tradition and Language in the Evolution of Scottish Unionism: A Case Study, Paisley 1886–1910', in *Unionist Scotland 1800–1997*, Edinburgh: John Donald, 64.
43. D. W. Urwin (1965), 104.
44. D. W. Urwin (1965), 109.

3

'A Birth, a Marriage or a Funeral'?
1911–1924

Although Scottish Conservatives and Liberal Unionists had co-operated since the dramatic political events of 1886, the two parties maintained separate organisations. By 1911, however, the revived prospect of Home Rule for Ireland (the *Parliament Act* of that year having removed the House of Lords' veto power) encouraged a movement formally to merge the Conservatives and Liberal Unionists at both constituency and national level.

England made the leap first. In May 1912 a formal merger of the two parties created the 'Conservative and Unionist Party'. 'We agreed that we could not bind the Scottish organisation in any way,' recalled Austen Chamberlain (a Liberal Unionist) in his memoirs, 'that the cause of Scotland must be separately treated, and that the Scotsmen must settle it for themselves'.[1] Fusion in Scotland was keenly supported by the Canadian-Scottish Leader of the Opposition at Westminster, Andrew Bonar Law,[2] the Conservatives and by West of Scotland Liberal Unionists, but not the *Scotsman*, which took 'a very strong view against complete fusion'.[3] A joint committee representing the National Union of Conservative Associations for Scotland (NUCAS), the East and North of Scotland Liberal Unionist Association (ENSLUA) and the West of Scotland Liberal Unionist Association (WSLUA) was nevertheless convened under the presidency of Sir George Younger. It recommended unification.

This proposal was adopted by special conferences in Glasgow and Edinburgh on 5 December 1912, seven months after the merger south of the border. Both Liberal Unionists and Conservatives adopted the resolution 'that it is desirable that the present Central Conservative and Liberal Unionist organisations in Scotland should be united to form one consolidated Scottish Unionist organisation'. This was to be known as the 'Scottish Unionist Association'.[4] Thus the term 'Conservative', which in a Scottish context was considered 'a label with a regrettable past and, as far as could be told, an unpromising future', was abandoned.[5]

Following luncheon at the Scottish Conservative Club (later a Debenhams department store) on Edinburgh's Princes Street, Sir George Younger explained the twin rationale behind the fusion: 'It would tend to greater economy of administration', and he hoped 'it would result in what they all earnestly desired, in sending into the wilderness at the earliest moment a party and a Government of which most people were heartily sick'. Similarly, at the final meeting of the ENSLUA, also in Edinburgh, its chairman argued that the merger enabled the two parties to present 'an unbroken front to the common enemy', which was, of course, H. H. Asquith's Liberal government.[6]

The WSLUA, meanwhile, met at the Christian Institute in Glasgow, where one speaker, Mr J. Cumming, argued that not only had the Liberal Unionists 'carried on the principles of the true Liberal party, but they had brought their Conservative friends a good deal in their direction'. He continued:

> The word 'Tory' was all that remained of the old Tory, who revered things that existed simply because they existed, [and] was as dead as the dodo. Personally, he was a Unionist because he was a Liberal. Unionism meant not only the union of Scotland, England and Ireland, but the union of all classes of the Empire, and also the union of all classes of the community in a homogenous whole.[7]

This pitched the new Scottish Unionist Association as a 'national' party, albeit one that was more liberal than conservative. The secretary of the WSLUA wrote 'A BIRTH, A Marriage or a Funeral' on his minute of his final meeting.[8] Organisationally, the SUA still closely resembled the old Scottish Conservative Party, with power invested in two divisional Councils (Eastern and Western) which controlled their own campaigns and funds, and out of which a political secretary was funded. The Edinburgh-based Eastern Division covered the eastern Highlands and half the central and Border counties, while the Glasgow-based Western Division covered the South-West, the Clydeside industrial region and part of the western Highlands. Indeed, the 'only alteration which is thought to be necessary in the Rules and Constitution of this Association, is the substitution of the name "Unionist" for "Conservative"'.[9]

But given the Liberal Unionists' strength in Scotland,[10] politically it was the reverse. While in England, judged Michael Fry, 'the Conservatives absorbed the Unionists, in Scotland it was, at length, to be the other way round'.[11] The merger 'filled' the Scottish Unionist Party 'with enough of the old Liberalism to carry it through to the 1920s', the Liberal concern with land, education and local government reform giving the new party a 'radical edge'.[12] Its inflections, as Colin Kidd has observed, 'were neither English nor metropolitan, but rather those of an embattled presbyterian provincialism somewhat distrustful of the motives of the English core of the United Kingdom'.[13]

This proved to be no bad thing. As Alvin Jackson has observed, the (former) Liberal Unionists 'taught Scottish Tories how to address an electorate beyond the Protestants of Glasgow or the landed proprietors of the New Club'.[14] Clubs were important to Scottish Unionists. To mark the amalgamation, members and delegates from all over Scotland were given lunch by the Scottish Conservative and Scottish Unionist clubs. Bonar Law visited the former in the evening, after 'addressing a great demonstration in the King's Theatre',[15] at which more than 3,000 people had been present. These events followed the first Scottish Unionist Association conference on 24 January 1913, attended by 600 delegates and 'the utmost enthusiasm' marking the proceedings. The former Lord Advocate, Charles Scott Dickson, was elected the president of the Scottish Unionist Association, A. J. Balfour having declined.[16]

Shortly before the merger, Sir George Younger had briefed Bonar Law on 'the position so far as Scotland is concerned', telling his leader that 'a most decided change of opinion' meant the new party's prospects at the next election would be 'extremely hopeful', but only if the party at Westminster avoided any fiscal surprises:

> The work in Scotland for the last fourteen months has been very hard, and it has been extremely difficult to fill the seats with candidates without too seriously burdening the Central Fund [but if an] open door be left, we shall gain many seats, I am equally certain that our chances may be ruined there if any mistake is made now. It doesn't appear to me that we can hope to have a working majority unless some fifteen or sixteen seats are won in Scotland ... the

position is an extremely critical one from the Scottish point of view, and that a great part of the work which has been so laboriously carried out during the past eighteen months runs the risk of being wasted.[17]

The new party's early years were however dominated by events in Ulster, the part of Ireland in which opposition to Home Rule was strongest.[18] But in what Hutchison called a 'curious colourlessness' to pre-war Scottish Unionism, there was a more muted reaction in Scotland than many anticipated. Not only was Home Rule rarely cited as a prominent factor in by-election results between 1910 and 1914, but when Sir Edward Carson led an Ulster Unionist deputation to stir up opposition on the mainland, an estimated 100,000 turned out in Liverpool but only 8,000 in Glasgow.[19] Carson also inaugurated the official British anti-Home Rule campaign at the city's St Andrew's Hall.[20] Thousands of West coast Unionists signed the 'British Covenant in Support of Ulster', although doing so made some uneasy. The former Scottish Secretary, Lord Balfour of Burleigh, for example, was 'afraid of finding myself committed to opposing things for Ireland, when I would take them for my own country, and would [thus] be in an impossible situation so far as Scotland is concerned'.[21]

This reflected the emergence of an idea which became known as 'Home Rule all round', the argument being that rather than granting devolution to Ireland alone, the same autonomy ought to be extended to Scotland, England and perhaps even Wales. Indeed, Home Rule for Scotland remained a commitment of the Scottish Liberal Association and would later be advanced, from a more radical perspective, by Labour. This compelled Scottish Unionists to clarify their own thinking, which was rather restricted by the party's founding ethos as a *Unionist* organisation.

In a wide-ranging essay, 'Nationality and Home Rule', A. J. Balfour, the former Scottish Secretary and Prime Minister, analysed his 'combination of different patriotisms'; 'for the communities which compose the British Empire, for the United Kingdom of which I am a citizen, and for Scotland, where I was born, where I live, and where my fathers lived before me'.[22] Balfour had captured the three central elements of Scottish Unionism – Imperial, British and Scottish – a definition of Scottish patriotism the historian Sir Robert Rait, something of a court historian for Scottish Unionists, did much to legitimise. Rait viewed the 1707 Union as the 'greatest and wisest measure ever passed by the Parliament of Scotland', while also questioning the assumption, 'less common now than it was fifty years ago, that national progress must always be measured by constitutional advance'.[23]

In May 1914, Sir George Younger, who remained the Scottish Unionist Whip at Westminster, sent Bonar Law a memorandum prepared 'by a small committee of the Scottish Unionist Association' entitled 'Scottish Home Rule'. 'Scottish National sentiment is a strong force in all ranks of Scottish life', it declared, something its authors believed might 'either be turned to good account or bad'. The 'Radicals' (i.e. Liberals) were attempting to channel it into 'narrow political Scottish nationalism' which wanted a Scottish Parliament, and therefore it fell to Unionists 'to turn it into good'.[24]

The memo had three recommendations for Unionist candidates, to (a) 'show a full appreciation of the fine worth and patriotic importance of Scottish National sentiment when directed into legitimate channels', (b) 'to expose the fallacies of ... Parliamentary severance of Scotland from the other parts of the United Kingdom' and, beyond this, (c) 'point to the important part which Scottish National patriotism has played and must still play in the wider patriotism of the whole British Empire'. There were also policy suggestions: 'some form of Imperial Council' to relieve the UK Parliament of its legislative backlog as well as 'delegation of certain matters of more exclusively local concern' from Westminster to local bodies in 'the several countries of the United Kingdom'. It also suggested overhauling the 29-year-old Scottish Office, adding 'at least two' under-secretaries, granting 'greater administrative powers' and gathering together various boards and departments 'in one building' situated in Edinburgh. The party, however, declared itself resolutely opposed to the sort of legislative devolution envisaged by the Liberals.[25] They would consider everything short, as Sir George Younger characterised it in the House of Commons, of 'a Government at Edinburgh with an executive responsible to a Scottish Parliament'. 'At that', he added conclusively, 'we draw the line.'[26]

As a briefing for parliamentary candidates, however, the SUA memo proved academic, for the general election expected in 1914 was postponed on account of the First World War and

Unionist associations put into 'cold storage' for the duration.[27] The thirteenth Unionist *Campaign Guide*, issued in advance of the election which never came, denigrated the 'sentimental' argument for a Scottish Parliament and encouraged Unionist candidates to 'strenuously oppose' any devolution scheme, although they were encouraged to support 'any reasonable project for introducing more decentralization and elasticity into administration'.[28] As Colin Kidd has observed, the widespread desire to answer the Irish Question had 'created some ideological space within Unionism for a measure of Scottish home rule'.[29]

When H. H. Asquith formed his short-lived (wartime) coalition government in 1915, Scottish Unionists worked in partnership with Liberals at local and national level. In 1916 Asquith was succeeded as Liberal leader by David Lloyd George, who now led another Liberal–Tory coalition government which lasted until 1922. When a general election finally came at the end of the Great War in 1918, and with the *Representation of the People Act 1918* having significantly increased the franchise,[30] Scottish Unionists had become 'the patriotic party of the "Anglo-Scottish" Empire',[31] with dozens of its candidates boasting military titles.[32] The party's literature embraced 'a wide spectrum of approaches to Scottish self-government',[33] while it made considerable efforts to woo newly enfranchised female voters, generally older and quite affluent. Coalition Scottish Unionists gained 28 of Scotland's 71 seats, leaving them 'poised both to exploit the wartime divisions within Liberalism by making a bid for the middle-class vote, and to challenge Labour for the support of the Protestant working classes'.[34]

Scottish Unionists were aided by *The Bulletin*, which was launched in 1915 as a stablemate to the *Glasgow Herald* and just as pro-Unionist. Four years later, the *Sunday Post* and *Sunday Mail* added two more Unionist-supporting newspapers to the mix and since 1913 Scottish Unionists had even produced their own news-sheet, *People's Politics*, which appeared three times a year.[35] After 1918, the Church of Scotland remained 'unequivocally Unionist', one might say the 'Unionist Party at Prayer', while Scotland's distinct legal profession shifted its allegiance from Liberal to Unionist: between the wars 24 advocates would sit as Unionist MPs.[36]

The Scottish Unionist Party's brief flirtation with legislative devolution, however, died with a Speaker's Conference on devolution and the dregs of 'Home Rule all round' as enshrined in the *Government of Ireland Act 1920*. This, paradoxically, gave to 'Northern Ireland' what most of its inhabitants did not want: legislative autonomy. Unionist policy then 'switched rather suddenly from defence of the Union to defence of Ulster',[37] with the Anglo-Irish Treaty agreed on 6 December 1921 granting Dominion status to the 'Irish Free State'.

Although this troubled many in the party, there was surprisingly little opposition from party 'die-hards', even in the West of Scotland. As Cameron noted, there 'were still Unions to be defended', that between Great Britain and Northern Ireland and the Anglo-Scottish Union of 1707, which were not under any immediate threat.[38] As Michael Fry has observed, Scottish Unionism had long 'outgrown its origins in the Irish crisis of 1886 and developed an outlook relevant to its own circumstances'. Having helped negotiate the Treaty (its ratification completed, ironically, by the vehemently anti-Home Rule Bonar Law), the party

> ignored howls of protest from the Orangemen and, when they broke off relations, coolly left them to it. Unionism's stock as a defence against Irish disloyalty and subversion was not to be so easily exhausted. Yet its Ministers at the Scottish Office adopted notably progressive policies in education, housing and welfare, all on public monies won from London, which were of special benefit to the depressed Catholic community and indeed began its eventually successful integration.[39]

As most of Ireland detached itself from the United Kingdom, Conservatives separated themselves from their Liberal coalition partners, although Scottish Unionists proved more reluctant than their English counterparts. Only five Scottish Unionist MPs (including the Ayr MP Sir George Younger) joined the famous Carlton Club revolt in October 1922, while 17 (including the Scottish Whip, Sir John Gilmour) supported Sir Austen Chamberlain's plea to maintain the coalition. Younger was 'furious' with Gilmour but nevertheless offered him the Scottish Office in the new Conservative government led by Bonar Law. 'It was loyal of him to refuse it,' wrote the Earl of Crawford in his diary. 'The Scottish members are independent of London, and a large majority of the Unionists are anxious to maintain the coalition understanding.'[40] Indeed, Sir Robert Horne, the Unionist

MP for Glasgow Hillhead and Chancellor of the Exchequer, stated in his election address that

> I regard co-operation with the National Liberals – with whom we share a common policy – as vital to the interests of the nation ... I am glad to think that in Scotland the Unionist party takes the view which I hold.[41]

Similarly, Sir William Raeburn in Dunbartonshire told his electors he had been 'against the Carlton Club decision, and voted accordingly along with the great majority of my Scottish colleagues; but what was done then cannot be undone.'[42] Other candidates made it clear they were Unionists rather than Conservatives. Sir Aylmer Hunter-Weston said he was not a 'Unionist' in the old party sense, but because he supported 'the union of all classes and all interests in the Nation'.[43] 'I never was a Tory,' Sir Patrick Ford wrote privately to Austen Chamberlain, 'but from 1907 when I entered politics as a Liberal Unionist I have held to that view, only accepting Toryism as modified by it.'[44] Reverting to the designation 'Conservative', as the party in England looked set to do, would be 'repugnant to the great body of Unionists in Scotland'.[45]

The term 'Unionist' conveyed what Hutchison called 'a double appeal', wooing the 'Orange-inclined working-class element, as well as retaining the Liberal Unionist identity'.[46] As Alvin Jackson has observed, Unionist ideology during this period 'continued to be inflected by religious bigotry',[47] although there is a general consensus that this had been (and indeed continued to be) exaggerated by political opponents who 'wished to identify Toryism with sectarianism'. As Gerald Warner has observed:

> Where it existed, it was on a very temporary basis at purely local level, in a tiny number of Scottish constituencies. It was never endorsed by the leadership: as early as 1889, the Council of the National Union had refused affiliation to the Protestant Confederacy and Patriotic Union. All that the links with Orangeism amounted to was a few local politicians succumbing to the temptation to garner much-needed votes from Irish Protestant immigrants at a time when Labour was harvesting the votes of Irish Catholic immigrants.[48]

Indeed, the Glasgow Conservative Association's Orange representative left in 1922 over Unionist support for the Anglo-Irish Treaty. A separate 'Orange and Protestant Party' was formed in protest but made few inroads, usually instructing its adherents to back Unionists against 'socialist' candidates.

Nevertheless, caution if not outright prejudice was certainly present when Sir George Younger considered alternatives, given John Gilmour's reluctance to become Scottish Secretary. Sir George told Bonar Law he found

> it is not thought wise to appoint [Lord] Lovat. He is an able fellow and would, I think, fill the post very well, but it is believed that it would greatly inflame Scottish feeling if a Catholic occupied the position. [Viscount] Novar would be an excellent man and a most typical Scotchman, if we could induce him to accept Office. He has been absolutely with us ever since he returned from Australia [where he had been Governor-General], and if we could secure him, it would be rather a score.[49]

When Bonar Law unveiled his Cabinet in November 1922, Novar among them, the Earl of Crawford was incredulous, not least because the new Scottish Secretary was 'a lifelong Liberal who though reticent on political matters during the last year or two has never declared himself a Conservative. A truly amazing appointment showing our poverty in Scotland. While he joins us ... there are still practical proofs of coalition!'[50]

Indeed, despite the recent collapse of the coalition, the Scottish Unionist Association's Eastern Division chose not to oppose incumbent National (or coalition) Liberals, and when the National Liberals reciprocated in Unionist-held seats, the two parties ended contesting roughly the same constituencies as in 1918. But despite operating a pact in 46 seats at the general election of November 1922,[51] the Scottish Unionists won just 13 seats, fewer than Labour and even Asquith's Liberals. The SUA Central Council considered this 'a serious set-back', something it blamed on the coalition having 'hampered the growth of Unionist organisation, which almost vanished during the war ... it was not easy for Unionists to remain loyal to their allies and at the same time construct an effective Party machine'.[52] Indeed, before the election the SUA's new political secretary, an advocate and Great War veteran called Patrick J. Blair, had privately observed that for all its electoral success

> one sometimes has the feeling that the party in Scotland is not quite what it should be. Perhaps the ideal is a little high. People who should take an interest do not; people who do seem to carry

weight in it are really 'light horsemen', and hot air and futility sometimes prevail.[53]

As Scottish Secretary, Novar quickly fell into line with Unionist policy as he grappled with industrial unrest on the Clyde. In May 1923, Bonar Law resigned on health grounds after just 209 days as premier. His successor, the Anglo-Scottish Stanley Baldwin, did not rate Novar and kept him out of the loop. 'Great anxiety about Scotland,' wrote the Earl of Crawford. 'Jack Gilmour told me last week that the party organisers at Edinburgh had never been consulted, and this evening George Younger said that Novar had never heard of a comprehensive scheme of tariff reform until he read the report of Baldwin's Plymouth speech.'[54]

Despite a clear majority in the House, Baldwin felt bound by Bonar Law's pledge that there would be no new tariffs without a further election and asked the King for a dissolution of Parliament. Presciently, Novar told Baldwin that a snap general election risked handing the government over to socialists. 'I should say that I cannot well see how our chief industries in Scotland, Engineering, Shipbuilding, Linen etc can be assisted by Protection,' he added, 'and I anticipate therefore that Protection will receive little support there.'[55] Indeed, in 1920 the *Glasgow Herald*, 'the voice of business Unionism', had 'assumed an attitude of strong hostility to the Government's fiscal policy', running a series of articles predicting that many Scottish industries faced ruin if protection were implemented.[56]

Although the SUA's Eastern Divisional Council had reported 'signs of renewed activity among the Unionists of many constituencies' since the last election, the 'chief obstacle' remained 'the apathy of the mass of professing Unionists, who, though ready to criticise the policy of the Party and its organisation, will not rouse themselves to work, or pay for the essential staff work'.[57] In the December election of 1923, the party secured just 14 MPs, one more than in 1922 but eight fewer than the Liberals.[58] Patrick Blair had been under orders from London to find a candidate for every constituency in Scotland, even Liberal strongholds the party had long ago given up on. Robert Boothby, for example, was despatched to Orkney and Shetland without even the pretence of a selection committee.[59] The result showed that Unionists were not yet the repository of choice for middle-class Scottish voters, although isolated victories such as that in West Aberdeenshire came despite Unionists having little or no local organisation.

Now deprived of a clear majority (Conservatives had won a total of 258 seats in the House of Commons), Stanley Baldwin resigned as Prime Minister in January 1924 after losing a confidence vote on the King's Speech. Labour, as Viscount Novar had predicted, then formed its first administration, although that was to prove a useful catalyst in turning the minority Scottish Unionist Party into a more popular vote-winning machine. The editor of the staunchly Unionist *Scotsman* had recently stressed to Sir John Gilmour the dangers of the party becoming perceived as reactionary. 'The Die-hards have already made it very hard for us in Scotland,' he wrote. 'If their influence prevails in the future as it has in the past, Unionism in Scotland will be ruined.'[60] Scottish Unionists took note of this reality and embraced moderation.

NOTES

1. Sir A. Chamberlain (1936), *Politics from the Inside: An Epistolary Chronicle 1906–1914*, London: Cassell, 156.
2. Bonar Law's father was a Free Church of Scotland Minister from Coleraine in what would become Northern Ireland. He grew up in Glasgow and attended the High School of Glasgow before becoming a successful businessman in the Glasgow iron trade and entering politics.
3. C. Burness (2003), *'Strange Associations': The Irish Question and the Making of Scottish Unionism, 1886–1918*, East Linton: Tuckwell Press, 210.
4. *Scotsman*, 6 December 1912.
5. M. Fry (1991), *Patronage and Principle: A Political History of Modern Scotland*, Aberdeen: Aberdeen University Press, 130.
6. *Scotsman*, 6 December 1912.
7. *Scotsman*, 6 December 1912.
8. Scottish Conservative & Unionist Association Papers, Acc 10424/22, Edinburgh: National Library of Scotland. The minute added that there 'is a crisis in the political world and, on the advice of our leaders, we are joining with the Conservatives, under the common name of "Unionists," believing that the main shock of the battle of Home Rule has yet to come, and that it can best be met and defeated by a solid front'.
9. Acc 10424/10.

SCOTTISH CONSERVATIVE AND UNIONIST PARTIES

10. Both parties were weak: in 1912 there were seven Conservative
MPs and four Liberal Unionists.
11. M. Fry (2013), *A New Race of Men: Scotland 1815–1914*,
Edinburgh: Birlinn, 308.
12. J. G. Kellas (1980), *Modern Scotland* (Revised Edition), London:
George Allen & Unwin, 136–8.
13. C. Kidd (2008), *Union and Unionisms: Political Thought in
Scotland, 1500–2000*, Cambridge: Cambridge University Press, 14.
14. A. Jackson (2012), 'Sociability, status and solidarity: Scottish
Unionism in the era of Irish Home Rule, 1886–1920', in D.
Torrance (ed.), *Whatever Happened to Tory Scotland?*, Edinburgh:
Edinburgh University Press, 18.
15. Scottish Conservative & Unionist Association Papers, Acc
11368/2, Edinburgh: National Library of Scotland.
16. Scottish Conservative & Unionist Association Papers, Acc
10424/10 (iii). Scott Dickson was raised to the bench as Lord
Justice Clerk in 1915.
17. Sir George Younger to Andrew Bonar Law, 6 November 1912,
Bonar Law Papers, BL/27/4/7, London: The Parliamentary
Archives.
18. For more on the 'numerous individual Conservative linkages' connecting Scotland and Ulster, see A. Jackson (2012), 'Sociability,
status and solidarity: Scottish Unionism in the era of Irish Home
Rule, 1886–1920', in D. Torrance (ed.), *Whatever Happened to
Tory Scotland?*, Edinburgh: Edinburgh University Press, 14–28.
19. I. G. C. Hutchison (2001), *Scottish Politics in the Twentieth
Century*, Basingstoke: Palgrave, 18.
20. Scottish Conservative & Unionist Association Papers, Acc
10424/10 (iii).
21. Lord Balfour of Burleigh to Walter Long, 2 February 1907, Walter
Long Papers, Add MS 62411, f70, London: British Library.
22. A. J. Balfour (1913), *Nationality and Home Rule*, London:
Longmans, Green & Co., 9–23.
23. Sir R. Rait (1914), *History of Scotland*, London: Thornton
Butterworth, 239, 243.
24. Memo entitled 'Scottish Home Rule', Bonar Law Papers
BL/32/3/30, London: The Parliamentary Archives. In a covering
letter, Sir George Younger made a point of emphasising that the
memo had 'not in any way been prepared or influenced' by the
Scottish Unionist Whip's Office (then based at St Stephen's House
in Westminster), but was rather 'quite a spontaneous effort on the
part of the Edinburgh people'.
25. Memo entitled 'Scottish Home Rule', Bonar Law Papers
BL/32/3/30.

26. HC Deb 15 May 1914 Vol. 62 c1549.
27. Of the wartime truce, J. T. Ward remarked: 'The trouble with "gentlemen's agreements" (as Tories discovered in both Wars) is that they require "gentlemen" on both sides' (J. T. Ward, 1982, *The First Century*, 25). Leith Burghs had been narrowly gained by a Unionist at a by-election in February 1914.
28. SUA (1914), *Campaign Guide* (Thirteenth Edition), Edinburgh: Scottish Unionist Association, 133–41.
29. C. Kidd (2008), 18.
30. The 1918 Act added women above the age of 30 to the electoral register and increased the number of males entitled to vote by 50 per cent. The Scottish electorate rose from 779,012 at the 1910 election to 2,205,383.
31. C. Harvie (1992), 'Scottish politics', in A. Dickson and J. H. Treble (eds), *People and Society in Scotland Volume III 1914–1990*, Edinburgh: John Donald, 247.
32. I. G. C. Hutchison (2001), 44. Half the Unionist MPs elected in 1918 had military titles compared with one-tenth of Liberal Members.
33. M. Arnott and C. M. M. Macdonald (2012), 'More than a name: The Union and the un-doing of Scottish Conservatism in the 20th Century', in D. Torrance (ed.), *Whatever Happened to Tory Scotland?*, Edinburgh: Edinburgh University Press, 47.
34. A. Jackson (2012), 25. Non-coalition Unionists also won two seats in Scotland.
35. *People's Politics* was suspended for the duration of the First World War, reappeared in 1918 and finally ceased publication in 1921.
36. I. G. C. Hutchison (1998), 'Scottish Unionism between the two World Wars', in C. M. M. Macdonald (ed.), *Unionist Scotland 1800–1997*, Edinburgh: John Donald, 82.
37. I. McLean and A. McMillan (2005), *State of the Union: Unionism and the Alternatives in the United Kingdom since 1707*, Oxford: Oxford University Press, 121.
38. E. A. Cameron (2010), *Impaled Upon a Thistle: Scotland since 1880*, Edinburgh: Edinburgh University Press, 165.
39. M. Fry (2002), *The Scottish Empire*, Edinburgh: Birlinn, 386.
40. J. Vincent (ed.) (1986), *The Crawford Papers: The Journal of David Lindsay, 27th Earl of Crawford and 10th Earl of Balcarres, 1871–1940*, Manchester: Manchester University Press, 455.
41. Scottish Conservative & Unionist Association Papers, Acc 10424/122, Edinburgh: National Library of Scotland. Horne refused to join the incoming Conservative government under Bonar Law.
42. Acc 10424/122.

43. See E. McFarland (2014), 'A Slashing Man of Action': The Life of Lieutenant-General Sir Aylmer Hunter-Weston MP, Oxford: Peter Lang.
44. I. G. C. Hutchison (1986), A Political History of Scotland 1832–1924: Parties, Elections and Issues, Edinburgh: John Donald, 227.
45. C. Burness (2002), 'The making of Scottish Unionism, 1886–1914', in S. Ball and I. Holliday (eds), Mass Conservatism: The Conservatives and the Public since the 1880s, London: Frank Cass, 32.
46. I. G. C. Hutchison (2001), 15.
47. A. Jackson (2012), 15. A Scottish Unionist publication had recently warned that a Scottish Parliament would be led not by Scotsmen 'but a more ignorant type of Irish voter, Lithuanians, and other aliens, working in or about the mines and factories in the industrial areas of the West' (see D. Torrance, 2020, 31–2).
48. G. Warner (1988), The Scottish Tory Party: A History, London: Weidenfeld & Nicolson, 186.
49. Memo dated 21 October 1922, Bonar Law Papers BL/109/1/26a, London: The Parliamentary Archives. Younger appeared unaware that the Marquis of Lothian, a Conservative Scottish Secretary appointed in 1887, had also been Catholic.
50. J. Vincent (1986), 460–1.
51. This was nearly two-thirds of Scottish constituencies, vis-à-vis under a fifth in England. The Solicitor General for Scotland feared that 'Scottish Conservatives could run great risk if they went forward as pure Conservatives' (I. G. C. Hutchison, 1986, 314).
52. I. G. C. Hutchison (1986), 321. The Unionist Whip complained that 'our organisation is often the only organisation'.
53. A. Jackson (2011), The Two Unions: Ireland, Scotland, and the Survival of the United Kingdom, 1707–2007, Oxford: Oxford University Press, 249. Appointed in 1921, Blair remained political secretary for a remarkable 39 years. J. T. Ward recalled 'an outstanding character, a dedicated organiser who could also deliver a major speech or write policy documents' (J. T. Ward, 1982, 29).
54. J. Vincent (1986), 487.
55. D. Torrance (2006), The Scottish Secretaries, Edinburgh: Birlinn, 100.
56. I. G. C. Hutchison (1986), 322.
57. SUA Central Council report for 1922–3, Scottish Conservative & Unionist Association Papers, Acc 11368/77, Edinburgh: National Library of Scotland.

58. C. Cook (1975), *The Age of Alignment*, London: Macmillan, 131. The issue of tariff reform prevented any such arrangement.
59. For an account of the campaign, see R. Rhodes James (1991), *Bob Boothby: A Portrait*, London: Hodder & Stoughton, 50–4.
60. I. G. C. Hutchison (1986), 322.

4

Unionist Scotland:
1924–1945

During the 1920s 'it devolved upon the Scottish Tories, hitherto a small band without many personalities or traditions or indeed much hope, to provide the main opposition to the Socialists'. Writing in 1957, Sir Robert Boothby judged that:

> On the whole they succeeded remarkably well; and this was largely due to the enthusiasm and unquestioned brilliance of a great political teacher, the late Noel Skelton. Sir Robert Home, as the effective spokesman of big business, and Walter Elliot with his diversified interests, ministerial preoccupations and doubtful political antecedents – had he not been a Socialist at Glasgow University? ... Fortified by the pawky humour of Fred Macquisten – a 'card' if ever there was one – the Scottish Unionists put up a good show in the Twenties; and held their own, better than their English colleagues, in the General Election of 1929.[1]

Part of their contribution was intellectual. Not only did the Duchess of Atholl's *Women and Politics* and Walter Elliot's *Toryism and the Twentieth Century* ensure that 'Conservatism between the wars was British rather than English',[2] but Noel Skelton, an advocate and the Unionist MP for Perth, provided the English and Scottish parties with a lively political philosophy: the pursuit of a 'property-owning democracy', the division of land into smallholdings, co-partnership in industry and the use of referendums to resolve constitutional disputes. Originally columns for the *Spectator*, these were published in January 1924 as *Constructive Conservatism*, a pamphlet which had a lasting impact on three future premiers: Sir Anthony Eden, Harold Macmillan and Sir Alec Douglas-Home. Skelton's strategic goal was to coax Unionists (and Conservatives) into competing with the Labour Party on its own terms.[3]

The timing was prescient given the minority government, Labour's first, formed in early 1924. The ministry was a curious mix of working-class socialists, aristocratic Liberals and even a Scottish Unionist Lord Advocate.[4] But the experience of – and indeed the fear generated by – the mere existence of a Labour government proved the catalyst required for Scottish Unionists to become a truly 'national' party. Between 1923 and 1924, the SUA Central Council had been 'glad' to report 'a general and marked improvement throughout the whole country, not only in organisation, but in general activity and in the spirit of members of the Unionist Party'.[5] And having capitalised on the circumstances of Ramsay MacDonald's fall – including fears of a communist plot – at the end of 1924 Stanley Baldwin was returned to office with a landslide majority of 223 and, for once, a gratifying result in Scotland: Scottish Unionists won 36 seats, 22 more than in 1923, their best result since 1900.

Labour, despite also increasing its share of the vote, was pushed into second place north of the border. Unionists took around a dozen seats from each of their main rivals (the Liberals had recently reunified, although were wiped out beyond the Highlands). Even in Glasgow, as the *Daily Record and Mail* reported, Unionists had gained two seats from Labour, thus removing 'its unenviable reputation as "The Red City"'.[6] Fittingly, a former woodturner called Willie Templeton was returned as a Unionist MP in Banffshire,[7] one of only four working-class Unionist candidates despite the Scottish Unionist Association having resolved in 1922 to field more.[8] Of the 36 Unionists elected, 11 were lawyers, eight landowners, nine service officers and seven businessmen. They were also 'more firmly rooted in Scottish society than the Liberals': seven of the 12 1924 burgh Unionists had attended a Scottish university while nine of the 11 lawyers practised in Scotland.[9]

Baldwin's decision to abandon the policy of Protection had enabled Unionists to capture middle-class votes in the West of Scotland, something also aided by the final demise of the Liberals as a party of government (a Unionist had defeated Asquith in Paisley). Robert Boothby's East Aberdeenshire constituency, for example, was 'not really a Conservative seat' but rather 'a curious and unique mixture of relaxed Scottish nationalism, local pride, liberalism, and the type of Conservatism that regards change with deep suspicion'.[10] Liberal Scotland had been tamed and co-opted; the inter-war years would instead represent Unionist Scotland.

Stanley Baldwin cited the party's showing in Scotland as one of several reasons for not reappointing Viscount Novar as Scottish Secretary:

> You were so acceptable to Scotland and such a loyal colleague that my regret was intensified on personal grounds. But I have always felt it a weakness not to have the Scottish Secretary in the Commons and after the popular verdict in Scotland I regard it as more than ever essential. You will believe me when I say that Cabinet making is the most difficult, troublesome, and painful task to which man is called to put his hand.[11]

Novar did not believe a word of it, scrawling on Baldwin's letter (for the benefit of Lord Rosebery, an old Liberal ally): 'This is weak but his best line of argument.' He responded formally, and more contritely, on 12 November 1922:

> I only joined the Conservative Party in 1922 and I did so then because I thought the safety of the country was at stake and that everyone should back Mr. Bonar Law and you in your efforts to bring the Coalition to an end and to keep out the Socialists. Your reference to 'loyalty' is welcome as showing that you understand my opposition to Protection and to the Dissolution of 1923 ... I recognise that my original nomination was due to the friendship of Mr. Bonar Law and not to party claims. It was an interesting episode and I have every confidence that my successor will carry out many of the reforms I had hoped to initiate, but which had to be deferred on account of our weakness, last year, on the Scotch Grand Committee.[12]

Novar's successor was to be Sir John Gilmour, the 48-year-old second baronet of Montrave who had declined office two years earlier.[13] He was to become one of the most substantial Scottish Unionist politicians of the inter-war period, a 'ginger-headed soldier', noted the Earl of Crawford, 'who will be most useful'.[14] It helped that Gilmour sat for what was now said to be the safest Unionist seat in Scotland, the Pollok Division of Glasgow, a constituency he had won in 1918 and held until his death in 1940. This in itself demonstrated the party's new electoral vitality, while Gilmour's restoration to the government benches was a sign Baldwin intended to heal old wounds between coalitionists (such as Gilmour) and those responsible for the 1922 Carlton Club rebellion. With a Scottish mother and an English father, Baldwin himself proved adept at presenting himself as a truly 'British' premier. In 1928 he narrowly beat the Scottish nationalist Robert Cunningham Grahame to the rectorship of Glasgow University, claiming that 'the things that make Scottish Nationalists anxious are matters in which they have my full sympathy'[15]

Another feature of the inter-war Scottish Unionist Party was its moderation. Most Unionist MPs were now drawn from the party's liberal wing, with only a few (Fred Macquisten, Thomas Moore and Archibald Maule Ramsay) constituting 'die-hards'.[16] Hutchison has identified housing as 'the centrepiece of the Unionists' progressive policy programme' during this period.[17] As Scottish Secretary, Sir John Gilmour championed housing subsidies and established the Second Scottish National Housing Company, which was tasked with building 2,500 new homes. A scheme involving cheap steel-framed houses provided by the Scottish industrialist Lord Weir, however, foundered upon trade union opposition. In August 1927, Gilmour issued a state-of-the-nation press release, boasting that while in 1924 only 4,000 houses had been built, that figure had increased to almost 13,000 in 1926, with an expected total of up to 17,000 in 1927. Rosslyn Mitchell, a Labour MP, even lauded Gilmour. 'Your actions so little resemble the Toryism of my youth', he told the Scottish Secretary, 'I believe the rigidity of party lines is slackening.'[18]

The adoption of an interventionist approach was central to the Scottish Unionist appeal, not only because it allowed the party to reassure middle-class Liberals that Conservatives (at least in Scotland) were not reactionaries but because it could appeal to working-class voters or 'underdogs', one of its main objects being 'to raise the standard of life of the people'.[19] Finlay has argued that this equipped the Unionists with structural appeal:

> First, the highly individualistic nature of many of the skilled working class may have felt equally at home in the Conservative fold as with Labour, whose collectivism went against this fundamental tenet. Second, maintaining the skills hierarchy, especially in heavy industries, may have encouraged some workers to adopt a traditional and therefore Conservative political outlook. Third, the small-scale unit of production may have helped notions of paternalism to survive.

Fourth, the development of large-scale trade unions that predominantly represented the unskilled and semi-skilled workers may have been seen as a threat to traditional skill and craft differentials.[20]

To Hutchison, the transformation of Scottish Unionists from the 'bedraggled rump of pre-war Scotland into the ascendant party between the wars' owed much to its success in policy matters and in 'reacting adroitly to social processes'.[21]

Conscious that quality of life was not the only source of political appeal, in 1926 Stanley Baldwin elevated the Secretary for Scotland to one of His Majesty's principal Secretaries of State after years of lobbying from what would later be called 'civic Scotland'. In return, Baldwin was presented with the Freedom of Edinburgh and hailed as 'the man of the hour' as a result of his handling of the General Strike.[22] The Prime Minister did not waste an opportunity to big up Scottish Conservatism. 'I think you could not get five more typical and better men in their several walks from Scotland than now occupy the five posts in the Government peculiarly connected with Scotland,' he told a crowd of 1,500 at Edinburgh's McEwan Hall, 'and I am glad it has fallen to me to introduce into Parliament that Bill which will convert my old friend Sir John Gilmour into a Secretary of State.'[23] Walter Elliot, who was upgraded to under-secretary of state at the Scottish Office, praised the government for granting Scotland 'a status unknown since the '45'.[24]

Such sentiment reflected the growing confidence of Scottish Unionism, not least its easy congruence with the Scottish nation, a connection which had not existed for most of the 19th century. Hutchison regarded the 'two master strokes' of Unionist organisation as laying in its 'mobilisation of women and young people'.[25] The first 'All Scotland's Women's Conference' on 22 October 1926 was 'a gratifying success'.[26] The Duchess of Atholl had become the first female Conservative minister in 1924[27] and in 1928, when the Unionist MP and former Scottish Office minister James Kidd died, the party nominated his daughter Margaret to succeed him, although despite 'a strenuous contest' the seat fell to Labour.[28] When the *Representation of the People (Equal Franchise) Act 1928* granted women electoral equality with men, the SUA's Central Council warned that there existed 'no moral excuse for those who set themselves against its authority'.[29] The Eastern Division Council also reported that three 'ladies, who wish to take up politics as a profession' were receiving 'instruction' from Central Office in 'the practical work of organisation' as well as 'general political knowledge'.[30] Lady Findlay of Aberlour, whose husband Sir John was proprietor of the Unionist-supporting *Scotsman*, was in 1927 elected president of the Scottish Unionist Association, the first woman to hold the office.[31] At the 1931 general election, meanwhile, two more female Unionist MPs joined Atholl in the Commons – Florence Horsbrugh in Dundee and Helen Shaw in Bothwell.[32]

Unionists also cultivated the working class – the Workers League was a strong organisation 'with lodges in many parts of the country supplying Party workers, speakers and canvassers'[33] – and especially future voters. By 1929 there were around 90 Junior Unionist Association branches in the East of Scotland with some 7,000 members. It was particularly active during the 1930s (like the SUA, it had two divisions, East and West). In 1933 the Edinburgh University Unionist Association affiliated to the SUA, followed by Aberdeen University in November 1934, while the party would also make a point of 'running young men, men in their early twenties who have either private means or else unusual merit in scholarship or athletics, as Parliamentary candidates'.[34] The Junior Imperialist Union also held its inaugural meeting in Edinburgh during April 1933, although it later ditched the word 'Imperialist', it having become 'for many people a connotation with a somewhat sinister meaning' and 'far from the views and principles of the Unionist Party with regard to the "Empire"'.[35]

But as Fry has observed, the party 'was Unionist because it was imperialist; it was imperialist because its prosperity was bound up with Empire.'[36] But it went much deeper. During the 1920s Scottish Unionism 'thrived by cultivating Scottish institutions, administrative devolution, and making patriotic appeals within the wider framework of union'.[37] The three interlocking strands of Unionism – Scottish, British and Imperial – were repeatedly emphasised (Finlay thought 'locality' might be a fourth[38]), meaning it rather than Labour or the Liberals 'had probably the best claim to be a nationwide party'.[39] Underpinning this was the visibility of Scottish Unionist figures on the UK and Imperial stages. Several served as UK party chairman: Sir Arthur Steel-Maitland (1911–17), George Younger (1917–23), J. C. C. Davidson (1926–30) and John Baird (1931–40).

There had also been a short-lived Prime Minister (Andrew Bonar Law), a Chancellor of the Exchequer (Sir Robert Horne), a Home Secretary (Sir John Gilmour), two Agriculture ministers (Gilmour and Walter Elliot) and one Health Secretary (Elliot). When Sir Lewis Shedden retired following half a century as secretary of the Glasgow Unionist Association, it was noted with pride that he had served under '11 Prime Ministers – five of them Scotsmen, and two of them businessmen from our own midst in Glasgow'.[40]

The party's Scottishness was jealously guarded. The 1929 Scottish Unionist Association conference resolved that the use of the word 'Conservative' was 'injurious to the interests' of the Scottish party and agreed with Lord Balfour that the word 'Unionist' expressed better the things in which we 'most passionately believe'.[41] Balfour had stated in 1927 that he preferred the expression Unionist 'partly because so much of my life was spent in attempting to preserve in its full sense the union with Ireland' and partly because a 'very large fraction of the future felicity of the world depends upon the union of classes within the Empire'.[42] But while SUA conferences of the 1920s were 'democratic enough', they were also 'overwhelmingly middle-class through being held on working days and given to dim "debates" on obsequious motions'.[43]

There was also organisational instability. Senior Agents had departed in 1923 and 1924, while Sir Leith MacLachlan turned out to be 'obstructive ... particularly bad at organising the women's vote' and 'most unpopular'. Only in 1928 did Robert Topping, the last principal agent, bring some consistency.[44] Hutchison cautioned against placing too much emphasis on superior organisation when it came to explaining the inter-war success of Scottish Unionism. The existence of a paid organiser was 'not a necessary prerequisite for political success'. The Cathcart Unionists, for example, managed to retain a seat gained in 1922 despite not having a paid organiser until 1926.[45]

The Scottish Unionist Members Committee (SUMC) was constituted in March 1932, a sort of party within the Westminster Conservative caucus. A 'well-disciplined body, which was taken seriously by ministers', it 'served as a buffer between government and a wide range of Scottish interests'.[46] Philip Norton regarded it as a 'national' rather than 'regional' committee of the Conservative Parliamentary Party,[47] and indeed it regularly clashed with the voluntary wing in Scotland (the SUA). The existence of the SUMC also provided a stepping stone to the party's UK-wide 1922 Committee. During the Second World War, two Scottish Unionists (Alexander Erskine-Hill and John McEwen) were elected chairman of the influential backbench committee, whose executive also included Allan Chapman and Sir Douglas Thomson.[48]

Sir John Gilmour, meanwhile, embarked upon a long-overdue modernisation of the machinery of government in Edinburgh, a city punctuated with a myriad of boards, commissions and offices, many of them lacking any ministerial oversight. The innocuous-sounding Reorganisation of Offices (Scotland) Bill, however, sparked a backlash from Labour and Liberal MPs who were also intent on 'standing up for Scotland'. When they accused the Scottish Secretary of substituting English civil servants for Scottish autonomy, Gilmour retreated, withdrawing the Bill and reintroducing it the following year with a more patriotic emphasis. He also announced plans for what would become St Andrew's House in Edinburgh, a modernist consolidated home for modern Scottish administration.

The consolidation of local government in Scotland also proved controversial. This was a Unionist-free zone, with 'anti-socialist' voters instead backing 'moderate' or 'progressive' candidates in an inefficient panoply of 869 parish councils, 201 town councils, 98 district councils, 37 education authorities, 33 county councils and 27 district boards of control.[49] Gilmour proposed abolishing parish and district councils, education authorities and the district boards of control, their functions absorbed by reconstituted county councils. Although he anticipated strenuous opposition from the soon-to-be ex-authorities, Sir John concluded a Cabinet memo with the observation that the 'results in the selected counties' would also be 'satisfactory from a ratepayer's point of view'.[50] Not all Unionist MPs agreed. Noel Skelton, whose father had served as vice-president of the Local Government Board for Scotland, was a vehement critic, while Sir Henry Keith even claimed the reforms violated the 1707 Treaty of Union.[51]

Certain Orangemen also took 'strong exception' to the proposals, particularly those concerning 'the co-option of members to local bodies on religious grounds and to the abolition of elective parish councils'. Having been 'among the most prominent supporters of Unionist or Conservative candidates' in the past, 'in pursuance of their principles and out of loyalty to the Union', the Grand Lodge issued a warning: 'If the Unionist Government wants the support of the Catholics, then let them have it, but they cannot have the support of both Catholics and Protestants – and Scotland is still a Protestant country.'[52] Indeed, despite the SUA having long kept such concerns at a safe political distance, many leading Unionists were active Orangemen, including Sir Charles Cleland of the Glasgow Unionist Association, the MP Archibald McInnes Shaw (grand master of the Order in Scotland) and Sir John Gilmour, Scottish Secretary between 1924 and 1929.[53]

So, when Cardinal Bourne, the Archbishop of Westminster, made anti-socialist statements shortly before the general election of 1929, Scottish Unionists distributed a leaflet with quotes from Bourne 'at all Chapels and places where the Catholics congregate'. 'I think it would be quite useful,' suggested Sir Patrick Ford, 'particularly in the West of Scotland.' This activity was to a degree covert, the Scottish Unionist organiser Lewis Shedden suggesting a poster 'be displayed and distributed judiciously and anonymously where there is a substantial Roman Catholic population'. In response, the Labour Party claimed the material was a forgery, while the *Glasgow Observer and Catholic Herald* railed against the Unionist candidate in North Lanark, Lord Scone, who was associated with the Scottish Protestant League.[54] Indeed, Scone had told the House of Commons that there was 'in the west of Scotland a completely separate race of alien origin'.[55] Catholic Unionist candidates were rare, although Maurice Bloch, a prominent businessman and vice-president of the Glasgow Unionist Association, would contest the Gorbals constituency in 1929 and again in 1931 and 1935, on every occasion without success.

The party's secular activity varied, in the words of J. T. Ward, from

> grand fetes to hear prominent politicians to humble tea or coffee parties and whist drives, from earnest debates to trips 'doon the water'; from grand balls to youthful 'hops', from Ayr's 12-guinea jaunts to Paris to street-corner 'shows' by the 'Unionist Cinema Talkie Van', or 'magic lantern' demonstrations in Glasgow by Andrew Strang and Commander Harvey of the Navy League. And there were Empire Day marches and musical evenings, with jazz performers or Anniesland's 'Temple Unionist Band'.[56]

'Cinema vans' were particularly popular, used to bring Unionist propaganda to a wider audience; a May 1929 speech by Winston Churchill was even 'relayed' from Glasgow's St Andrew's Hall to eight different locations around Scotland. The printed press also aided the Unionist cause, but with a string of recent by-election defeats having hinted at growing Labour strength in Scotland, the 1929 election saw Unionists lose a substantial 16 seats. Labour once again formed a minority government.

The economic backdrop of the late 1920s, particularly in industrial parts of Britain such as Scotland, had contributed, while Sir John Gilmour's administrative reforms had stirred up considerable resentment (although his majority in Pollok actually increased). A paper later prepared by the Scottish Unionist Whip's office blamed 'misrepresentation' of the *Local Government (Scotland) Act 1929* for losing a considerable number of votes in several constituencies. More broadly, the memo also criticised the lack of a 'definite and attractive future policy' which could be grasped by the Scottish electorate.[57] At least, noted the SUA's Central Council, Scotland had 'not been subject to the violent fluctuations which took place south of the Tweed'.[58] To Mitchell, the party had peaked in 1924 'by default' and had failed 'to consolidate their position by stressing any peculiarly Scottish dimension to their platform'.[59]

Between 1929 and 1931, Scottish Unionists reaffirmed their rejection of 'Conservative' nomenclature as 'injurious to the interests of the party'[60] and immersed themselves in intensive campaigning activity.[61] Stanley Baldwin addressed a large meeting at Edinburgh's Usher Hall, while each month 20,000 copies of the *Scottish Unionist*, issued jointly by the EDC and WDC, were circulated throughout Scotland. This had folded by 1930 due to dwindling interest and was replaced in 1935 by *Scotland Illustrated*, which as its title suggested eschewed political content for attractive photographs.

In the late 1920s the Western Divisional Council had sent delegates to the English (and Welsh) National Union of Conservative and Unionist Associations (NUCUA) conference for the first time, while by 1931 this had been augmented by non-voting Scottish representatives on the National Union's Executive and Central Council (the Ulster Unionists in Northern Ireland had similar representation). 'These arrangements are welcomed as providing a means of liaison and co-operation between the Party's Organisations in Scotland and in England,' noted the 1931 SUA Central Council report,[62] although in reality it represented 'a compromise between those who wanted a complete merger and those who wanted no contact at all'.[63] Nevertheless, it is striking the degree to which the Scottish party viewed itself as a completely separate organisation; one report even referred to 'the English Conference' taking place in Birmingham in October 1933. For the first time since the war, meanwhile, Scottish Unionist finances were volatile. In the late 1920s, the WDC reported a 'falling off instead of an increase in the year's income', while by 1931 its books were only balanced due to assistance from 'some good friends of the Party'.[64] Yet as Hutchison has observed, this instability came as the party reached even greater electoral heights.[65]

While the formation of a 'National' government in 1931 'blurred distinctions' on the centre-right and brought National Liberals into the arms of the Unionists[66] – 'National' Unionists won an unprecedented 48 seats in the October election that followed[67] – Liberal MPs were still appointed Secretary of State for Scotland, something which irritated ambitious Unionist MPs in a way it had not a decade earlier. The writer and Combined Scottish Universities MP John Buchan regarded the appointment of the publisher Sir Godfrey Collins in 1932 as 'simply preposterous' and wrote to Stanley Baldwin in rather desperate terms:

> I do not speak overmuch in the House – there is no need for it – but I do a great deal of speaking up and down the country, especially in Scotland, where I think I have a good deal of influence. Politics have always been my chief interest, and I have a good deal of administrative experience ... and, as you know, I can work pretty hard. So I would like to be considered when posts are being filled, for I am no longer as young as I was, and I want to do some useful public work before the Guard comes to take the tickets.[68]

Buchan would play a part in a new fault line within Scottish Unionism, between proponents of 'administrative' and 'legislative' devolution.[69] Prominent in this respect was the advocate Andrew Dewar Gibb, who as a Unionist had contested seats at the general elections of 1924 and 1929. A strong legal nationalist, his 1928 SUA conference resolution on 'the increasing provincialization of Scotland' had been rejected by the party leadership, although Buchan agreed with Dewar Gibb that

Unionists ought to support 'what is sane in the Nationalist movement'.[70] The SUA's political secretary, Colonel Patrick Blair, even rebuked Dewar Gibb for his interest in Scotland's economic decline, saying such questions lay outside the party's purview.[71]

Dewar Gibb also lobbied Stanley Baldwin, urging him to recognise 'the new spirit alive in Scotland' with a 'definite Conservative policy for Scotland' (he suggested a Royal Commission on the constitution), something he believed would benefit both Scotland and the Scottish Unionist Party. His book, *Scotland in Eclipse*, caught the zeitgeist and the *Daily Telegraph* observed that the author saw 'nothing incompatible in a blending of stout Scots nationalism, on fresh, statutory, but resourceful lines, and British Conservatism'.[72] *Scotland in Eclipse* also argued that Scotland's place in the Empire had been compromised by her subordinate status within the UK, a radical break with mainstream Scottish Unionist thought. Dewar Gibb and the polemical journalist George Malcolm Thomson instead argued for a Habsburg-style 'dual monarchy' in which Scotland would assume its rightful place in the Imperial metropole.[73]

Following the logic of such arguments, Dewar Gibb and Thomson joined the new Scottish (Self-Government) Party, which was intended as a counterpoint to the more left-wing National Party of Scotland and mainly comprised former Unionists. There were other straws in the wind. Shortly before the 1931 general election, the popular writer and Nationalist Compton Mackenzie had beaten the Scottish Unionist grandee (and former Chancellor) Sir Robert Horne to become Lord Rector of Glasgow University. This kept discussion of Home Rule firmly on the political agenda, to the extent that at the beginning of 1932 Stanley Baldwin, now Lord President and *de facto* Prime Minister given Conservative dominance of the National Government led by Ramsay MacDonald, felt it necessary explicitly to rule out a Home Rule Bill, there being no evidence 'that the creation of small units makes for the prosperity of the world'.[74]

In the spring of 1932 the Scottish Unionist Whip's Office produced a pamphlet entitled, simply, *Scottish Nationalism*. This drew heavily upon previously published material from the 1920s but was notable for referring to 'Independence' rather than 'Home Rule', just as 'Separatist' would shortly replace

'Nationalist' in Scottish Unionist discourse. Its central thesis was the by now familiar defence of Scottish distinctiveness and an attempt to hedge constitutional bets: 'The necessity for further devolution may become a practical question, and Scottish Unionists would not refuse to consider the matter carefully; but any scheme hitherto proposed contains more disadvantages than gains for Scotland.'[75]

In June 1932, however, the 'large and prosperous' Glasgow Cathcart Unionist Association 'suddenly severed its connection with the Tory Party and declared that it stood for Scottish Home Rule and Imperial Federation'.[76] The 'Imperial Committee of the Unionist Association of Cathcart' even issued a manifesto, emblazoned with a Union Jack, saltire and lion rampant. It declared that measures of 'Dominion government' for Scotland, England and Wales were 'essential for the better government' of those nations and the Empire, as well as 'to realise the Aspirations and preserve the Characteristics of the Scottish Nation'. The Scottish Unionist Association's response was 'swift ... well organised and decisive', with three important meetings contrived to isolate the association and minimise the political fallout.[77] Fifteen Glasgow Unionist associations, meanwhile, condemned Cathcart's 'divisive, disloyal and unconstitutional procedure'.[78]

Nevertheless, the Cathcart secession clearly worried the Scottish Unionist leadership, not least because the sentiment was 'emanating from traditional middle-class quarters', something reinforced by the media, intellectuals and businessmen who had noticed a widening economic gap between Scotland and England. Lord Beaverbrook's *Scottish Daily Express* even said it 'should be the ultimate intention to capture the Unionist Party for the home rule project'.[79] The party, therefore, began to refashion its Unionist ideology to 'acknowledge the legitimacy of nationalist sentiment' but 'without encouraging political separatism'.[80] This included a day-long Commons debate on Scottish affairs – during which John Buchan boldly declared that 'every Scotsman should be a Scottish Nationalist'[81] – and the book *A Scotsman's Heritage*, a sort of Scottish Unionist manifesto published in 1932 as a response to Andrew Dewar Gibb's polemical tracts. Contributors included Lord Macmillan on the superiority of Scots law, and Walter Elliot, who praised the Church of Scotland as *the* 'national' institution.[82]

The *Church of Scotland Act 1921* had formalised the independence of the Kirk and thus laid a legislative path to its 1929 reunion with the United Free Church, after which the divisions which had once coloured 19th-century Scottish politics receded. Some Unionists even dreamed of unifying the Church of Scotland with the Anglican Church of England.[83] As ever, the Unionist leadership kept its distance from more extreme Protestant elements. When Kirk and United Free Church leaders lobbied the Scottish and Home secretaries regarding Irish immigration, they were curtly informed that official figures showed this to have declined significantly since the 19th century. Not only that, but Irish families were in receipt of considerably fewer public relief funds than native Scots.[84]

Some of this religious prejudice was carried by Unionist supporters of legislative devolution into the new Scottish National Party (SNP) formed in 1934, although some – such as the prolific writer James A. A. Porteous – continued to try and nudge the Scottish Unionist Association in a devolutionary direction. His lengthy 1935 book *The New Unionism* urged his colleagues to reach a 'compromise with separatism where National and Imperial interests require that course'.[85] Another notable rebel was James Graham, the 6th Duke of Montrose, who somehow managed to retain the Conservative whip in the House of Lords despite being a founder member of the SNP. 'No lasting good in my opinion can result until we are granted decentralized government, with a Legislature in Scotland,' he wrote to Lord Halifax, the Conservative leader in the Upper House. 'I have endeavoured for a long time to interest the Unionist Party in this question; but have met with nothing but opposition.'[86] James Kellas, meanwhile, noted 'a curious tinge of Scottish nationalism' in Scotland's 16 representative peers, who continued to be 'elected' from among the Scottish peerage during a picturesque ceremony at the Palace of Holyroodhouse concurrently with each general election.[87]

But as Matthew Cragoe has observed, with 'an apparently sound administrative structure in place, and a membership that, on paper at least, was numbered in the tens of thousands, the Tories encountered nationalism from a position of some strength in the 1930s'.[88] At the general election of 1935, National Unionists (supporters of the National Government) won 35 seats in Scotland, with closely aligned National Liberal candidates gaining seven. A Unionist even gained Orkney and Shetland for the first time since 1900.[89] Growing Unionist strength meant that when the Liberal Scottish Secretary Sir Godfrey Collins died in late 1936, a Conservative could once again be appointed Secretary of State. Indeed, Unionists refused to accept either of the candidates offered by the Liberals in the subsequent Greenock by-election and insisted on fielding a 'National' candidate of their own. Amid this disharmony, Labour won the seat on a swing of 7.5 per cent.[90]

The Scottish Office, meanwhile, was filled by Walter Elliot, hitherto Minister for Agriculture and a popular under-secretary at Dover House. As Secretary of State, he built upon the moderate policies he and Sir John Gilmour had pursued in the 1920s, not only in terms of housebuilding but also growing industrial intervention.[91] Elliot announced a long-expected inquiry into Scottish governance under the chairmanship of Sir John, who had recently served as Home Secretary. The 'Gilmour Committee' reported in October 1937 and proposed four new departments – Agriculture, Health, Education and 'Scottish Home' – to be headed by civil servants and based at the soon-to-be-constructed St Andrew's House.

In a Cabinet memo, Elliot cautioned against magic bullets, warning that Gilmour's proposals

> will not in themselves dispose of the problems upon whose solution a general improvement in Scottish social and economic conditions depends. It is the consciousness of their existence which is reflected, not in the small and unimportant Nationalist Party, but in the dissatisfaction and unease amongst moderate and reasonable people of every rank.[92]

Elliot was, like many Unionist MPs, a cultural nationalist. In March 1937 he and Lady Elgin cut the first sod at Bellahouston Park in Glasgow for what was to become the Empire Exhibition of 1938: an ostentatious expression of Scotland's achievements within a UK and Imperial context. Elliot also showed his commitment to Scotland's heritage by introducing a Bill to improve the upkeep of historical records and allow for the return of documents 'borrowed' by England centuries before.[93]

By early 1938, Elliot was increasingly concerned about developments on the Continent, but while he considered resignation he was instead promoted to the Ministry of Health in a May

Cabinet reshuffle. In Kinross and West Perthshire, meanwhile, the Duchess of Atholl's Unionist association had become weary of the 'Red Duchess', a sobriquet acquired on account of her support for Republicans in the Spanish Civil War,[94] and deselected her in 1938. She fought the subsequent December by-election on an independent Unionist anti-appeasement ticket with the support of Winston Churchill (for which he was strongly rebuked) but lost to William McNair Snadden, a local farmer.[95]

Walter Elliot was succeeded by industrialist David John Colville, a Unionist steelmaker who would steer the Scottish Office into the Second World War and a new decade. He was also the first Secretary of State to occupy St Andrew's House, which opened on the eve of the conflict. Although it was not clear at the time, administrative devolution had come to maintain 'the rationale of the home rule case', for if Scotland, asked Kellas, 'deserved so much administrative devolution, how could legislative devolution be denied, with a democratically elected body in Scotland to hold the Scottish Office to account?'[96] Unionist Northern Ireland, after all, had the bicameral Stormont parliament.

Thus, Scottish Unionists unwittingly encouraged a 'ratchet-like effect' within the territorial constitution of the United Kingdom. They might have believed they had successfully fixed, to paraphrase Charles Stewart Parnell, the 'boundary' of the Scottish nation, which was to be administrative and no further, but in fact they had helped unleash political forces which occasionally looked beyond their control.

With the outbreak of war in 1939, the SUA's Western Divisional Council 'resolved to suspend all purely party activities ... and to divert the energies of the Organisation to useful forms of war work'.[97] The 1939 Scottish Unionist Association conference was also cancelled and did not take place again until 1942. During this political 'truce', by-elections were meant to be uncontested, although the SNP ignored this convention. Nevertheless, in Argyll in 1940 Major Duncan McCallum scored 'a fine victory over a Scottish National opponent who had the support of various anti-Government forces, both inside and outside the constituency'.[98] Between 1914 and 1918 the Unionist organisation had been 'given official tasks which served to some extent to preserve its framework' but, crucially, there was to be no such arrangement in 1939.[99]

The war also prompted a *mea culpa* from Colin Thornton-Kemsley, who had held Kincardine and Western Aberdeenshire after the incumbent, Malcolm Barclay-Harvey, was appointed Governor of South Australia. A Neville Chamberlain loyalist who had engineered a vote of censure against Winston Churchill by the Epping Conservative Association, he apologised at the outbreak of hostilities. 'I certainly think that Englishmen ought to start fair with one another from the outset in so grievous a struggle,' was Churchill's response, 'and so far as I am concerned the past is dead.'[100] Less apologetic was the proto-fascist Captain Archibald Maule Ramsay, the Unionist MP for Peebles and Southern Midlothian, who was interred in 1940 but allowed to resume his Commons seat after being released in September 1944.[101] He was deselected by his constituency and did not attempt to contest the 1945 election.[102]

In 1941, meanwhile, the Scottish Unionist Association established a 'Reconstruction Committee' in order to prepare its post-war programme.[103] When it came to the social reforms under consideration by the Liberal MP Sir William Beveridge, most Scottish Unionists simply advocated a return to the pre-war status quo, with three of the seven members of the Progress Trust, formed in opposition to Beveridge's proposals, being Scottish Unionist MPs.[104] The Renfrewshire West MP, Henry Scrymgeour-Wedderburn, was the only Scottish member of the radical backbench Tory Reform Committee. A minute recorded him observing that all political parties would have to discard some of their former political prejudices in order to promote the spirit of goodwill and co-operation which would be essential if the immense post-war problems of reconstruction were to be successfully tackled. He envisaged a planned economy, involving some measure of continuation of wartime controls. It was the lack of foresight in this matter of planning, he believed, which was responsible for many of the troubles which arose after the last war.[105]

Despite this division of opinion, by 1944 the Western Divisional Council maintained that the party's 'past record of achievement in the field of social reform is a guarantee that it will not be behind in post-war efforts to ameliorate the conditions of the people'.[106]

At a bad-tempered meeting of the SUA's Central Council in February 1942, several Unionists expressed concerns that the party's lack of policies was making it electorally vulnerable. F. C. Watt warned that if the Unionist Party did not put 'its house in order with a view to reconstruction' then 'we would sooner or later have to face the country without any policy at all ... we were going to face a Labour Party saying "Look what we did for you!"'. Sir William Maxwell agreed that 'too little attention had been given to the larger question of formulating a policy on such matters as Highlands and Islands, housing, religious education, etc'.

These fears competed with long-standing concerns regarding party organisation, several associations having 'dwindled to skeleton proportions during the war period'.[107] Major E. G. R. Lloyd believed Unionists 'had interpreted the party truce much too narrowly' and to their 'great disadvantage':

> We had assumed that we must not hold no meetings in constituencies, and consequently the whole Party was ceasing almost entirely to function ... We had been leaving it all to the Prime Minister ... People were asking why should they be interested in the Unionist Party if they had not got a programme. We must therefore have a programme for post-war years, and something must be done to stimulate interest in the Unionist Party and its organisation.

One activist pointed out that this was not a new problem – 'Unionist organisation was not efficient before the war' – while Sir Douglas Thomson (MP for Aberdeen South) claimed provocatively that the party was 'living in an absurd world of appeasement', a reference to a general feeling 'among Unionists that they were being ousted'. Alexander Erskine-Hill (Edinburgh North) reminded those present that the Scottish Office comprised 'all Socialists' and, naturally, 'they preferred their own friends' when it came to public appointments.[108] 'In all the Committees and Commissions appointed since the war,' claimed the SUA chairman, 'Unionists had been studiously avoided', the constitution of a Hospitals Committee having caused particular resentment. 'We might be caught napping,' concluded Sir Douglas Thomson. 'The Party might well be defeated at the next Election, and this might, or might not, be a bad thing.'[109]

Two years later, the WDC complained of having 'lost some of our most experienced Organising Secretaries',[110] something that clearly concerned the party leadership 'in view of the possibility of a General Election within a year':

It cannot be too much impressed upon those responsible for maintaining the Party organisation that on the strength of the Unionist Party depend the safety and welfare of Great Britain and of the British Empire. All in the Party organisation must co-operate together; there can be no opposing interests of east and west, of men and women, of seniors and juniors, of central offices and constituency associations – all are working together for the Unionist Party in Scotland, and this is work of which they may well be proud.[111]

The WDC believed the main responsibility for 'restoring confidence must rest with the leaders of the Party and Members of Parliament': 'It will not be done by placating opponents at the expense of supporters. Such a policy can be carried too far, even in the name of national unity.'[112]

Adding to Scottish Unionist woes was rising nationalist sentiment, something obvious from the SNP's showing in a succession of wartime by-elections. The SUA's John Cranna wrote to the Scottish Unionist Members Committee to express concern at the hitherto Unionist-supporting *Bulletin* having 'taken up the cause of the Scottish Nationalists'. 'Our Propaganda Committee considers that its attitude is harmful to our interests,' he added. 'Coming from the stable it does, we should expect otherwise, and would like to do something about it.'[113] The SUMC asked Colonel Blair, the SUA's political secretary since 1922, to prepare a new pamphlet enabling MPs 'to deal with Nationalist points when they arose'.[114] This was prescient, for on 12 April 1945 Dr Robert D. McIntyre became the first SNP MP following a by-election in Motherwell. Indeed, Unionists were conscious that McIntyre had attracted support from among its usual voters.[115] Two weeks later, Blair distributed copies of *The Answer to the Scottish Nationalists*, noting in a covering letter that the main nationalist grievances were the failure to construct a Forth Road Bridge and designate Prestwick an international airport. But Blair had little else to offer beyond suggesting that Unionist MPs stress that 'full weight' was given in Parliament to 'Scottish interests', and that any failure to achieve 'desirable advantages' could not be 'attributable to the existence of the Union'.[116]

At the 1945 general election, nearly half the Scottish Unionist candidates 'discussed the problems of Scottish government' in their election literature,[117] but while the fears regarding policy and organisation articulated in 1942 and 1944 proved unduly gloomy, Colonel Blair's prediction of securing between 41 and 52 seats in Scotland owed more to wishful thinking than judicious analysis.[118] While the UK Conservative vote fell to 39.8 per cent (from 47.7 in 1935), in Scotland the decline was less marked, falling from 42 to 40.3 per cent. Together, the Unionists and National Liberals and Conservatives had 27 seats to Labour's 40.[119] One of the Unionist casualties was former Scottish Secretary Walter Elliot in Glasgow Kelvingrove.[120]

NOTES

1. *Spectator*, 30 May 1957.
2. P. Ward (2005), *Unionism in the United Kingdom, 1918–1974*, Basingstoke: Palgrave Macmillan, 27.
3. For a full study of Skelton, see D. Torrance (2011), *Noel Skelton and the Property-Owning Democracy*, London: Biteback.
4. See Lord Macmillan (1952), *A Man of Law's Tale: The Reminiscences of Lord Macmillan*, London: Macmillan, 81–100.
5. Central Council report for 1923–4, SCUA Papers, Acc 10424/27(iv), Edinburgh: NLA.
6. *Daily Record and Mail*, 31 October 1924. Following the election, the SUA resolved 'to meet the Socialists on their own ground by the provision of working-men speakers and the immediate distribution of pamphlets and literature' (SCUA Papers, Acc 10424/7).
7. In 1909 Templeton had become organising secretary of the Unionist Workers' League, and two years later he stood without success as the Liberal Unionist candidate in Ross and Cromarty.
8. I. G. C. Hutchison (1986), *A Political History of Scotland 1832–1924: Parties, Elections and Issues*, Edinburgh: John Donald, 324.
9. M. Dyer (1996), *Capable Citizens and Improvident Democrats: The Scottish Electoral System 1884–1929*, Aberdeen: Scottish Cultural Press, 165.
10. R. R. James (1991), *Bob Boothby: A Portrait*, London: Hodder & Stoughton, 61–2.
11. D. Torrance (2006), *The Scottish Secretaries*, Edinburgh: Birlinn, 101.
12. D. Torrance (2006), 101.
13. The first John Gilmour had been created a baronet in 1897 as a reward for his presidency of the Scottish Union of Conservative Associations.
14. J. Vincent (ed.) (1986), *The Crawford Papers: The Journal of David Lindsay, 27th Earl of Crawford and 10th Earl of Balcarres, 1871–1940*, Manchester: Manchester University Press, 201.

15. See G. Ward-Smith (2001), 'Baldwin and Scotland: More than Englishness', *Contemporary British History* 15, 61–82.
16. I. G. C. Hutchison (1998), 'Scottish Unionism between the two World Wars', in C. M. M. Macdonald (ed.), *Unionist Scotland 1800–1997*, Edinburgh: John Donald, 73–99.
17. I. G. C. Hutchison (2001), *Scottish Politics in the Twentieth Century*, Basingstoke: Palgrave, 51.
18. I. G. C. Hutchison (2001), 53.
19. I. G. C. Hutchison (2001), 50.
20. R. J. Finlay (2012), 'Patriotism, paternalism and pragmatism: Scottish Toryism, Union and Empire, 1912–65', in D. Torrance (ed.), *Whatever Happened to Tory Scotland?*, Edinburgh: Edinburgh University Press, 36.
21. I. G. C. Hutchison (2001), 44.
22. A Private Member's Bill from the die-hard Unionist MP Fred Macquisten to 'restore the individual freedom of the working man' by removing the political levy paid to trade unions had prompted the Prime Minister's 'peace in industry' speech.
23. *Scotsman*, 8 June 1926.
24. *Scotsman*, 28 July 1926. For an analysis of Elliot's Unionism, see P. Ward (2005), *Unionism in the United Kingdom*, 21–40.
25. I. G. C. Hutchison (1998), 'Scottish Unionism between the two World Wars', in C. M. M. Macdonald (ed.), *Unionist Scotland 1800–1997*, Edinburgh: John Donald, 76.
26. Central Council report for year ending 30 June 1927, Acc 10424/27(iv).
27. For a joint memoir of the Atholls, see K. Atholl (1958), *Working Partnership*, London: Arthur Barker.
28. This deprived Scottish Unionist MPs of their clear majority on the Scottish Grand Committee.
29. SCUA Papers, Acc 10424/27(v).
30. SCUA Papers, Acc 10424/27(v).
31. Findlay's eldest son, also Sir John, succeeded to the baronetcy and proprietorship of the *Scotsman* and was the Scottish Unionist MP for Banffshire during the Second World War.
32. Horsbrugh became the first Scottish female Privy Counsellor and in 1936 was the first woman to give a reply to the King's Speech. Helen Shaw campaigned for modernisation of the Lanarkshire coal mines.
33. SCUA Papers, Acc 11368/85(v).
34. C. de B. Murray (1938), *How Scotland is Governed*, Edinburgh: Moray Press, 51.
35. Meeting of Scottish Unionist Members on 6 September 1944, Scottish Unionist Members Committee Papers, SUMC 1/9, Oxford: Bodleian.

36. M. Fry (1987), *Patronage and Principle: A Political History of Modern Scotland*, Aberdeen: Aberdeen University Press, 110.
37. A. Jackson (2011), *The Two Unions: Ireland, Scotland, and the Survival of the United Kingdom, 1707–2007*, Oxford: Oxford University Press, 279.
38. R. Finlay (2012), 30.
39. E. A. Cameron (2010), *Impaled Upon a Thistle: Scotland since 1880*, Edinburgh: Edinburgh University Press, 163.
40. Acc 10424/10(viii).
41. Acc 11368/97(ii).
42. J. Mitchell (1990), *Conservatives and the Union: A Study of Conservative Party Attitudes to Scotland*, Edinburgh: Edinburgh University Press, 9.
43. J. T. Ward (1982), *The First Century: A History of Scottish Tory Organisation 1882–1982*, Edinburgh: SCUA, 33.
44. J. T. Ward (1982), 29.
45. I. G. C. Hutchison (1998), 79–80.
46. A. Jackson (2012), 141.
47. P. Norton (1994), 'The parliamentary party and party committees', in A. Seldon and S. Ball (eds), *Conservative Century: The Conservative Party since 1900*, Oxford: Oxford University Press, 115.
48. 'One Scotsman succeeds another,' noted the *Scotsman* approvingly, 'since the former Chairman was Mr W. P. Spens, who sits for Ashford but is a member of a well-known Scottish family' (*Scotsman*, 26 October 1940).
49. Two Junior Unionists had won seats on Glasgow City Council in 1936.
50. I. Levitt (1992), *The Scottish Office: Depression and Reconstruction 1919–1959*, Edinburgh: Scottish History Society, 349–50. An amendment at the Bill's committee stage spared the parish and district councils.
51. *Glasgow Herald*, 27 August 1928. Article 21 of the Treaty of Union had provided for the protection of the rights of Scotland's royal burghs.
52. *Evening Times*, 21 January 1929.
53. J. J. Smyth (2003), 'Resisting Labour: Unionists, Liberals, and Moderates in Glasgow between the wars', *Historical Journal* 46:2, 375–401.
54. File of papers 'concerning the Roman Catholic vote', Acc 10424/8(v).
55. D. Seawright (1999), 75.
56. J. T. Ward (1982), 35.
57. Gilmour Papers, GD383 29/30, Edinburgh: National Archives of Scotland.

58. Central Council report for year ending 30 June 1929, Acc 10424/27(v).
59. J. Mitchell (1990), 43.
60. G. Warner (1988), *The Scottish Tory Party: A History*, London: Weidenfeld & Nicolson, 192. The English party had ditched the name 'Unionist' in 1925.
61. Elected in the 1930 East Renfrewshire by-election was the future 14th Duke of Hamilton. See M. Peel (2013), *The Patriotic Duke: The Life of the 14th Duke of Hamilton*, London: Thistle.
62. Central Council report for year ending June 1931, Acc 10424/27(v).
63. S. Ball (2013), *Portrait of a Party: The Conservative Party in Britain 1918–1945*, Oxford: Oxford University Press, 247.
64. Central Council report for year ending June 1931, Acc 10424/27(v).
65. I. G. C. Hutchison (1998), 79–80.
66. L. Bennie, J. Brand and J. Mitchell (1997), *How Scotland Votes: Scottish Parties and Elections*, Manchester: Manchester University Press, 222.
67. J. Kellas (1994), 'The Party in Scotland', in A. Seldon and S. Ball (eds), *Conservative Century*, 677.
68. A. Lownie (2002), *John Buchan: The Presbyterian Cavalier*, London: Pimlico, 221–2. Buchan was later made Lord High Commissioner to the General Assembly of the Church of Scotland in 1933 and Governor-General of Canada in 1935.
69. For a full discussion of 'administrative devolution', see J. Mitchell (2003), *Governing Scotland: The Invention of Administrative Devolution*, Basingstoke: Palgrave Macmillan.
70. D. Torrance (2020), *'Standing Up for Scotland': Nationalist Unionism and Scottish Party Politics, 1884–2014*, Edinburgh: Edinburgh University Press, 36–7.
71. J. Wales (2021), *Scottish Unionist Ideology 1886–1965: Political Thought, Ecclesiology and Historiography*, Baden-Baden: Nomos, 165.
72. D. Torrance (2020), 37.
73. See G. Malcolm Thomson (c. 1930), *The Kingdom of Scotland Restored*, Humphrey Toulmin.
74. HC Deb 4 May 1932 Vol. 265 cc1107–8. Home Rule had crept into the party's *Campaign Guide* for 1929 but had disappeared by 1931.
75. SUWO (1932), *Scottish Nationalism*, Edinburgh: Scottish Unionist Whip's Office, 5–16.
76. J. M. MacCormick (1955), *A Flag in the Wind: The Story of the National Movement in Scotland*, London: Victor Gollancz,

64. For other accounts of the Cathcart secession, see J. Mitchell (1990), 44–8 and G. McKechnie (2013), *George Malcolm Thomson: The Best-Hated Man – Intellectuals and the Condition of Scotland Between the Wars*, Glendaruel: Argyll, 160–5.

77. J. Mitchell (1990), 202.

78. J. T. Ward (1982), 34.

79. G. McKechnie (2013), 163.

80. R. Finlay (1996), 'Scottish Conservatism since 1918', in M. Francis and I. Zweiniger-Bargielowska (eds), *The Conservatives and British Society 1880–1990*, Cardiff: University of Wales Press, 114–16.

81. HC Deb 24 November 1932 Vol. 272 cc262–3.

82. Duke of Atholl (ed.) (1932), *A Scotsman's Heritage*, London: Alexander Maclehose & Co., 58, 64, 87–8 & 100.

83. J. Wales (2021), 76–7.

84. J. Wales (2021), 114–15.

85. J. A. A. Porteous (1935), *The New Unionism*, London: George Allen and Unwin, 25, 87–9. Porteous ultimately quit the Scottish Unionists, later becoming the SNP's economic adviser.

86. Duke of Montrose (1952), *My Ditty Box*, London: Jonathan Cape, 192–3.

87. J. Kellas (1994), 672.

88. M. Craigoe (2006), 'Conservatives, "Englishness" and "civic nationalism" between the wars', in D. Tanner et al. (eds), *Debating Nationhood and Governance in Britain, 1885–1945*, Manchester: Manchester University Press, 202.

89. Noel Skelton, who had moved from the Perth constituency to the Combined Scottish Universities, was in the unusual position of being elected posthumously.

90. I. G. C. Hutchison (2001), 47.

91. For an admiring account, see C. Coote (1965), *A Companion of Honour: The Story of Walter Elliot in Scotland and in Westminster*, London: Collins.

92. R. Finlay (1997), *A Partnership for Good? Scottish Politics and the Union since 1880*, Edinburgh: John Donald, 112.

93. D. Torrance (2006), 142.

94. As Kellas has observed, Atholl's 'socialism' in this context was 'less ideological than strategic', for she feared the effect of a Franco victory on British security, 'since this might give rise to a Spanish-German-Italian Fascist alliance against Britain' (Kellas, 1994, 688).

95. See S. Ball (1990), 'The politics of appeasement: the fall of the Duchess of Atholl and the Kinross and West Perth by election, December 1938', *Scottish Historical Review* 69, 49–83, and

S. J. Hetherington (1989), *Katharine Atholl 1874–1960: Against the Tide*, Aberdeen: Aberdeen University Press, 186–218. Atholl rejoined the Scottish Unionists in 1940. McNair Snadden held the Kinross and West Perthshire seat until 1955.

96. J. Kellas (1994), 684–5.
97. Acc 10424/7(viii).
98. Acc 10424/7(viii).
99. WDC report on constituency organisation dated 8 September 1944, SUMC 1/9.
100. C. Thornton-Kemsley (1974), *Through Winds and Tides*, London: Standard Press, 26–36.
101. See G. Bowd (2013), *Fascist Scotland: Caledonia and the Far Right*, Edinburgh: Birlinn, 214–25, 238–9.
102. S. Ball (2013), 358.
103. Only two rather vague pamphlets were published by the Reconstruction Committee of the Scottish Unionist Association, both in 1944, one entitled *Scottish Local Government* and the other *Scottish Agriculture*.
104. I. G. C. Hutchison (2001), 75.
105. I. G. C. Hutchison (2001), 74.
106. 1944 WDC report, Acc 10424/27(viii).
107. 1945 WDC report, Acc 10424/27(viii).
108. Boothby had written to Churchill in May 1940 to report Scottish Unionist unhappiness 'at the appointment of an Englishman as Secretary of State [for Scotland] – for the first, and it is to be hoped the last, time in history. They take the view, unanimously, that it is nothing short of a public insult to Scotland at the most critical moment in her proud history' (Robert Boothby to Winston Churchill, 14 May 1940, Churchill Papers, CHAR 20/4a, Cambridge: Churchill Archives Centre).
109. SUA Central Council, 27 February 1942, Acc 10424/54.
110. Meeting of WDC in Glasgow, 17 March 1944, SUMC 1/46.
111. SUMC 1/9.
112. SUMC 1/9.
113. John Cranna to Beattie, 26 March 1945, SUMC 1/13.
114. Minute dated 20 February 1945, SUMC 1/47.
115. P. Somerville (2013), *Through the Maelstrom: A History of the Scottish National Party, 1945–1967*, Stirling: Scots Independent, 4.
116. Letter from P. J. Blair dated 28 May 1945, SUMC 1/47. The pamphlet included recycled quotes from the historian Robert S. Rait (who had died in 1936) and a 1932 speech from Sir Robert Horne.
117. *Scotsman*, 10 April 1947. In 1945 Fred Douglas of the Scottish

Committee of the Communist Party published a polemic entitled
The Scottish Tories: A Political Exposure (Glasgow: SCCP).
118. J. Ramsden (1995), *A History of the Conservative Party: The Age
of Churchill and Eden, 1940–1957*, London: Longman, 86. Blair
did protest that a lack of information rendered a 'forecast with
any pretence of confidence with regard to its accuracy' as 'quite
impossible'.
119. One Independent Unionist was also elected.
120. Elliot returned to the House of Commons in a Combined Scottish
Universities by-election a year later. Elected in South Edinburgh
in 1945 was Sir William Y. Darling, former Lord Provost of
Edinburgh and great uncle of Alastair, later the Labour MP for
Edinburgh Central (see Sir W. Darling, 1952, *So It Looks To Me*,
London: Odhams Press).

5

'Scottish Control of Scottish Affairs': 1945–1964

The 1945 Labour landslide came as less of a shock in Scotland than England, for the 'socialists' – as Unionists always called them – had long been a major electoral force north of the border. 'Unionists did not feel themselves crushed,' judged Michael Fry, 'on the contrary, they saw Scotland as an anti-socialist stronghold.'[1] Indeed, as the Scottish Unionist Association's Western Divisional Council put it, 'it was the West of Scotland which amid the Socialist landslide of 1945 stood steadfast for the Unionist cause'.[2] Clement Attlee's nationalisation agenda also helped refashion Scottish Unionism for the 1950s. Menaced, as Matthew Cragoe put it, 'from opposite sides by the competing ideologies of socialism and nationalism',[3] the party began to navigate what Harold Macmillan might have called a 'Middle Way' between those twin political threats.

In August 1946, the *Scotsman* carried a 'Statement of Conservative Policy' which laid claim to a long-standing policy of 'administrative decentralisation' which 'in the interest of the United Kingdom' it now believed ought to be extended until 'all matters solely of Scottish concern' were 'administered in Scotland'. Labour policy, the party explained, had not only resulted in 'unnecessary delays and inefficiency', but in 'a great loss of Scottish prestige'.[4] And rather than playing down 'growing resentment' over the government's 'indifference' regarding Prestwick Airport and a Forth Road Bridge, as it had during the war, another Unionist publication now made those grievances its own.[5]

When Walter Elliot, who had lost his seat at the 1945 election, contested what was to be a final Combined Scottish

Universities by-election in November 1946, he stressed that the legislative Union between Scotland and England 'was never meant to entail, and should not entail, a complete swamping of the economic identity of the Northern Kingdom such as is now being conducted in the name of nationalisation'. This transfer of Scottish industrial control to Westminster was not nationalisation, he added in a memorable phrase, but amounted to 'denationalisation'.[6] Also elected to the Commons that month was Lady Grant of Monymusk, who as Lady Tweedsmuir would champion Scotland, Britain and the Commonwealth over her long career in both Houses of Parliament.[7]

Unionist representatives, meanwhile, engaged with the 'Scottish National Assembly' (SNA), a product of John MacCormick's Scottish Covenant Association, when it met in Glasgow during 1947. The Unionist MP for Perth, Colonel Gomme-Duncan, expressed his 'hearty belief that Scotland was having and had had, an exceedingly raw deal' and that in future it 'should be recognised as a partner and not occupy the position of office boy'. The Earl of Selkirk, meanwhile, said the interests of the UK 'as a whole were by no means always identical with those of Scotland', while Lord Polwarth, a Unionist industrialist, supported the idea of a Royal Commission on Scottish affairs, something that would later form part of Unionist strategy.[8] Particularly influential was a memorandum by the advocate and Unionist MP James Latham Clyde, later published in several parts by the *Scotsman*.

Following the Assembly, the Earl of Selkirk wrote to Patrick Blair, the SUA's political secretary, saying it was of 'very great importance that it should be clear in Scotland that the Unionist Party is a distinct entity, however closely it may be associated with the Conservative Party in England'.[9] Colonel Blair agreed 'very strongly', observing in his reply to Selkirk that 'the Scottish Unionist Members of the House of Commons do preserve a very distinct entity, and their Committee, everyone must agree, has done great service to Scotland'.[10]

The organisational autonomy to which Selkirk and Blair referred was further bolstered by the routine substitution of 'Unionist' for 'Conservative' in party literature emanating from London; the Eastern Divisional Council (EDC) even inserted pictures of SUA leaders to give one leaflet 'a distinctive Scottish character'.[11] The following year the EDC also suggested using 'distinctively Scottish' 'national symbols' on Unionist posters.[12] The official logo of the Scottish Young Unionists was changed to a large Scottish thistle. With Scottish voters increasingly alive to national symbolism, this diligence with propaganda perhaps contributed to a claimed increase of about 40 per cent in Unionist association membership between June 1947 and June 1948. The SUA secretary, Alan Beaton, said it was 'the busiest season I have known in my 30-odd years connection with the Party'.[13]

'As well as marking out a distinct position in relation to Labour,' concluded Hutchison, 'the Tories used this anti-Whitehall posture to counter the threat of Scottish nationalism and pull back Liberals into the fold.'[14] Liberals allied with the Unionists continued to stand under 'National Liberal', 'Liberal Unionist', 'National Liberal and Conservative' or 'Liberal and Conservative' banners, but after 1945 these titles did not mean they were 'anything other than a Conservative'.[15] Speaking at the Scottish Liberal Club in February 1946, the National Liberal MP for East Fife, James Henderson-Stewart, had suggested the time was ripe for an 'all-round, sincere reconciliation among true Liberals':

> I see gradually emerging, before this Parliament has completed its term, a realisation that Labour rule is a menace which at all costs must be ended; and out of that realisation a coming together of enlightened Conservatives (of whom there are a great many in this new House), of vigorous Independents, of disillusioned Right Wing Labour men and Liberals of all groups. There, could it be fashioned, is the democratic force of tomorrow; there, if we but act wisely, is the future vehicle of true constructive Liberalism![16]

After the war, the Scottish Liberals had instigated reunification talks with the National Liberal Party in Scotland, although these came to nothing, particularly after Henderson-Stewart wrote to *The Times* suggesting a merger with the Conservatives instead.[17]

Drafting a detailed account of the 'new' (liberal) Unionism, however, proved problematic. A draft by Colonel Blair highlighted the usual grievances regarding 'authorities in London which have little knowledge of Scottish conditions and Scottish interest', but its implication that devolution of the sort enjoyed by Northern Ireland *would* be acceptable if it could match Stormont's generous financial settlement made the SUMC nervous.[18] Drafts of a separate pamphlet – 'SCOTLAND and THE UNION' – by the Tory propagandist Colm Brogan added to these nerves by denying 'disadvantages ascribed by the Nationalists to the Union without sufficiently pointing out the many advantages that have accrued to Scotland from the Union'.[19]

Crucially, however, the Unionist 'offer' was in advance of that published by the governing Labour Party in early 1948. This – largely procedural in nature – was greeted with general derision, and later that year the Unionists attempted to take advantage of Labour's discomfort by supporting the Scottish Convention candidate, John MacCormick, in the Paisley by-election caused by the elevation of Oliver Baldwin (Stanley's son) to the House of Lords.[20] 'So complete was Unionism's domination of the centre-right', judged Mike Dyer, 'that its clients had come to include the most significant figure in the Scottish nationalist cause.'[21] The Labour candidate, Douglas Johnston, however, comfortably beat MacCormick and held the seat.

The Scottish Unionist Association conference in Perth, meanwhile, unanimously urged the party leadership to give 'serious consideration' to 'a positive undertaking for a large measure of devolution for Scotland', although speakers emphasised that this did not mean 'a separate Parliament for Scotland'. The Earl of Mansfield revived the idea of a Royal Commission comprising 'eminent Scots men and women in all walks of life'.[22] Press reports that a review of Conservative Party organisation by Sir David Maxwell-Fyfe intended to end what one newspaper called the Scottish Unionist Association's 'home rule' were therefore unhelpful.[23] Senior Unionists moved quickly to kill the story and it even prompted a rebuttal from UK party chairman Lord Woolton, who pointed out that Maxwell-Fyfe's committee had no jurisdiction over party organisation in Scotland:

> There has never been any suggestion of ending Scotland's political independence. Why shouldn't they be independent if they want to be? … I am anxious that both in England and Scotland it [the Tory organisation] should work more effectively, but I have no desire to impinge on the right of the Scottish Unionist Association to control their own affairs.[24]

This threat to Unionist independence was soon forgotten when in early 1949 the Kirriemuir Plebiscite Society found 92.3 per cent support for a Scottish Parliament (and 23.3 per cent for independence) in a strongly Unionist part of

Scotland. When the Scottish National Assembly and some sections of the media began to lobby for a national referendum, the Scottish Unionist Members Committee began to panic. A meeting on 15 February 1949 found Unionist MPs canvassing a range of options, including legislative devolution, to meet what they considered to be an obvious demand from voters, including their own.[25]

At the SUA conference a few months later, a resolution calling for a 'large measure' of devolution was once again passed without dissent. Addressing a huge crowd at Glasgow's Ibrox Park Stadium, Winston Churchill described the 'whole process of nationalisation' as particularly 'detrimental and offensive to Scotland', affecting not only its 'prosperity' but the 'independence' it had 'exercised in so many fields'. He promised 'separate' Scottish boards for rail transport and electricity, as well as the prospect of additional under-secretaries to aid the Secretary of State for Scotland. In short, a future Conservative government would take steps to 'see that Scotland is no longer treated as though she were some province or appendage of England'.[26]

Usefully, the major statement of post-war Conservative policy, *The Right Road for Britain* (1949), spoke of creating a society 'decentralised, diversified, neighbourly, resourceful and resolute',[27] which dovetailed neatly with *Scottish Control of Scottish Affairs*, the Scottish Unionist Association's policy statement published in November 1949. The Act of Union, it declared, had 'never contemplated' such an 'unnatural state of affairs' in which management and control of state-owned industries were being transferred to Whitehall. It was therefore Unionist policy, 'while maintaining the Union of the two countries', to ensure that 'responsibility for managing Scottish Affairs in a manner best suited to the desires and the traditions of the people of Scotland' was retained, 'where it belongs, in the hands of Scotsmen'.

There was to be a 'Deputy to the Secretary of State for Scotland' with Cabinet rank and usually based in Scotland, an additional under-secretary, a Royal Commission on Scottish Affairs, separate Scottish boards for nationalised industries, closer liaison between UK departments and the Scottish Office, more 'freedom' for local authorities and, when necessary, separate Scottish Bills in Parliament.[28] Unlike in the 1920s, however, there was not even the hint of an open mind when it came to legislative devolution. 'The Unionist Party in Scotland will probably never support the idea of a Scottish Parliament', Norman Brook wrote, slightly inappropriately for a civil servant, to Prime Minister Clement Attlee in late 1949, 'since it could not hope to secure a majority in it.'[29]

Speaking at a press conference on the proposals, Walter Elliot said the Royal Commission's remit ought to be 'as wide as possible' while excluding legislative devolution. John Cameron, a prominent supporter of the Scottish Convention and Dean of the Faculty of Advocates, found this curious:

> To have gone so far and to have stopped at the logical and, indeed, democratic conclusion seems strange because such a large measure of administrative autonomy – in administration, both governmental and industrial – would seem to demand for coherence that there should also be side by side with administrative autonomy, control of domestic finance exercised through an equally separable and recognizable legislative machine.[30]

A *Scotsman* editorial nevertheless praised the Unionist proposals as having the 'merit of being consistent',[31] while *The Times* commended them for appealing to those who did not desire 'startling change' but rather 'clearer signs that Scottish affairs are considered and decided in Scotland by those who know the special conditions of the country'.[32] Speaking in Edinburgh on 14 February 1950, Churchill even argued that should England become 'an absolute Socialist state' then Scotland should never 'be forced into the serfdom of Socialism as a result of a vote in the House of Commons', an argument that anticipated the 'no-mandate' cry of anti-Tory nationalists in the 1980s.[33]

At the 1950 general election this tactic of associating local 'nationalist' discontent with a broader campaign theme of combating centralisation appeared to serve the Scottish Unionist Party (and its National Liberal or Liberal Unionist allies) well. In North Angus and Mearns, Colin Thornton-Kemsley beat the actor James Robertson Justice (Labour) by more than 7,000 votes, partly due to support from 'life-long Liberals', for Thornton-Kemsley 'still held the view, formed twenty-five years earlier, that there was nothing in the basic tenets of the two great historic parties ... which was sufficiently divisive to prevent them uniting to oppose State socialism'.[34] In all, Unionists added four MPs to their 1945 total.

Correctly anticipating that another election would not be far off, Churchill replaced the old London-based 'Scottish Whip' with a new 'Chairman of the Unionist Party in Scotland'. This was to be James Stuart, previously UK chief whip and, in a doubtless conscious piece of historical symbolism, a descendant of Scotland's early Stuart monarchs. His political secretary – the SUA's senior official – remained Colonel Patrick Blair, who had kept a 'tight rein' on Unionist politics since 1922.[35]

In 1950 *The East of Scotland Year Book* ('being a political reference annual for the year 1950') was published, the first of a series of almanacs issued by the Scottish Unionist Association over the next decade and a half. This took care to stress that the SUA was 'financially and in its organisation independent of England', although it was also represented on the National Council of Conservative and Unionist Associations. The annual SUA conference still took place alternately in the East and West of Scotland.[36] As in the 1920s and '30s, the Eastern and Western Divisional Councils, which 'took into account the differing political cultures within Scotland',[37] remained all-powerful. In 1949 the SUA had changed its constitution to enable their respective convenors to serve on its Executive and Central Council *ex officio*.[38]

The 1951 Conservative Party manifesto, *BRITAIN Strong and Free*, once again played 'the nationalist card to full effect',[39] detailing 'measures designed to give Scotland greater control of Scottish affairs and to enable her to maintain and develop her own national way of life'.[40] On polling day, not only were Churchill's Conservatives returned to office, but in Scotland the Unionists and their allies secured an additional three seats and almost 40 per cent of the popular vote. Even in safe Labour seats like Aberdeen North, the Unionists had campaigned vigorously, boasting as many local members as their rivals and superior organisation.[41] Given the new government's slim overall majority of 17, this gave added weight and influence to the Scottish party. Scottish nationalism appeared to have been 'harnessed' by Scottish Unionists 'to the anti-socialist chariot'.[42]

James Stuart, the new Secretary of State for Scotland, was a close ally of Winston Churchill and had recently been appointed the first Scottish Unionist chairman. Although Walter Elliot had hoped for a return to office, he had annoyed Churchill by not publicly condemning appeasement in the late 1930s.[43]

Having the Prime Minister's trust meant Stuart got free rein when it came to choosing his ministerial team. This included a new Minister of State, and to fill it Stuart wanted the Earl of Home. The Prime Minister was unimpressed (Home had been Neville Chamberlain's parliamentary private secretary during the Munich crisis) but eventually relented, remarking drolly: 'Very well, Home Sweet Home it shall be.'

Home's appointment fulfilled part of the 'Scottish Control of Scottish Affairs' agenda, in that he would deputise for Stuart and attend Cabinet when necessary. 'Go and quell those turbulent Scots,' Churchill told Home upon his appointment, 'and don't come back till you've done it.'[44] The rest of the Scottish Office team reflected an electorally successful Unionist alliance. Two of Stuart's under-secretaries were National Liberals, James Henderson-Stewart and Niall Macpherson (Dumfriesshire). Churchill also considered appointing Lady Tweedsmuir, but Stuart disliked the idea of women as ministers.[45] Finally, the Edinburgh North MP Lord Clyde (one of the architects of the party's Scottish policy) became Lord Advocate while in a then unusual move the Solicitor-General for Scotland, William Milligan, was appointed from outside Parliament (although he later became a Unionist MP in early 1955).[46]

That both Stuart and Home were impeccably aristocratic reflected the demographic of Scottish Unionism in the early 1950s, with the party's representatives generally comprising 'knights of the shire' or prosperous industrialists. As the third son of the 17th Earl of Moray, Stuart had been an equerry to the Duke of York (later King George VI) and had fancied his chances with Lady Elizabeth Bowes-Lyon (later Queen Elizabeth). Instead, he married Lady Rachel Cavendish, fourth daughter of the 9th Duke of Devonshire, which meant that one of Stuart's brothers-in-law was the future Prime Minister Harold Macmillan.

As Scottish Secretary, Stuart proved to be another moderate. Together with Macmillan (who was Minister for Housing), they doubled the government's housing subsidy, and for the first time in three decades, housing construction and occupancy rose in Scotland. The Earl of Home also kept Highland Liberals happy by establishing a Crofters Commission to develop Scottish crofting through the provision of grants and loans, while the *Hydro-Electric Development (Scotland) Act* raised that board's borrowing limit.[47] Within a month of the 1951 election, Home had also announced a committee on the financial and economic relations between Scotland and the rest of the United Kingdom, to be chaired by Lord Catto. This reported in July 1952 and recommended a 'Revenue and Expenditure' white paper, which was published in January 1954.[48] Unionists had no qualms when it came to the financial benefit Scotland derived from the 250-year-old Union.

The Scottish Office also worked hard to diversify Scotland's industrial base, its aim being to improve the standard of living and satisfy consumer demand, both key in terms of maintaining Scottish Unionist support. James Stuart led the campaign for a fourth (steel) strip mill to be located in Scotland, which became the totemic Ravenscraig, a name which became more closely associated with Mrs Thatcher than Mr Churchill. Construction of a Forth Road Bridge, meanwhile, was given the green light, lancing one of several pre-war nationalist grievances.

When John MacCormick, Rector of Glasgow University and the Unionist-backed candidate in the 1949 Paisley by-election, contested the numerical accuracy of 'Queen Elizabeth II' (who acceded to the Throne in February 1952), it fell to Lord Cooper to consider its constitutionality. Cooper's obiter remarks, thereafter much quoted by Scottish nationalists, that 'the principle of unlimited sovereignty of Parliament is a distinctively English principle' with 'no counterpart in Scottish constitutional law', reflected both the Lord President's legal nationalism and his tenure as a Scottish Unionist MP. He went on to criticise those who acted 'as if all that happened in 1707 was that Scottish representatives were admitted to the Parliament of England'.[49] Scottish Unionist MPs subsequently lobbied for the 'II' to be omitted from Scottish pillar boxes (a few having been blown up), and Winston Churchill acquiesced in stipulating that the Royal cypher in Scotland should be 'ER' rather than 'EIIR'. 'Nationalist unionism' lived.

In February 1952, the Cabinet had also considered the 'Stone of Scone', upon which Queen Elizabeth was to be crowned in June 1953. It had been removed from Westminster Abbey more than a year earlier by four students, and Scottish Unionist MPs were acutely conscious that its recovery and future use would have to be handled with care. On 26 February 1952, for example, the Scottish Unionist Members Committee informed the media that while it believed the Stone 'should be available for use at the Coronation Service ... there was no unanimity as to where it should be kept at other times'.[50] Scotland's 'representative' peers, always more nationalist than their elected colleagues, had expressed support for repatriating the Stone during a House of Lords debate on 9 May 1951. The Countess of Airlie, a Royal courtier, even wanted to hold a separate Scottish coronation ceremony.

The new monarch's 'State Visit' to Edinburgh in June 1953, meanwhile, proved a masterclass in 'official' Scottish nationalism. In his foreword to the official souvenir programme, the Secretary of State for Scotland said the 'Honours of Scotland' to be carried before Her Majesty were 'symbolic but striking proofs' of the 'special place' Scotland held in relation to the Crown and Commonwealth. It was also repeatedly emphasised that the young Queen was 'sensitive to the alert national consciousness of her Scottish subjects', having personally requested that the Honours 'be borne before her'.[51]

Even John MacCormick acknowledged that Churchill's government had begun to 'show signs of activity in Scotland in response to the pressure of [nationalist] propaganda', most significantly in delivering on its late-1940s promise to establish a Royal Commission on Scottish Affairs. With that, judged MacCormick, 'the wind was taken out of our sails'.[52] A 1954 Scottish Unionist Association pamphlet quoted a speech from the senior Conservative Rab Butler, in which he claimed the government had 'cut back those infringements on Scottish nationhood' which had been 'so marked and keenly felt' after the war:

We have fulfilled our pledge to strengthen and reorganise the Scottish Office. We have kept our promise to establish a Royal Commission to advise on administrative and other problems. We are providing in transport, in broadcasting and now in electricity, better Scottish control over public corporations north of the border.[53]

The Royal Commission reported in early 1955, having considered only 'administrative' (rather than legislative) devolution. It made only modest proposals: transfer of responsibility for roads to the Scottish Office, the appointment of justices of the peace from the Lord Chancellor, and animal health from the Ministry of Agriculture. Lord Balfour, the Commission's chairman, diplomatically attributed any ill feeling to 'needless

English thoughtlessness' and 'undue Scottish susceptibilities'.[54] Perhaps conscious there were no 'earth-shaking recommendations', Stuart urged a speedy response in order to 'prevent a possible public campaign in which the Royal Commission's recommendations, as well as procrastination by the Government, would be called in question'.[55]

In April 1955 and aged 80, Churchill finally bowed to pressure (including from James Stuart) and retired as Conservative leader and Prime Minister. Buoyed by goodwill and favourable polls, Sir Anthony Eden, his successor, called a general election. And however weak its recommendations, the Royal Commission allowed Unionists to campaign on the basis of having met its earlier manifesto pledges. As in 1950 and 1951, the 1955 Conservative manifesto, *United for Peace and Progress*, devoted a substantial section to 'Scottish Affairs' (three times as long as that in 1950). The Secretary of State, it declared, was to assume 'care of Scottish roads and bridges' and where 'further measures of this kind' were shown to be 'in the best interests of Scotland', then Conservatives would 'not hesitate to adopt them'.[56]

The 1955 *Year Book for Scotland* (previously the *East of Scotland Year Book*) also drove home the message that Unionists, rather than Labour MPs, were the guardian of Scottish interests within the Union, so that 'allegations of neglect by the Government of Scottish affairs are clearly unfounded and misleading'.[57] The *Scotsman* judged that in terms of 'administrative devolution the Unionists have indisputably gone farther than their predecessors', and while it 'may not have been wholly fulfilled', they had 'applied the principle, whereas the Socialists cannot get away from centralised control'.[58]

On polling day, the Scottish Unionists were rewarded with a unique result for a political party in Scotland: a majority of both seats and (albeit narrowly) the popular vote.[59] A gain of one seat, Central Ayrshire ('and a majority of two over the Socialists'), was credited to the leadership of Sir Charles McFarlane, although to the party's 'great regret' and 'after one of the most gallant of all the contests', he only just failed to capture Glasgow Provan from Labour.[60]

In the months that followed, Unionists continued to play the Scottish card. Lord Home spoke 'of Scotland as a country' joined now for 250 years 'in friendly union with a great and powerful neighbour', while he also invoked Sir William Wallace, 'who in the 13th century, first rallied his countrymen to resist a forceful union with England'.[61] In 1953 a cross-party group of Scots, including several Unionists, had proposed a London memorial for Sir William. Walter Elliot's papers reveal concerns of 'too strong a Scottish Nationalist element' creeping into the project, thus Elliot was drafted in to give reassurance that it was backed 'by people whose patriotism has sanity as well as sincerity'. The 1956 unveiling in Smithfield (the location of Wallace's execution) was marred by a protest, the chairman of the London branch of the SNP calling those present 'traitors to Scotland' for daring to sing the (UK) National Anthem. He proceeded to jump onto the platform, but the elderly Elliot sent 'him flying to the back of the platform with a tackle worthy of a Border Rugby forward'.[62]

There had been less vigour when it came to reducing public expenditure, at least from the point of view of Unionist activists. Such complaints had first surfaced in 1953, but the grievance was increasingly expressed after the 1955 election. Patrick Blair reported that Unionist voters were beginning 'to say that it does not matter which party is in office – they are equally bad'. This was frustration at what became known as 'Butskellism', a general consensus between the two main parties when it came to maintaining full employment, the welfare state and public expenditure. By 1956 the SUA president William Sinclair 'found himself continually defending the Government not against recognised opponents but against declared Unionist Electors, some of whom were threatening to withdraw their support from the Party'.[63] A true believer in this sense was Ralph Harris (later Lord Harris of High Cross), a St Andrews lecturer and early 'monetarist' who had unsuccessfully contested Edinburgh Central in 1955.[64]

There was also much grumbling either side of the election regarding the state of Unionist organisation in Scotland. In June 1954 the Scottish Unionist Members Committee had recorded its 'sense of general dissatisfaction and concern', critical articles having appeared in the Unionist-supporting *Glasgow Herald* and *Bulletin*.[65] In February 1956 the SUMC held a more substantial meeting on the same topic, which was full of unfavourable comparisons between the 'badly run' Edinburgh office and 'the organisation in London built up by Lord Woolton'. Colonel Blair was deemed 'excellent for inside work' but 'was not good at public relations'. And with the Eastern and Western

Divisional Councils 'invariably working in different directions' there were calls for a 'central Scottish Office'. As the Secretary of State for Scotland was based in London, it was not realistic for him also to act as party chairman in Edinburgh.[66] James Stuart had been struggling to combine the two positions since 1953 but the SUA unanimously opposed the creation of a 'deputy chairman', fearful that it would erode its autonomy. The party was not as professional as it could have been. At the 1955 election only 28 of the 64 Unionist associations had certified agents, although by 1957 this had risen to 54.

Some Unionists also argued that the maintenance of a distinct party identity north of the border was not necessarily to its advantage. At the 1956 Scottish Unionist Association conference, the East Renfrewshire Association submitted a resolution seeking to change the name of the party in Scotland to 'Scottish Conservative and Unionist', arguing that the expression 'Unionist' had 'lost much of its original significance'. Others, however, believed this 'would not be advisable' as the word 'Unionist' involved 'an important matter of principle'.[67] 'The word "Conservative"', protested the National Liberal MP Colin Thornton-Kemsley, 'conveys an excessive fondness for the past, a reluctance to change, and a disharmony with ideas of progress!'[68] The Unionist MP for Stirling and Falkirk, J. S. C. Reid, believed that not only should Unionists ostentatiously 'appeal to the sentiment of the Scottish nation' but also 'stress our individuality as a Unionist party in Scotland apart from the Conservative party'.[69]

In response to those who believed the word 'Unionist' to be 'out of date', the 1957 *Year Book for Scotland* argued that it now possessed a 'new connotation' unconnected with Home Rule for Ireland, adding that it may be taken to mean 'the unity of all classes in a property-owning democracy and the unity of the Commonwealth'. To many, it added, Unionist was preferable to 'Conservative' in that it more fully captured 'Unionist philosophy' as epitomised by Edmund Burke, chiefly the 'disposition to preserve with the ability to improve'.[70] On this basis the party feared that fielding 'Unionist' candidates in local government elections 'would split the anti-Socialist vote, and that many moderates would refuse to vote for Unionist candidates'.[71] Although a Unionist had defeated a 'Socialist' in Largs in 1959, only in the early 1960s were concerted efforts made in Port Glasgow, Rutherglen and East Kilbride by Unionist or Conservative groups.[72] In Edinburgh and Glasgow, Unionists styled themselves 'Progressives', the best-known example being Teddy Taylor in Cathcart between 1959 and 1964.[73] Three Young Unionists had also been elected as Progressives in Glasgow in 1957.

James Stuart, meanwhile, was sanguine about the Suez crisis which ultimately ended Sir Anthony Eden's premiership. 'I did not object to our going IN,' he recalled in his memoirs. 'What I did object to was our coming OUT.'[74] On the other hand, the Unionist MP for Lanark, Patrick Maitland, had been opposed full stop, explaining in his 1959 election address that his 'stand ... was due to the Scot in him and his desire to secure a foreign policy worthy of Scotland's partnership with the English'.[75] Michael Fry, meanwhile, blamed Stuart's 'languid inactivity' for many of the party's problems as the 1950s drew to a close:

> Nobody better illustrated how Unionism was cutting itself off from its roots, notably in choosing its MPs from the anglicised upper class. It began to lose the centre ground which it had held for thirty years ... Unionists had also attracted a large working-class vote, founded on the Protestant patriotism which had been part of their ideology since the outset [but] Unionism was to find itself ever more strictly confined to the counties and the bourgeois districts of the big cities.[76]

Illustrating this point had been the intervention of Derek Smith, a former Girvan provost and twice unsuccessful Unionist candidate for South Ayrshire, at the 1957 Scottish Unionist conference in Ayr. He alluded to what Urwin called an 'invisible and impenetrable barrier which separates Non-U Unionist from U Unionist candidates',[77] citing the filling of a vacancy in the Bute and North Ayrshire constituency with Brigadier Fitzroy Maclean:

> We woke up one morning and found that there was a candidate where we did not know a vacancy existed. I think the author of the book 'Eastern Approaches' should write another book called 'Northern Approaches' explaining how it is done. Was it to be wondered that people became cynical towards the Tory Party?[78]

At this point, Smith was called to order by the conference chairman. Two years later there was a rather despairing call from the Western Divisional convenor for associations to submit resolutions to the annual SUA conference, 'thus demonstrating that their organisation was alive'.[79]

Stuart himself was 'glad when it became possible for me to quit the Government in the following year. I had lost interest and was tired.'[80] He was later elevated to the House of Lords as Viscount Stuart of Findhorn and skirted over his five years at the Scottish Office in just 14 pages of his disappointing memoirs, entitled *Within the Fringe*.

'If I had ever been offered the Scottish Office,' declared the Scottish Unionist MP Sir Robert Boothby in the early 1960s, 'I should have asked for an official residence in Edinburgh':

> I should have driven round Scotland in an enormous black car, with the rampant lion flying proudly in the wind, and – if possible – outriders on motorcycles. I should have steamed round her coast every year in the fishery cruiser, rechristened a yacht for the purpose, with more flags. And all this not for the purpose of self-aggrandisement; but just to show that the Secretary of State for Scotland is, in his own right, a tremendous political figure whose presence at the British Cabinet table must be counted an honour to them.[81]

John Maclay, who succeeded James Stuart as Secretary of State for Scotland in 1957, was not quite this ostentatious. From a Liberal industrialist family – his father Joseph had served as Lloyd George's shipping controller between 1916 and 1921 – even as Scottish Secretary he did not really consider himself a Conservative, often declaring disarmingly: 'I'll have to find out what the Tories think.'

Indeed, in 1957 Maclay also became 'leader' of the six Scottish National Liberal MPs, all of whom took the Unionist whip in the Commons. These Members were 'elected with the combined support of Liberals and Conservatives and Unionists in their respective constituencies' and thus a curious hangover from the coalition or 'national' governments of the 1910, '20s and '30s. The grouping's support remained remarkably steady, returning the same number of MPs at the 1951, 1955 and 1959 general elections, thus sustaining Unionist hegemony while ensuring 'Liberal influence' was 'brought to bear on Conservative thinking'.[82]

Maclay basically continued his predecessor's industrial strategy, but a worsening economic backdrop in the late 1950s made life politically difficult. In his foreword to the 1958 *Year Book for Scotland*, the SUA president Philip Christison warned that

'Unionists, Conservatives, and National Liberals, must stand united to prevent our country falling once more into Socialist hands with all that entails'[83] – quite a statement only a few years after that coalition had secured more than 50 per cent of the Scottish vote. Some MPs, inevitably, blamed the media, the SUA chairman expressing concern that letters to the *Scotsman* 'seem to indicate among some people a misapprehension' that 'Scotland is being unfairly treated and is being mulcted of money for the benefit of England'.[84]

Although in the 1950s pragmatic Scottish Unionism had 'effectively adapted some of Labour's statist policies for its own ends',[85] particularly when it came to public housing and support for New Towns, during the 1955–9 Parliament the economic boom that manifested itself in other parts of the UK was not as pronounced in Scotland. And given that Unionists had spoken the language of 'Scottish solutions' to Scottish problems, inevitably they ended up being held accountable. Walter Elliot's Kelvingrove constituency was lost to Labour in a 1958 by-election,[86] while discipline weakened among Scottish Unionist MPs. Patrick Wolrige-Gordon in East Aberdeenshire adopted the banner of 'Moral Re-Armament',[87] while in early 1959 Sir David Robertson (Caithness and Sutherland) resigned the Unionist whip in protest at what he alleged was government neglect of his constituency. In an attempt to project a more modern image of the party, meanwhile, the consistently overlooked Lady Tweedsmuir was asked to front one of the party's four BBC election broadcasts, the Prime Minister being anxious for 'a lady Member ... representing Scotland' to do so.[88]

At the general election in October 1959, Scottish Unionists lost five seats and around 14,000 votes (although it retained a lead over Labour in terms of the popular vote),[89] which in the context of steady advances since the 1920s most likely reflected negative economic developments which had not been present four years earlier.[90] Nationally, by contrast, the Conservative Party increased its majority over Labour to 100 seats. 'The Conservatives all but forgot Scotland in the 1959 election,' was Bill Miller's diagnosis,[91] while John Ramsden saw as a display of 'indifference' Harold Macmillan's promotion of one defeated Scottish MP to the Lords while allowing 'him to take the name of the constituency that had just refused to elect him'.[92]

George Younger, a young Unionist candidate unsuccessfully fighting North Lanarkshire, put the swing to Labour in the West of Scotland down to unemployment.[93] In response, John Cranna, the SUA's secretary, said the 'prosperity theme which worked so effectively in England had, as you say, rather a hollow ring in our black spots'.[94] In its annual report for 1959, the Western Divisional Council agreed that the 'prosperity theme ... was not quite in tune with conditions in West Scotland and other areas similarly affected by unemployment and under-employment'.[95] This growing economic gap doubtlessly contributed to a political one too. Between 1945 and 1955, Scottish election results had generally mirrored UK trends, but now there was a clear divergence. There was at least some consolation in the presence of 'keen new Scottish Members' such as Ian MacArthur, Betty Harvie Anderson, Patrick Wolridge-Gordon and Gordon Campbell.[96]

From a London perspective, the 1959 general election proved the last straw. 'The matter now brooks no further delay,' wrote Lord Hailsham. 'Their organisation is horrible.'[97] Urwin observed that as Scottish Unionism had emerged 'relatively unscathed' from the 1945 election and those that followed in the 1950s, 'the agitation for organizational reform in England' had lacked 'its counterpart in Scotland', thus much-needed 'soul-searching' had been delayed by a decade and a half.[98] The retirement of Sir Patrick Blair in 1960 provided

> an opportunity of modernisation that was not taken; instead his departure worsened the deteriorating relations between the Chairman's Office (in Edinburgh) and the Scottish Unionist Association (in Glasgow) which now made the adoption of any coherent strategy in Scotland more problematic, and [Harold] Macmillan had to appoint a series of peacemakers when rows erupted over both personalities and finance.

Still Unionist chairman despite his departure from the Cabinet, Viscount (James) Stuart succumbed to pressure from Scottish Unionist MPs and appointed Sir Alick Buchanan-Smith vice-chairman with Jack McDonald Watson his political secretary.[99] Although a minor reform, it upset the relationship 'between the Scottish Chairman's Office and the SUA on the one hand and the relationship between the English and Scottish Parties on the other'. And when the *Scotsman* described McDonald Watson as the 'Scottish Chief Agent', the SUA recoiled at this application of English party terminology, the incident confirming its suspicion that the Chairman's Office intended to erode the SUA's autonomy.[100] They were to be proved correct.

Rab Butler suggested to the Prime Minister that Jack McDonald Watson might succeed Stuart as chairman, as he was 'considered highly efficient'. 'This is urgent,' added Butler. 'It is evident in the House of Commons that one of our most vulnerable points is the position in Scotland [but] we are keeping this quiet to stop the Scots resenting it.' Diplomatically, however, Butler rejected the idea of revised nomenclature during his speech to the 1960 SUA conference:

> You are called 'Unionists'; we in England call ourselves since Peel's time 'Conservatives'. I have been asked whether we need or want a new title, and what are our aims. I reply: to conserve, to unite, and to construct. We wish to conserve the best of our past heritage, to unite the country and ourselves with our Commonwealth, and to create or to construct new vistas for our future. We need no new name but our creed is clearly pointed. We are the constructive Conservative and Unionist Party.[101]

At the same gathering, according to D. W. Urwin, the EDC and WDC had recommended

> improvements in the status, remuneration and conditions of service of constituency agents; improvements in the salary and conditions of service of trainee agents; the introduction of political education for party workers and the general public; an increase in subscriptions; greater representation of Young Unionists at higher levels; reorganization of the Chairman's Office.

It was also argued that the party should make sterner efforts to secure the best possible office-bearers at all levels, since 'that was where the party failed'.

Moving a motion for such organisational reform was the Perth and East Perthshire MP Ian MacArthur. He suggested that as many party facilities were highly developed in England, then Scottish Unionists ought to make more use of them. In a veiled attack on the two Divisional Councils, MacArthur suggested that a 'single central body' ought to be responsible for 'general direction or guidance, the formulation of policy and the control of party finance'.[102]

Despite broad support, most of the proposed reforms were left unexecuted and the EDC and WDC maintained their separate existence. This inactivity, meanwhile, made Harold Macmillan 'rather concerned about the condition of the Party in Scotland':

> The organisation is old-fashioned and semi-feudal. I have decided to call 5 or 6 ministers and Scottish notabilities together for a discussion. James Stuart will, I know, help; but he is now not well enough to be very active. He is still nominally chairman. We had originally intended Alec Home to succeed him. But now that he has gone to the F[oreign] O[ffice], this plan is impossible.[103]

Scottish Unionist MPs were increasingly of the view that the Eastern and Western Divisional Councils had to go and the SUMC lobbied Conservative Central Office accordingly. 'Scotland will not accept the right solution', a deputy chairman called Toby Law told Rab Butler, 'which is that Central Office should be given control over the whole of Great Britain.'

Macmillan's meeting finally took place on 16 November 1961. Present were the Prime Minister, Lord Kilmuir (Lord Chancellor), Lord Home and two whips (chief and Scottish). Kilmuir – one of Macmillan's peacemakers – had found the convenors of the EDC and WDC 'polite, friendly and immoveable'. The SUA insisted that Buchanan-Smith and McDonald Watson had to go. 'It seems that a handful of educated people are determined to make a scene because they don't like two people,' mused Viscount Stuart in February 1962, 'and if they are prepared to go so far as to lose the next General Election in Scotland, then it is very bad.' The SUA got its way, at least for the time being. Buchanan-Smith departed with a peerage and was succeeded by Sir John Gilmour, son of the 1920s Scottish Secretary.[104]

John Maclay, meanwhile, remained at the Scottish Office before he was among those sacked by Macmillan in his infamous 'night of the long knives', thus signalling 'the termination of a style of politics', i.e. a 'Heath-Robinson coalition of Unionists, National Liberals and Associates', that had brought the centre-right 'unique electoral success'.[105] Maclay was replaced by Michael Noble, the youngest son of a baronet who once cheerfully informed an official that he had only stood as a Unionist in a 1958 by-election because most of his friends were Conservatives.[106] He also succeeded the elderly Stuart as Scottish Unionist chairman and appointed a public relations officer in an attempt to give the party a more professional edge. Lord Aldington still believed 'the organisation in Scotland looks ghastly from here [London] and when you get there it is worse'. He appealed to activists in the National Union to 'help Scotland wherever possible', but as John Ramsden sardonically observed, quite 'what Sussex or Staffordshire Tories were meant to do for the Scots which Central office could not do was not explained'.[107] At the 1962 West Lothian by-election, the Unionists lost their deposit for the first time in 42 years.

Although Noble's relative youth and enthusiasm was an attempt to revitalise both the party in Scotland and Macmillan's Cabinet, within months of the reshuffle he lost one of his ministers in a messy spy scandal known as the 'Vassal affair'. The Glasgow Unionist MP Thomas 'Tam' Galbraith was replaced by Lady Priscilla Tweedsmuir, daughter-in-law of the novelist John Buchan. 'At last', wrote Margaret Thatcher, 'the powers that be have done what they should have done as far back as 1951.'[108] Lady Tweedsmuir would remain a high-profile Scottish Conservative and Unionist figure for the next decade.[109]

The Scottish economy dominated Noble's tenure just as it had Stuart's and Maclay's. The influential Toothill Report caught the zeitgeist for central government 'planning', something enthusiastically embraced by the Butskellite Scottish Secretary. Scotland's New Towns were designated 'growth areas' and St Andrew's House reorganised to include a new Scottish Development Department. Noble also engineered the transfer of the Post Office Savings Bank to Glasgow following a last-minute Cabinet intervention, the first major government agency to leave London.[110] It appeared to do little good. Tam Galbraith, now a backbench MP in Glasgow Hillhead, reported a conversation with his agent to the SUMC. 'He is worried about the general lack of enthusiasm which he says is due to the fact that people don't know what the Gov[ernmen]t is trying to do [economically]. He says morale couldn't be worse.'[111] 'The economic situation in Scotland is rather difficult,' agreed the Prime Minister in his diary in June 1962. 'But, more serious, the Scots are losing their nerve and engaging in a spasm of self-pity.'[112]

Macmillan might have been referring to the Unionist-dominated Scottish Council (for) Development and Industry

(SCDI), where prominent figures like the Lords Polwarth and Clydesmuir were edging towards support for legislative devolution out of frustration at the London-centric nature of economic decision-making.[113] In response, Scottish Unionists pointed to its ostentatious centrism. It was wrong, protested one publication,

> to describe the Unionist Party as being upon the Right in the political scale. It is not 'reactionary'. It is not out to 'exploit'. Rather it is on the Middle Road, between two extremes – the extremes of laissez-faire and Socialism. The Unionist Party realises the need for a synthesis of these two fundamental ideas of human individuality and of service to others and to the community. Remember that the Unionist Party initiated or supported most of the social reforms and the social services.[114]

But even by the late 1950s 'there was a sense that elements of Scottish political culture and Unionism were beginning to diverge'.[115] Not only did the 'wind of change' blowing across Africa and other parts of the British Empire threaten Unionism by imperilling 'the ideology and weakened the glue of barely articulated popular Unionism',[116] but the 'almost institutional connection between the Kirk and the Unionists' in the 1920s had 'melted away'.[117] Perhaps conscious of this, in the late 1950s the party explored (but did not carry through) the idea of Church of Scotland representation in the House of Lords, something the Conservative Research Department agreed would 'greatly please the Church of Scotland, which carries throughout Scotland a good deal more influence and prestige than does the Church of England throughout England'.[118]

Scottish Unionists were not entirely inactive. A scrapbook of SUA activity between 1950 and 1965 at the National Library of Scotland testifies to a vast array of speeches, events and publicity drives during that period.[119] In December 1960 the Scottish Young Unionists (SYU) celebrated their half century at the Glasgow Conservative Club. Indeed, by the early 1960s the SYU boasted 62 branches within the Western Divisional area alone. Young Scottish Unionists were profiled in the *Glasgow Herald* and given airtime on the BBC and Scottish Television, while its activists held weekend schools, a 'Jazz Ball' and even a 'Miss Scottish Young Unionist' contest.[120] But despite the party's best efforts – six Young Unionists had contested seats at the 1959 election – there had been no Lord Woolton-like figure 'to stir sluggish constituencies into action' and make Young Unionists a force to be reckoned with, as the Young Conservatives were in England.[121] In 1963 plans for a new structure were discussed, something prompted by a dearth of resolutions submitted to the movement's annual conference.[122]

On 15 August 1963, the Scottish Office minister and MP for Kinross and West Perthshire, William Gilmour Leburn, collapsed and died while walking on the moors. George Younger – great-grandson of the former Scottish Whip and UK party chairman Sir George Younger – was selected to replace him in 'what amounted to a job for life'.[123] Polling day was set for 7 November, but when Harold Macmillan resigned as Prime Minister on grounds of ill health and the 14th Earl of Home emerged as his preferred successor, the new Scottish Unionist chairman Sir John George,[124] the MP for Glasgow Pollok and a former miner, informed Younger that he would 'do your duty for your country and your party' and stand aside so that Home, about to become plain old Sir Alec,[125] could legitimise his premiership with a seat in the House of Commons. Younger reluctantly obliged on Sunday 20 October. 'It is highly unusual for the ... Unionist Party', observed a contemporary account, 'to conduct political business on the Sabbath. But this was an emergency, and for once rules had to be broken.'[126] The Prime Minister retained the seat with a majority of 9,328.

Sir Alec naturally offered to do what he could to find Younger an alternative constituency, but such were the party's declining fortunes in Scotland there 'was nothing they could offer'.[127] Eventually he accepted the nomination for Ayr, a constituency which had also provided Younger's great-grandfather with a political career. But the seat was not as safe as it had once been, neglected by the incumbent (and Father of the House) Sir Thomas Moore and situated in the very part of Scotland which had swung strongly to Labour in 1959. As the 1964 election approached, Anne Noble, the irrepressible wife of the Scottish Secretary, campaigned on Younger's behalf. 'We want people to know that Unionists are not just political bores like Mr Younger,' she quipped during a meeting in Alloway. 'People should know Unionists are nice people,' she added amid laughter, 'that they are fun and amusing, and lead a good life in every sense of the word.' The press latched on to Anne Noble's description of herself as the Conservative Party's 'horror comic'.[128]

In the run-up to polling day there was a sense the Unionists – their representatives, reputation and even their name – had come to be regarded as something of a joke. The *Daily Record*, which had switched to supporting Labour in the early 1960s, took to caricaturing its new opponents, something David Seawright reckoned might have given 'public portrayal to the negative image of the Tory Party in Scotland as the "Hooray Henrys" of the grouse moor'.[129] 'In Britain, 1964, while Sir Alec enjoys a day's shootin' on the empty moors,' observed one article on the eve of the election, 'old folks go hungry and young folk seek vainly for a job.'[130] In Central Edinburgh, the Labour candidate even distributed material contrasting the castle inhabited by Tory candidate and QC Nicholas Fairbairn with slum housing in the Scottish capital.[131]

The 1964 Conservative Party *Campaign Guide* made strenuous efforts to combat this image, highlighting economic advances since the last election ('Scotland's economy is at present undergoing a transformation') and reviving its 'Scottish Control of Home Affairs' slogan.[132] Lady Tweedsmuir also emphasised the 'modernising' role of Sir Alec Douglas-Home as party leader and Prime Minister:

> I saw him last at [the] opening of the Forth [Road] Bridge, which is symbolic of the Scotland now being created. Modernisation [is] not a catch phrase but a fact. The power stations, nuclear and conventional, the new factories and industries coming into the growth areas at an increasing pace, and the miles of new roads, are transforming the face of Scotland and building her economy on a stronger and more varied basis.[133]

But Lord Dalkeith, the Unionist MP for Edinburgh North, worried that party literature placed 'insufficient emphasis' on what he felt was the 'essential difference' between the two major parties – that the Unionists (unlike Labour) did not regard 'the individual as a cog in the great state machine planned and controlled by the all-knowing man in Whitehall'.[134] As Malcolm Petrie has observed, the 'fragmenting' of the Unionists' anti-socialist coalition in the late 1950s and early 1960s had created an opportunity for both Liberals and the SNP 'to present alternative renderings of this individualist appeal, and to emerge as credible political alternatives'. Not only that, but individual liberty was beginning 'to be understood in constitutional rather than economic terms'.[135]

At the 1964 election, Scottish Unionists (although many now called themselves Conservatives) lost another six seats, meaning the party had shed a fifth of its vote and a dozen MPs since its electoral high-water mark in 1955. Michael Noble was re-elected in Argyllshire with a reduced majority,[136] while George Younger held on to Ayr with a majority of 1,701 in a straight fight with Labour. Particularly alarming was the loss of Glasgow Pollok, which pointed to the decline of a once-solid working-class vote. Part of the blame was pinned on the poor quality of Unionist literature, the Scottish version of the manifesto being 'the wrong colour; it was a mistake to put Sir Alec's photograph on the front; it was too verbose and not sufficiently constructive'.[137] So the result was blamed, 'a little too glibly, on organizational weakness'. 'Still separate from its English sister,' judged Michael Fry, 'the party was certainly in a mess, badly off, burdened with an amateur and fractious machine, lacking facilities for research or policy-making and generally incapable of coherent action.'[138] There was one glimmer of hope, for this further electoral setback would finally stimulate a long-overdue reorganisation of what was about to become the Scottish Conservative and Unionist Party.

NOTES

1. M. Fry (1987), *Patronage and Principle: A Political History of Modern Scotland*, Aberdeen: Aberdeen University Press, 192–3.
2. Credit for this was given to John Cranna, the long-standing secretary of the Western Divisional Council (SCUA Papers, Acc 10424/9, Edinburgh: National Library of Scotland).
3. M. Cragoe (2015), 'Defending the constitution: The Conservative Party and the idea of devolution, 1945–74', in C. Williams and A. Edwards (eds), *The Art of the Possible: Politics and Governance in British History, 1885–1997: Essays in Memory of Duncan Tanner*, Manchester: Manchester University Press, 163.
4. *Scotsman*, 19 August 1946. This article was also published and distributed as '20 REASONS for joining the Unionist Party'.
5. CPS (1946), *Notes on Conservative Policy*, London: Conservative Parliamentary Secretariat.
6. Election address for the Scottish Universities by-election, SUMC Papers 1/51, Oxford: Bodleian Library.
7. For a discussion of Lady Tweedsmuir's Unionism, see P. Ward (2005), *Unionism in the United Kingdom, 1918–1974*, Basingstoke: Palgrave Macmillan, 57–71.

8. *Scotsman*, 24 March 1947.
9. Earl of Selkirk to Patrick Blair, 26 March 1947, SUMC 1/51.
10. Patrick Blair to the Earl of Selkirk, 28 March 1947, SUMC 1/51.
11. SCUA Papers, Acc 10424/44.
12. Minute dated 8 April 1949, SCUA Papers, Acc 10424/44.
13. *Edinburgh Evening Dispatch*, 14 October 1948.
14. I. G. C. Hutchison (2001), *Scottish Politics in the Twentieth Century*, Basingstoke: Palgrave, 78.
15. J. Kellas (1994), 'The Party in Scotland', in A. Seldon and S. Ball (eds), *Conservative Century: The Conservative Party since 1900*, 674. Allan Stewart, later a Scottish Conservative MP, claimed in his memoirs to have been 'brought up in a Liberal Unionist household' (A. Stewart, 1996, *The Long March of the Market Men*, Glendaruel: Argyll, 97).
16. D. Dutton (2008), *Liberals in Schism: A History of the National Liberal Party*, London: I. B. Tauris, 148–9.
17. See D. Torrance (2022), *A History of the Scottish Liberals and Liberal Democrats*, Edinburgh: Edinburgh University Press, 88–90.
18. Patrick Blair, 'The Unionist Party's policy regarding Scottish Affairs', SUMC 1/51.
19. Letter from Patrick Blair, 29 November 1947, SCUA Papers, Acc 11368/80(iii).
20. Oliver Baldwin, a homosexual Labour MP, had inherited his Conservative father's hereditary Earldom.
21. M. Dyer (2003), '"A Nationalist in the Churchillian Sense": John MacCormick, the Paisley By-election of 18 February 1948, Home Rule and the crisis in Scottish Liberalism', *Parliamentary History* 22:3, 300, 307.
22. *Scotsman*, 29 May 1948.
23. *Daily Graphic*, 19 October 1948.
24. *Daily Telegraph*, 20 October 1948.
25. Minute dated 15 February 1949, SUMC 2/4.
26. SCUA Papers, Acc 11368/80(iii). Churchill's speech was later published as *The Days Ahead* (London: Conservative and Unionist Central Office).
27. CUP (1949), *The Right Road for Britain: The Conservative Party's Statement of Policy*, London: Conservative and Unionist Party, 26.
28. SUA (1949), *Scottish Control of Scottish Affairs: Unionist Policy*, Edinburgh: Scottish Unionist Association, 2–10. The party's approach to Wales was much weaker. The *Conservative Policy for Wales and Monmouthshire* (drafted by Enoch Powell), also produced in 1949, was the first attempt by any of the major par-

ties to develop a distinct approach to Welsh affairs but merely envisaged a Minister for Welsh Affairs attending Cabinet.

29. Norman Brook to Clement Attlee, 14 December 1949, PREM 8/1517, London: The National Archives. By way of contrast, Glasgow University's study of the 1950 general election found discussion of Home Rule was 'often coupled with an expressed fear that a devolved Scotland would be permanently Conservative' (S. B. Chrimes, ed., 1950, *The General Election in Glasgow: February, 1950*, Glasgow: Jackson, Son & Company, 25).

30. J. Mitchell (1990), *Conservatives and the Union: A Study of Conservative Party Attitudes to Scotland*, Edinburgh: Edinburgh University Press, 29.

31. *Scotsman*, 29 November 1949.

32. *The Times*, 29 November 1949.

33. R. Rhodes James (ed.) (1974), *Winston S. Churchill: His Complete Speeches, 1897–1963: Volume 8, 1950–63*, New York: Chelsea House, 7937–8.

34. C. Thornton-Kemsley (1974), *Through Winds and Tides*, London: Standard Press, 229.

35. J. Kellas (1994), 205.

36. EDC (1950), *The East of Scotland Year Book 1950*, Edinburgh: Eastern Divisional Council, 21.

37. M. Dyer (2001), 'The evolution of the Centre-right and the state of Scottish Conservatism', *Political Studies* 49:1, 41.

38. C. J. Stevens (1990), 'Scottish Conservatism – A failure of organization?', in A. Brown and R. Parry (eds), *The Scottish Government Yearbook 1990*, Edinburgh: Edinburgh University Press, 78.

39. J. Mitchell (1990), 27.

40. CUP (1951), *Britain Strong and Free*, London: Conservative and Unionist Party, 33.

41. I. G. C. Hutchison (2001), 74.

42. V. Bogdanor (1980), 'Devolution', in Z. Layton-Henry (ed.), *Conservative Party Politics*, London: Macmillan, 78.

43. Elliot received some compensation by succeeding Stuart as chairman of the Scottish Unionist Members' Committee in the House of Commons.

44. A. Douglas-Home (1976), *The Way the Wind Blows: An Autobiography*, London: Collins, 103.

45. A. Seldon (1981), *Churchill's Indian Summer: The Conservative Government, 1951–55*, London: Hodder & Stoughton, 133.

46. A. Seldon (1981), 140. Milligan succeeded Clyde as Lord Advocate in December 1954. His successor as Solicitor-General, William Grant, was also a non-MP until the 1955 general election.

47. D. Torrance (2006), *The Scottish Secretaries*, Edinburgh: Birlinn, 222–3.
48. A. Seldon (1981), 130. This showed that Scotland contributed 9.7 per cent of British revenue while receiving a 12.3 per cent share of 'local' expenditure.
49. *MacCormick v Lord Advocate* [1953] SC 396.
50. Minute dated 26 February 1952, SUMC 2/6.
51. *State Visit to Scotland: Her Majesty the Queen and His Royal Highness The Duke of Edinburgh*, June 1953, Edinburgh: Pillans and Wilson, 11, 16.
52. J. MacCormick (1955), *The Flag in the Wind: The Story of the National Movement in Scotland*, London: Victor Gollancz, 185–6.
53. SUA (1954), *Scotland under the Unionist Government*, Edinburgh: Scottish Unionist Association, 1.
54. Lord Balfour (1954), *Royal Commission on Scottish Affairs 1952–1954: Report*, Cmnd 9212, Edinburgh: HMSO, 74.
55. 'Note for Record' dated 6 July 1954, T222/686, London: The National Archives.
56. CUCO (1955), *United for Peace and Progress*, London: Conservative and Unionist Party, 28–9.
57. SUA (1955), *The Year Book for Scotland 1955*, Edinburgh and Glasgow: Scottish Unionist Association, 17.
58. *Scotsman*, 30 April 1955.
59. James Mitchell has called this 'an ahistorical reading of results that lumps together support for the Scottish Unionist Party . . . and other Unionists/Liberal Unionists', but the lumping was done by MPs and the contemporary media (see J. Mitchell and A. Henderson, 2020, 'Tribes and turbulence: The 2019 UK General Election in Scotland', in J. Tonge, S. Wilks-Heeg and L. Thompson (eds), *Britain Votes: The 2019 General Election*, Oxford: Oxford University Press, 143).
60. SUA (1955), 7.
61. Speech dated 10 November 1955, SUMC 1/25/1.
62. Correspondence relating to the Wallace Memorial, Walter Elliot Papers, Acc 6721 Box 2, Edinburgh: National Library of Scotland.
63. See M. Petrie (2018), 'Anti-Socialism, Liberalism and Individualism: Rethinking the realignment of Scottish Politics, 1945–1970', *Transactions of the Royal Historical Society* 28, 197–217.
64. C. Kidd (2012), 'Smithians, Thatcherites and the ironies of Scottish Conservative decline', in D. Torrance (ed.), *Whatever Happened to Tory Scotland?*, Edinburgh: Edinburgh University Press, 67.

65. Minute dated 15 June 1954, SUMC 2/6.
66. Meeting on 'The Party Organisation in Scotland', 14 February 1956, SUMC 2/16. Even in the late 1940s, the Galloway MP John McKie had suggested that the greatest contribution Colonel Blair could make to a Unionist victory in 1950 'would be to relinquish the post which he had held so long' (*Glasgow Herald*, 15 January 1949).
67. Minute dated 24 April 1956, SUMC 2/16.
68. G. Warner (1988), *The Scottish Tory Party: A History*, London: Weidenfeld & Nicolson, 205.
69. A. Jackson (2011), *The Two Unions: Ireland, Scotland, and the Survival of the United Kingdom, 1707–2007*, Oxford: Oxford University Press, 253–4.
70. SUA (1957), *The Year Book for Scotland 1957*, Edinburgh and Glasgow: Scottish Unionist Association, 25.
71. D. W. Urwin (1966), 'Scottish Conservatism: A party organization in transition', *Political Studies* 14:2, 158.
72. For a short history of Unionist engagement with local government, see SCUCO (1967), *The Year Book for Scotland 1967*, Edinburgh: Scottish Conservative and Unionist Central Office.
73. See E. M. Taylor (2008), *Teddy Boy Blue*, Glasgow: Kennedy & Boyd, 57–78, for an entertaining account of Taylor's career as a Progressive councillor.
74. J. Stuart (1967), *Within the Fringe: An Autobiography*, London: Bodley Head, 176.
75. SCUA Papers, Acc 10424/133. Maitland lost to Labour's Judith Hart. He had succeeded the Earl of Home in 1951, who had been disqualified from the Commons a few months before the general election after succeeding to his father's peerage. Maitland's daughter Olga served as a Conservative MP between 1992 and 1997.
76. M. Fry (1987), 199.
77. D. W. Urwin (1966), 154. Eighteen of the 36 Scottish Unionist & National Liberal MPs elected in 1955 had attended English public schools (Eton accounted for six of them) and nine Scottish public schools.
78. *Bulletin*, 13 April 1957. The headline was '"Jobs for the boys" anger a Scots Tory'. See also F. McLynn (1992), *Fitzroy Maclean*, London: John Murray, 323–4.
79. I. G. C. Hutchison (2001), 108.
80. J. Stuart (1967), 177.
81. B. Boothby (1962), *My Yesterday, Your Tomorrow*, London: Hutchinson, 139–40.
82. EDC (1951), *The East of Scotland Year Book 1951*, Edinburgh: Eastern Divisional Council.

83. SUA (1958), *The Year Book for Scotland 1958*, Edinburgh and Glasgow: Scottish Unionist Association, 7.
84. Note dated 11 September 1959, SUMC 1/54.
85. A. Jackson (2011), 261.
86. Elliot's ebullient wife Kay unsuccessfully tried to hold her late husband's seat. Instead, she joined the House of Lords via the *Life Peerages Act 1958*.
87. The backing of this global spiritual movement divided Wolrige-Gordon's local Unionist association into two camps and attempts at compromise were 'nothing more than wasted Saturday afternoons' (D. W. Urwin, 1966, 153).
88. P. Ward (2005), 59.
89. Patrick Maitland (Lanark), Douglas Spencer-Nairn (Central Ayrshire) and Jack Nixon Browne (Glasgow Craigton) all lost their seats. The Independent Unionist Sir David Robertson was re-elected in Caithness and Sutherland, where he had been unopposed by an 'official' Unionist candidate.
90. Mike Dyer's analysis suggests Unionists did better than expected in 1959, 'the fear of Labour, with its promises of higher direct taxes [being] even more pronounced in Scotland' (M. Dyer, 2001, 33).
91. W. L. Miller (1981), *The End of British Politics? Scots and English Political Behaviour in the Seventies*, Oxford: Clarendon Press, 29.
92. J. Ramsden (1996), *A History of the Conservative Party: The Winds of Change: Macmillan to Heath, 1957–1975*, London: Longman, 135.
93. Younger later confessed to naivety for assuming that 'supportive exhortations of keep the other side out' meant Labour rather than Catholics. See D. Seawright (1999), *An Important Matter of Principle: The Decline of the Scottish Conservative and Unionist Party*, Aldershot: Ashgate, 81.
94. John Cranna to George Younger, 13 October 1959, George Younger Papers, Acc 13116/1, Edinburgh: National Library of Scotland.
95. WDC annual report, Acc 10424/27(ix).
96. Bellairs to Fraser, 22 December 1959, SUMC 1/56.
97. J. Ramsden (1996), 135.
98. D. W. Urwin (1966), 157.
99. D. Seawright (1998), 'Scottish Unionism: An East–West divide?', *Scottish Affairs* 23, 64–5. Blair had been knighted in 1958.
100. C. J. Stevens (1990), 82–3.
101. R. Butler (1960), *A Message to Scotland: Conserve–Unite–Construct*, Glasgow: Conservative Political Centre, 2.

102. D. W. Urwin (1966), 158.
103. P. Catterall (ed.) (2011), *The Macmillan Diaries Vol. II: Prime Minister and After 1957–1966*, London: Macmillan, 357.
104. C. Sutherland (2016), *The Decline of the Scottish Conservative Party*, Kibworth: Book Guild Publishing, 44–53.
105. M. Dyer (2003), 42. The National Liberals finally merged with the Conservatives in 1968.
106. D. Torrance (2006), 240.
107. J. Ramsden (1996), 135–6.
108. Margaret Thatcher to Lady Tweedsmuir, Tweedsmuir Papers Acc 11884/64, Edinburgh: National Library of Scotland.
109. Tweedsmuir's son-in-law, Lord James Douglas-Hamilton, also became a Scottish Conservative MP and Scottish Office minister.
110. D. Torrance (2006), 243.
111. Tam Galbraith to Bellaires, 10 January 1962, SUMC 1/56.
112. P. Catterall (2011), 480.
113. See J. Phillips (2008), *The Industrial Politics of Devolution: Scotland in the 1960s and 1970s*, Manchester: Manchester University Press.
114. SUA (1955), 13.
115. E. A. Cameron (2010), *Impaled Upon a Thistle: Scotland since 1880*, Edinburgh: Edinburgh University Press, 275.
116. I. McLean and A. McMillan (2005), *State of the Union: Unionism and the Alternatives in the United Kingdom since 1707*, Oxford: Oxford University Press, 10.
117. E. Cameron (2010), 265–6.
118. Notes dated 1 March 1957 and 22 January 1958, SUMC 1/54. The Royal Commission on Scottish Affairs had commended the claim of the Scottish National Church to 'an appropriate share in representation' in the House of Lords.
119. See SCUA Papers, Acc 10424/8.
120. SCUA Papers, Acc 10424/103 and Acc 10424/115.
121. I. G. C. Hutchison (2007), 'Scottish Young Conservatives: A local case study – Central Ayrshire Constituency, 1950–c.1979', in A. Murdoch (ed.), *The Scottish Nation: Identity and History. Essays in Honour of William Ferguson*, Edinburgh: Edinburgh University Press, 130–2.
122. I. G. C. Hutchison (2001), 109.
123. *Herald*, 4 March 1995.
124. Sir John George's appointment had finally broken the link between the party chairman and the Scottish Office while Conservatives were in office.
125. The *Peerage Act 1963* allowed Home to disclaim. The same Act extinguished Scotland's 16 representative peers, many of them

Unionists. Instead, all Scottish peers became UK peers, which allowed them to sit in the Upper House as of right.

126. A. Howard and R. West (1965), *The Making of the Prime Minister*, London: Jonathan Cape, 96.
127. *Herald*, 4 March 1995.
128. See D. Torrance (2008), *George Younger: A Life Well Lived*, Edinburgh: Birlinn, 56–9.
129. D. Seawright (1999), 189.
130. *Daily Record*, 14 October 1964.
131. N. Fairbairn (1987), *A Life is Too Short: Aautobiography: Volume One*, London: Quartet, 124.
132. CUP (1964), *The Campaign Guide, 1964: The Unique Political Reference Book*, London: Conservative and Unionist Party, 362, 383–4.
133. P. Ward (2005), 60.
134. EDC minute dated 10 July 1964, Acc 11368/22.
135. M. Petrie (2018).
136. In 1970 Noble returned to the Cabinet as a short-lived President of the Board of Trade under Edward Heath.
137. I. G. C. Hutchison (2001), 107.
138. M. Fry (1987), 225.

6

Reaching Rock Bottom:
1964–1970

In all, 24 Unionists were returned in Scotland at the general election of 1964, a net loss of six. The president of the Scottish Unionist Association considered this 'a severe blow' but expressed hope that if it shocked the party 'into a real effort to improve our organisation without delay so as to be ready to fight back whenever the opportunity comes, we can profit from this sharp lesson'.[1] Having anticipated a bad result, the Scottish Unionist chairman Sir John George (who had not contested his Pollok constituency) had already laid the groundwork for what many considered a long overdue shake-up.

As David Seawright has written, 'the basic assumption was that the Scottish organisation would benefit from imitation and closer identification with the more professional and efficient centralised English party structure'.[2] On 9 June 1964 a rare meeting of the Westminster-based Scottish Unionist Members Committee and the Scottish Unionist Association took place. The former had long held the latter responsible for the party's organisational weakness and had briefed the *Sunday Telegraph* in advance of this meeting that the Scottish party was 'feudalistic' and that the Eastern and Western Divisional Councils caused damaging division. Both accusations were angrily rebutted by the SUA's president and the two divisional conveners.[3]

The WDC was however self-aware enough to conclude in December 1964 that the 'image of the party in Scotland was too aristocratic and Anglicised to be acceptable', indeed 'too remote from the lives of the ordinary people'.[4] At an election post-mortem conducted by the SUA's Central Council in November 1964, it was also reported that while in 1959 the EDC had 600 volunteers,

300 of them aged under 45, in 1964 there were just 200, only 17 of whom were under 45. The party leadership, meanwhile, was roundly blamed for the loss of three Highland seats to the Scottish Liberals, one activist claiming melodramatically that 'the party's magic circle of leadership would remain as remote from the mood and hopes and aspirations of the people of Scotland as the Government of Vietnam is from the people of Vietcong'.[5]

It proved relatively easy to bounce such a bad-tempered party into major structural reforms. By the end of 1964 the EDC and WDC had acquiesced in their own abolition, to be replaced with five regional councils (City of Glasgow, Highland, North-Eastern, Central and Southern, South-Western).[6] Most radical of all was the name change. The catch-all title of 'Unionist' engineered by Sir George Younger following the merger with Liberal Unionists in 1912 now became the 'Scottish Conservative and Unionist Association' (SCUA). 'We were looking for everything that could be wrong,' explained his great-grandson, also George. 'One of the things that to many of us was daft was to be calling ourselves Unionists ... We just thought, well, I'm not a Unionist actually, I'm a Conservative.'[7] Campaign material 'would no longer have to be changed from Conservative to Unionist at great expense'.[8] Younger also believed Sir John George had made a conscious decision to distance the party from the religious and sectarian overtones of 'Unionism'.[9]

The name change – long urged by younger party members – and structural reforms were announced in January 1965 and approved by what was to be the final Scottish Unionist Association conference in April that year. Urwin considered the 'most interesting reforms' to concern the 'professional' side of the organisation:

> The design was to create a pyramid of paid workers with the Chairman's Office at the apex, in line with the English model. Each regional council was given an agent who is appointed by and answerable to the Chairman of the Party. The old financial system was abolished and a single Scottish fund established, which would be controlled by the Chairman, while the National Treasurer, like the Chairman, is to be appointed by and responsible to the British party leader. In addition the staff and research department of the Chairman's Office has been greatly expanded and an overall policy committee created. Moreover, a Conservative Political Centre Officer for Scotland has been established for the first time.

But as Urwin cautioned, organisation was not everything. Not only did the Scottish chairman's office still lack direct authority over constituency agents, but the reforms seemed unlikely to 'bring to an end the intra-association disputes seemingly endemic in rural Scotland'. The deeper problem was that Scottish Conservatism appeared 'out of touch' with the changing 'social character and needs' of certain Scottish communities, as illustrated by Liberal gains in rural Scotland at the 1964 election:

> It is a new identification of Conservatism with these needs, rather than structural reform, which will enable the party to recover the ground lost very largely through complacency. The day-to-day responsibility thus rests with the local associations, which are perhaps still the determining factor in the party. Unless a majority of them accept the need for a revision of attitudes and internal policies and structure, it can legitimately be suggested that the structural reforms of 1965 will not have much serious effect on the relationship of the party with the electorate, and consequently that the problems which have faced Scottish Conservatism in the past will remain largely unsolved.[10]

Indeed, even as the reorganisation was being implemented, the party in Scotland continued to suffer further demoralising defeats. Roxburgh, Selkirk and Peebles fell to the 'Boy David' Steel (later Liberal Party leader) in a March 1965 by-election, the constituency having long stagnated under the incumbent Unionist MP Charles Donaldson. A few months later, Sir Alec Douglas-Home resigned as Leader of the Opposition and within days Edward Heath became the first UK Conservative Party leader formally elected by the Parliamentary Conservative Party. Conscious that something had to be done in Scotland, Heath quickly appointed George Younger (the MP for Ayr) the Scottish Conservative whip at Westminster.

When Harold Wilson called another general election at the end of 1966, the Labour Party romped home with an increased majority of 96. The Conservatives, as they now were, ended up with only 20 seats in Scotland, a further loss of four MPs, a sobering vindication of Urwin's warning that the party could not hide behind reorganisation. The result in 1964 had been bad enough; the outcome two years later was considered by many Conservatives to be terminal. 'We lost and heavily,' reflected the SCUA's president, Russell Fairgrieve. 'The fact that, in Scotland, we had a smaller swing against us than in other areas of the country is but poor consolation when our Party is out by a hundred seats.'[11] As the *Scotsman* observed:

> Ten years ago there were 36 Unionist MPs; now there are only 20, despite a drastic shake-up and despite the five super-agents. The grass roots are bewildered. Too much attention to organisation, too little attention to policies. Too much Eton and Oxbridge, too many irrelevant candidates. And, importantly, realists know that the Tories have not reached rock-bottom yet.[12]

Together with much soul-searching at 11 Atholl Crescent, the new Edinburgh home of the consolidated party operation, journalistic eyes turned towards the so-called 'young Turks' of the party. The *Scotsman* even tipped George Younger to become its next chairman. 'He has lived down his aristocratic connections with the beerage and the suspicion of dynasticism,' it claimed.[13] The 'new-style' Scottish Conservative, judged the *Glasgow Herald*, 'tends to rationalise the reasons for the party's decline by saying that the good work done for Scotland in the last five years of Conservative rule simply did not compensate for the inadequate policies of the previous five'.[14]

Figures within the party also began to look to Younger as a solution, or at least part of a solution. Ian McIntyre, a former BBC producer and now head of information and research at Scottish Conservative Central Office, spent the months after the 1966 election sounding out various party figures, which he distilled into a 'personal & confidential' letter to Younger dated 1 May 1966. In blunt terms, McIntyre believed the situation was 'much graver even than 20 seats out of 71 would indicate'. If sustained corrective action was not initiated soon, he argued, 'we shall become another Wales' (a reference to the 1964 election at which just three Tory MPs had been returned). In essence, McIntyre argued, it

> comes down to a lack of credibility. The Party as a whole just doesn't cut a convincing figure in Scotland any more, in spite of the efforts of 'the class of '59' and the arrival of people like Alick and Teddy [Taylor] and yourself. Perhaps even worse, the Central Office in Edinburgh doesn't convince candidates and others on the voluntary side that we are equipped to lead them out of this wilderness ... Hard as it is to face it is still not Michael Noble, or the class of '59 or you and Alick and Teddy and Hector [Monro] who furnish the stock

image of the Party in Scotland. It is the [Michael] Clark Hutchinsons, the [John] Brewises, the [Tam] Galbraiths, the [Earl of] Dalkeiths, [and] the Gilmours. They, by their silences, or by what they say when they do occasionally pipe up, destroy half the good you do.[15]

The newspaper leader writer James McMillan would later note that the proportion of Scottish Conservative MPs educated at English public schools had increased from two-thirds to four-fifths at the 1966 election, with only two of its MPs educated at Scottish day schools: Teddy Taylor (Glasgow High) and Norman Wylie (Paisley Grammar). Two more, Betty Harvie Anderson and Alick Buchanan-Smith, had attended Scottish public schools and two others, Esmond Wright and Wilfred Baker, English day schools. The remainder were products of Eton (8), Winchester (2), Wellington (3) and Cheltenham (1) and Canford (1). To McMillan, this illustrated the party's increasing 'Anglicisation' and reliance on a declining Protestant vote. Robin McEwan had been 'the only Catholic for many years to fight a seat for the Tories' (the 1965 by-election won by David Steel), while McMillan speculated that Robert Kernohan had failed to hold Pollok for the Unionists in 1964 because he had an Irish-sounding name.[16] Indeed, Budge and Urwin's groundbreaking study of Scottish political behaviour had revealed that Protestant working-class areas were still more likely to vote Conservative than their Catholic counterparts.[17]

Ian McIntyre, meanwhile, was equally frank in his assessment of what action was needed to arrest Scottish Conservative decline. Sir John Gilmour, he said, was not an 'effective or credible Chairman' and ought to be replaced by Younger with McIntyre as his deputy and 'specifically identified as the executive head of the office'. 'There comes a point beyond which it becomes tedious and embarrassing to be associated with failure on the Scottish Tory scale,' concluded McIntyre, 'and I am very close to that point.'[18]

On 12 January 1967, some of what McIntyre had recommended came to pass. Sir John Gilmour was removed as chairman of the Scottish party, but he was replaced by Sir Gilmour Menzies Anderson, a Glaswegian lawyer and Burma veteran, with George Younger as his deputy (he had recently masterminded a spirited campaign to 'Save the Argylls', the regiment with which he had served in Korea). Robert Kernohan was also recruited from running the *Glasgow Herald*'s London office to become director-general of Scottish Central Office in a further attempt to sharpen up the operation. McIntyre, despite his impatience, continued to head up information and research. A new 'House Style for the Conservative Party in Scotland' was rolled out during 1968, central to which was a new party logo which included 'a stylised segment of the Union flag, symbolising our position as the party of the Union'.[19]

There were soon noticeable improvements to morale as a result of the new party regime, which set about assembling an impressive team of candidates, not only for Westminster but to fight increasingly political local government elections (the 'Progressives' remained the equivalent of Conservatives in Scottish town halls, although polling suggested such labels repelled rather than attracted voters).[20] Two important by-elections put this to the test during 1967. The first, in March 1967, saw the academic Esmond Wright regain Glasgow Pollok for the Scottish Conservatives, while the second, in Hamilton seven months later, led to the triumphant election of the SNP's Winnie Ewing, only the party's second MP. This, rather than Pollok – where a strong SNP showing had allowed Wright to win – was a sign of Scottish politics to come.

To plan a response to the sort of nationalist sentiment which had spooked Scottish Unionists in the early 1930s and again in the late 1940s, Edward Heath summoned leading Scottish Conservatives to his London flat on 16 November 1967. Budge and Urwin had already identified the 'pervasiveness of Scottish national consciousness among Scottish electors', which they believed might 'set definite limits to the tactics politicians employ or the policies they advocate',[21] while a whole year before the Hamilton by-election the Opinion Research Centre (ORC) had detected a feeling of 'alienation and neglect' in Scotland and Wales, with the Conservative Party perceived as distant, 'a uniquely English party of the Squirearchy, the Establishment, the Church of England and Westminster'. The Scottish Conservatives in particular had an 'exceedingly bad image', being 'a bastion of "foreign" (English) privilege'. Strikingly, the survey found that a majority of Scottish voters would still support self-government even if they were left worse off.[22] Doubtless aware of this research, Heath later recalled:

Our party policy in March 1966 had been robustly opposed to the establishment of a Scottish assembly, a policy that I had inherited from a whole string of my predecessors ... But, in the light of the evident shift in opinion since that election, it would have been politically suicidal to stick to our guns. So, in June 1967, I set up a Scottish Policy Group with a completely open brief ... The suggestion for a Scottish Assembly would therefore come from the Scottish Conservative Party.[23]

The SNP's by-election win therefore acted to accelerate (rather than instigate) Heath's approach to the Scottish Question. The meeting at his London flat agreed that Conservatives would

show that we accepted that Scotland had protested against the present situation – had risen in dissent, but that we were the Party who was going to take note of this protest and meet the justifiable grievances of the Scots.[24]

It was a familiar refrain. In March 1968, the ORC completed some more market research which revealed that the Conservatives were 'the only Scottish Party which, on mention, often elicited mirthful or mirthless laughter'.[25] In tandem with the Scottish party's devolution policy group, Peter Goldman at the Conservative Research Department was also asked to investigate policy options. The result was notable in that it flagged the risk of any devolutionary policy being seen as 'an opportunistic volte-face' given that 'the broad history and tradition of the Party are anti-"home rule"'. Nevertheless, wrote Goldman, for Conservatives 'to become advocates and later architects of home rule, thus spiking the guns of Socialists, Liberals and Nationalists alike, is the most dramatic step we could take to retrieve this [electoral] strength'.[26]

Not everyone was as enthusiastic, not least the Scottish Conservative MP Betty Harvie Anderson, who led a delegation of MPs alarmed at the direction of travel. Jock Bruce-Gardyne, the Conservative MP for South Angus, believed that rather than pursuing independence or 'some intermediate solution masquerading under the slogan of devolution', the Conservative Party ought 'to reestablish belief and pride in Great Britain'.[27] Ahead of his speech to the May 1968 Scottish Conservative conference in Perth, meanwhile, Robert Kernohan cautioned Heath to present any proposals as 'part of the broad evolution of our existing policy'.[28] The Leader of the Opposition had already been briefed as to his policy group's conclusions, an indirectly elected 'Scottish Assembly' dealing with some stages of UK legislation that affected Scotland. This was signed off by the Shadow Cabinet on 8 May, and 10 days later in what became known as the 'Declaration of Perth', Heath proposed that 'a Constitutional Committee should be set up to examine proposals for the reorganisation of Scottish Government'. He then proceeded to pre-empt that committee's conclusion:

> What we have in mind is that this Scottish Assembly would be a single chamber, and would take part in legislation in conjunction with Parliament ... Let there be no doubt about this: the Conservative Party is determined to effect a real improvement in the machinery of government in Scotland. And it is pledged to give the people of Scotland genuine participation in the making of decisions that affect them – all within the historic unity of the United Kingdom.

Heath was also careful to place this policy in the context of what he called 'our basic principles':

> We find there two important strands. The first is that we have long been the Party of Union. Our fundamental belief is in the destiny of the United Kingdom ... The second strand is our belief in the devolution of power.[29]

The former Prime Minister, Sir Alec Douglas-Home, was appointed chairman of the committee, while George Younger was given the task of selling the new policy to the party at large. But in his haste to modernise the Conservatives as well as Scottish governance, Heath had ridden roughshod over the Scottish party with inadequate preparation and little attempt to take activists with him. 'We persuaded Heath it was a good idea,' recalled George Younger. 'But we were quite surprised by the strong reaction we got from the Old Guard after the declaration.'[30]

Visiting Scotland again a few months later, Heath listened as Scottish party 'notables' sounded off against the Assembly. 'This they do feebly, a poor lot, as the malt goes round,' recorded Douglas Hurd in his diary. Instead they told Heath of an alternative vision: 'Relieve surtax and appeal to the common man.'[31] At local government elections in May 1968, the SNP had continued their electoral success, doing particularly well in the New Towns championed by Unionists (and Labour) during the 1950s.

The SCUA had established its own 'New Towns campaign' in 1967, but the 1968 results had revealed its failure and the party's inability to woo upwardly mobile working-class voters.[32]

Catriona Macdonald has judged that the 'Declaration of Perth' was 'less of an aberration than a missed opportunity to take a long-held commitment to administrative devolution all the way to a legislative end',[33] and indeed, whatever its PR failings, Harold Wilson's government was compelled to follow suit, appointing a Royal Commission on the Constitution in April 1969. On a visit to Scotland, the Ulster Unionist Prime Minister of Northern Ireland, Terence O'Neill, extolled the virtues of the legislative devolution granted to the six counties of Ulster half a century earlier. He maintained that devolution did not mean 'spending more money than the English on a particular service, but doing it more intelligently, or in a way particularly suited to Scotland'.[34] Although ties between the two parts of the UK had weakened, fraternal visits between the Scottish and Ulster Unionists continued until the early 1960s.[35]

Most enthusiastic about devolution were a group of younger, generally moderate Conservatives who promoted a Scottish Assembly and other policies under the banner of a 'Thistle Group' formed in November 1967. The name was suggested by Malcolm Rifkind 'as something that was both Scottish and uncomfortable to tamper with'.[36] The group's first pamphlet ('A basic aim of the Thistle Group is to stir things up') was published prior to the Hamilton by-election but felt vindicated by its outcome. It had identified the Scottish party as failing on three fronts: its public image ('as presented though its policies'), the outlook of its candidates and, predictably, poor organisation. 'The Scottish Tory Party must not only be concerned with Scottish problems,' it declared, 'it must also be seen to be concerned.'[37] A second pamphlet suggested the adoption of a 'federal framework of government' in which fiscal 'independence' would be 'vital'.[38] The establishment of such a group to stress the Scottish dimension would not have been necessary even a decade earlier, but the formation of the Thistle Group demonstrated how quickly the party had lost its nationalist elan.

The Scottish Young Conservatives were just as critical. Their chairman, Victor MacColl, told the *Glasgow Herald* that the party did 'not speak the language of the Scottish people',[39] while he urged it 'to attack the old assumption of the working-class

voting Labour and the middle-class Conservative'. MacColl
even suggested it acquire 'a simple and direct political appeal
like the SNP'.[40] His was a voice of moderation compared with
the St Andrews Conservative Association, which as well as
promoting what would become known as 'monetarism' was
also preoccupied with maintaining white minority rule in
South Africa and Southern Rhodesia. In January 1970, Enoch
Powell addressed the Association's annual dinner and required
heavy police protection from a substantial crowd of student
protesters.[41] By contrast, when the chairman of the Central
Ayrshire Conservative association addressed its youth wing in
1969, he ignored international events and instead spoke about
his collection of snuffboxes. To Hutchison, 'the Young Tories
must have seemed dinosaurs'; only in 1967 had they abolished
formal dress for conference dances and compulsory church
attendance at weekend schools.[42]

Sir Alec Douglas-Home's report, *Scotland's Government*, was
finally published on 19 March 1970 and contained 34 recommendations. The most important was the creation of a 'Scottish
Convention' with approximately 125 members to consider the
second reading and committee stages of all exclusively Scottish
Bills, although importantly there was to be no separate 'executive' (or government), making it, in the view of James Mitchell,
'a mere talking shop'.[43] In spite of party uneasiness, two months
later the Scottish Conservative conference endorsed Sir Alec's
proposals by three to one. They also formed part of the first
separate Scottish party manifesto:

> Scotland, with its distinct identity, traditions and legal system, is par-
> ticularly conscious of these problems. The Report of the Committee
> set up under Sir Alec Douglas Home offers a new chance for the
> Scottish people to have a greater say in their own affairs. Its contents,
> including the proposal for a Scottish Convention sitting in Edinburgh,
> will form a basis for the proposals we will place before Parliament,
> taking account of the impending organisation of local government.[44]

Curiously understated was any Scottish Conservative case *for*
the Union, as opposed to some sort of devolution. In his contribution to a collection of essays on the 'Scottish Debate', the
Glasgow Pollok MP Esmond Wright complacently suggested it
was 'not the case for the United Kingdom that has to be made,
but rather the case against it':

The United Kingdom exists ... It is not, of course, without need of improvement, for no system is perfect. But any case for basic constitutional change needs to be made and proven beyond doubt ... For my part, with all its imperfections, I prefer the present order – amended, revised, and improved – to the revolutionary notions of political and economic separatism.[45]

Revolutionary notions were absent at the general election of 1970. Despite its late-1960s buoyancy, the SNP returned just a single MP, while the Conservatives experienced a modest increase in its vote share vis-à-vis 1966. This was enough to return 23 Scottish MPs, three more than at the last election, and although the swing to the Conservatives was smaller than in England (2.3 per cent and 5.6 per cent respectively), it at least indicated that the decline of the 1960s had been arrested. The party, meanwhile, returned to office for the first time since 1964. Gordon Campbell (a former diplomat) became Scottish Secretary, supported by George Younger, Alick Buchanan-Smith, Teddy Taylor and Lady Tweedsmuir as junior Scottish Office ministers.

A wartime injury had left Campbell's left leg in a calliper and he often had to rely upon two walking sticks in order to cover long distances.[46] Although a man of charm and bravery, he proved ill-suited to an increasingly tribal political atmosphere in Scotland, the usual cut and thrust of debate now underlaid with the then novel accusation that the Conservatives did not possess a 'mandate' with which to govern Scotland. Like Sir John Gilmour in the 1920s, Campbell tackled local government reform as Scottish Conservative candidates began to contest local elections for the first time. A two-tier system of nine 'regional' and 53 'district' authorities irritated activists and MPs, not least because the new 'Strathclyde' region was likely to consolidate Labour's hegemony in the West of Scotland.

Finding Campbell remote and studiously apolitical, ordinary party members aired their grievances with the increasingly disillusioned George Younger and Alick Buchanan-Smith. Following a special meeting in 1971, the Scottish Conservative and Unionist Association had voted to move its Glasgow headquarters to the same offices inhabited by the Scottish chairman in Edinburgh.[47] Party finances were also in a 'parlous state', its income in 1970 just £118,350, of which only £8,744 came from constituency associations (the target had been £16,000).[48]

The organisational reforms of 1965 also meant what was now the 'West of Scotland' area received only £10,500 of the party's annual income in 1973.[49] The annual 'Year Book for Scotland', once a fixture of the Scottish Unionist Association's activity, had ceased publication in 1967 as part of a previous economy drive.

The continuing erosion of support in urban areas also bolstered the 'grouse moor' image of Scottish Conservatives, their parliamentary ranks dominated by landowners and military men.[50] Kellas reckoned this opened up an urban–rural divide within the party, the 'Young Tories of the cities' blaming 'the domination of the party by lairds for [electoral] losses',[51] with the Stirling, Falkirk & Grangemouth Young Conservatives exploding 'against a lethargic Association' during 1971.[52] There were, however, also signs that a once-invisible barrier between 'U' and 'non-U' candidates was weakening. In late 1972, for example, Norman Wylie, the Lord Advocate and MP for Edinburgh Pentlands, primed the advocate James Clyde to succeed him at the next election. Clyde was keen, not least to advance his legal career (as had his father and grandfather, both Unionist MPs before becoming Lord President), but despite doing all that was asked of him – canvassing and speaking at meetings – the Pentlands association opted for another young advocate, the Thistle Group founder Malcolm Rifkind. Clyde was instead adopted for the virtually unwinnable constituency of Dundee East.[53]

Europe was another emerging fault line within both the Scottish and UK Conservative parties, although the former was broadly supportive of the UK joining the bloc (Clyde was particularly keen on developing a European legal fraternity). As the introduction to a June 1971 publication entitled *Scotland and Europe: Seven Viewpoints* observed:

> In some ways it is easier for us [Scots] to contemplate the partnership which the membership of the European Community would involve, for we ourselves inherit the experience and benefit of a political and economic community set up in 1707 – not, one should add, with universal support from the public opinion polls of the day. Our ability to retain our identity and evolve our institutions within this wider patriotism is not irrelevant in the debate about the alleged end of '1,000 years of history'. Hugh Gaitskell's phrase and attitude may be far-fetched for England. It is quite inappropriate for Scotland.[54]

The House of Commons voted on the UK's accession in October 1971, with Scottish Conservative MPs supporting entry by 18 to three, the refuseniks being a mixture of rural and urban: Michael Clark Hutchison in Edinburgh West, the Aden veteran Colin 'Mad Mitch' Mitchell in Aberdeenshire West and Teddy Taylor in Glasgow Cathcart.[55] Indeed, Taylor even resigned as a Scottish Office minister on this basis. Not yet an MP was the St Andrews graduate Allan Stewart, whose pungent campaign against the Common Market had prompted Jock Bruce-Gardyne to complain to Scottish Central Office regarding his defiance of party policy.

The Royal Commission on the Constitution appointed by the previous Labour government, meanwhile, finally reported at the end of October 1973. It recommended a directly elected Scottish Assembly just after the half-century-old Parliament of Northern Ireland (Stormont) had been abolished, whereupon Ulster Unionist MPs at Westminster had relinquished the Conservative whip, weakening the pan-UK ties to which Scottish Unionists had once contributed so much. Given that devolution had been a Scottish Conservative commitment since 1968, Gordon Campbell had come under repeated pressure to legislate. The need for local government reform initially provided some cover, but now the Royal Commission had reported he had nowhere to hide. Adding to Campbell's woes, the Scottish Conservatives were even more split on the issue than in 1968. At the 1973 Perth conference, a proposal calling on Heath's government to reaffirm its commitment to an Assembly had been heavily defeated on a show of hands. An alliance of Young Conservative delegates and the MP for Aberdeen South Iain Sproat (also Campbell's parliamentary private secretary) then led an attempt to kill off any residual commitment to devolution.

When the Prime Minister addressed the conference, he did not even mention the word 'devolution'. Privately, however, Heath's irritation at the corporate raids of Lonrho had 'fused with his natural antipathy to the hierarchy of the Scottish Conservative Party' to produce an angry speech at the pre-conference SCUA president's dinner in which the Prime Minister attacked what he called the 'ugly' (or 'unacceptable') face of capitalism.[56] The Scottish economic backdrop was grim. During the Upper Clyde Shipbuilders work-in of 1972, 'SCOTORY', an anonymous pamphleteer sponsored by the Thistle Group, had predicted that if Gordon Campbell did not alleviate present unemployment, then 'the Conservative Party will stand indicted not only for the present unemployment, but as the party of no compassion, of callous indifference, and of the jungle law of the survival of the fittest'.[57]

By the time Edward Heath called a snap general election in February 1974, asking 'Who Governs Britain?', the Conservative government had been worn down by industrial strife, an energy crisis and internal divisions over the Common Market. That neither Heath nor his Scottish Secretary were the most human of politicians did not help, a weakness the Prime Minister acknowledged by resurrecting the populist Teddy Taylor as a Scottish Office minister shortly before the campaign. Heath wanted him to shake things up in St Andrew's House and in the Scottish party, his vibrant constituency association in Cathcart having demonstrated that it was possible to cope with shifting demographics, in this case the construction of the Castlemilk housing scheme. Cathcart Conservatives were even summoned to party headquarters 'to explain to other constituency officials how an energetic and effective organisation could flourish'.[58]

What had once been rural Unionist heartlands badly needed a Teddy Taylor. In Moray and Nairn (James Stuart's old seat), Gordon Campbell was defeated on a 13 per cent swing by the SNP's Winnie Ewing, who had accused the Conservative government of having sold local 'fishermen ... down the European river'.[59] The loss of another seat gave Scottish Conservatives 21 MPs, barely an improvement on its 1966 tally. That Labour's Scottish vote share had declined by even more offered scant comfort, while the SNP's breakthrough with seven MPs and 21.9 per cent of the vote dominated the headlines. Hamish Watt, one of the seven but also a former Conservative candidate, claimed during the campaign that his party would not 'ask you to stop being Socialists, Conservatives or Liberals. We ask you to be Scottish Nationalists, Scottish Liberals, and Scottish Conservatives.'[60]

An updated Scottish Conservative manifesto attempted to reclaim the individualist 'freedom' mantle from both the SNP and Scottish Liberals, for it was in Scotland that 'centralising forces have had their most damaging impact':

Devolution is our policy and is the direct opposite of separatism. It can free Scotland from the frustrations of centralisation. Scottish Conservatives have a good record of devolution in the creation of departments at the Scottish Office free to take their own administrative decisions over a wide range of functions. And we have long recognised the need for matching devolution in the legislative and political field.

Income from North Sea oil was to be channelled into a Scottish Development Fund, which in turn would be used to abolish the tolls on the Forth, Tay and Erskine Bridges. Council tenants were to be given the opportunity to 'purchase their homes at one-third less than market value', while in the lifetime of the next Parliament a Conservative government would abolish domestic rating.[61]

But despite this attractive prospectus (elements of which would characterise the Thatcherite agenda of the 1980s), at a second general election in October the SNP made even more headway, winning 11 MPs. The Scottish Conservatives were reduced to just 16, its fewest since the early 1920s. Even worse, the SNP had beaten the Conservatives into third place when it came to share of the vote (30.4 to 24.7), which suggested that a lot of moderate Conservatives had supported the Nationalists. Despite this wave of what Nicholas Fairbairn called 'Nationalist dementia tartanica' sweeping over rural Scotland, in Kinross and West Perthshire he and the party kept it 'at bay' by 53 votes, Sir Alec Douglas-Home having chosen to retire.[62]

As the gloomy news poured into Atholl Crescent, George Younger (who was now Scottish Conservative chairman) admitted the party had 'taken a mauling' and blamed tactical voting by Tory supporters who had backed the SNP in order to topple Labour Members.[63] Six days after the election, Younger announced at a press conference that Conservative MPs would support the Labour government's scheme for a directly elected Scottish Assembly. Both 'Unionist' parties were now desperately trying to halt the onward march of the Scottish National Party. Younger was bombarded with memos and letters from activists across Scotland, many of them quite hostile. 'The main point which comes across', judged Russell Sanderson in November 1974, 'was that the loss of the October election was due almost entirely to the record of the Government 1970–74.'[64]

Southern Conservatives such as Douglas Hurd regarded the
Scottish party leadership with despair:

> Nice men with an excessive regard for hierarchy, they presided
> over a declining party with scant regard for what was happening
> outside their own playground ... they concealed political weak-
> nesses behind portentous titles and procedures. Their speeches were
> longer and their meals included more courses than their equivalents
> in England.[65]

In February 1975, Margaret Thatcher succeeded Edward
Heath as UK Conservative leader. 'I shall need a lot of advice
about Scotland but am ready and willing to take it,' she wrote
to George Younger, who she was about to appoint Shadow
Defence Secretary. 'I believe that the problem is the same as
further south – people lost *faith* in us and our job is to restore
it.'[66] Younger accompanied his new leader on her first, oddly
tumultuous, visit to Scotland a few days later. 'Mrs Supercool!'
screamed the *Daily Record* headline on 22 February.[67]

Mrs Thatcher's visit boosted morale among Scottish
Conservatives for the first time in years, telling activists in
Glasgow that they would

> not succeed, and would not deserve to succeed, if we sought the
> support of the people of Scotland by pretending to be, or seeming
> to be, partly a Liberal party, partly a socialist party and partly a
> Scottish national party. We stand as Conservatives for Conservative
> policies.[68]

'I shall never forget the warmth of that reception,' Thatcher
later gushed. 'Overnight, I became "Maggie"! And I've been
Maggie ever since.'[69] As for Mrs Thatcher's attitude towards
Scotland, one of her biographers suggested that she

> never understood Scotland, though she liked to think she did. She
> fancied she had a special affinity with the Scots, whom she imagined
> as thrifty, enterprising and inventive, a mixture of Adam Smith,
> George Stephenson and David Livingstone, hardy pioneers who had
> made the industrial revolution and built the British Empire. The
> reality was a persistent disappointment to her. Most Scots turned
> out to be unreconstructed working-class socialists with an egalitar-
> ian culture of public housing and an inbred hostility to Thatcherism;
> or tartan Tories, patrician, feudal, paternalistic and equally disdain-
> ful of her sort of southern stridency.[70]

When it came to devolution, although Thatcher realised the Scottish party 'was deeply split', she trod carefully, repeating the party's commitment to an Assembly 'as briefly as [she] decently could' at her first Scottish conference in May 1975 while gathering support for a change. 'Talking to people at the Conference brought home more clearly than ever the fact that there were some Scottish Tories who bitterly disagreed with their leaders about the whole question,' she recalled in her memoirs. 'My unease grew – and so did that of many other people.' As she explained in the second volume of her memoirs: 'Ted [Heath] had impaled the party on an extremely painful hook from which it would be my unenviable task to set it free.'[71]

George Younger stood down as Scottish party chairman in September 1975, after which he received a letter from John Davidson, a senior Scottish party official:

> Like you I am depressed by the state of the Party where friends in Scotland are serving us ill. Of even greater concern is the attitude of your colleagues in the South who may present the SNP with a huge and undeserved bonus by adopting a stance [that] could make the English Tories seem ignorant, insensitive and colonial in their attitude to Scotland. I fully share your views on devolution and it is up to you to stop our English MPs from fraternal assassination![72]

The 'friends in Scotland' to whom Davidson referred were a noisy and articulate band of Scottish Conservative MPs led by Teddy Taylor and which included Betty Harvie Anderson, who had resigned as Deputy Speaker in 1973 so she could campaign freely against devolution. Taylor had cooled on devolution, having previously viewed a Scottish Assembly as 'an invigorating and persuasive weapon' when it came to 'the transformation of the Scottish Conservatives [in]to a Scottish People's Party'.[73]

Many of the same MPs also opposed continuing UK membership of the EEC, which was put to the first UK-wide referendum in June 1975. The campaign group 'Scottish Conservatives Against the Treaty of Rome' had a 'distinctly Powellite flavour', and indeed Enoch attracted a large audience when he addressed a rally in Arbroath. Teddy Taylor also toured Scotland with the Labour MP Jim Sillars and the SNP's Margo MacDonald urging a 'No' vote. When he excoriated the 'Treaty of Rome', noted one newspaper, 'every Protestant who wears a Glasgow Rangers scarf knows what he [Taylor] means'.[74]

Margo MacDonald's stance served as a reminder that in the mid-1970s the SNP were anti-Europe and Scottish Conservatives broadly pro. An ORC survey in May 1975 found that more than two-thirds of SNP voters planned to vote to leave the EEC, compared with just a fifth of Conservatives.[75] Indeed, polling day revealed Scotland (where 58.7 per cent voted 'Yes') to be less enthusiastic about the EEC than England (68.7 per cent). Malcolm Petrie has argued that this allowed Nationalists to depict the Conservatives as 'anti-Scottish'. The SNP

> found its appeal to both individual and national freedom especially well-suited to this new political landscape. Conversely, Scottish Conservatives suffered the most acute losses, as the party's support for both Common Market membership and the restructuring of local government proved unpopular with large parts of the party's traditional support.[76]

Devolution thus assumed a lesser importance, not least because both the Conservatives and SNP were divided over that issue: the former through fears of weakening the Union and the latter because of concerns that a Scottish Assembly would dampen support for full independence.

The official Scottish Conservative position remained Lord Home's 1970 proposals, although no one expected those to survive undiluted. In November 1975, Malcolm Rifkind (now the MP for Edinburgh Pentlands) circulated a paper which supported an elected Scottish Assembly, albeit as an 'integrated' chamber of the UK Parliament and without an 'executive' of its own. But with the Labour government preparing to put its own devolution proposals to a Commons vote, Graham Wynn of the Conservative Research Department warned that if Mrs Thatcher came out firmly against an Assembly then the Scottish party 'would be split down the middle both in Parliament and in the country'.[77] Eleven Scottish Tory MPs were judged to be firmly pro-Assembly, including Younger, with only five deeply opposed. Broadly speaking, judged Charles Moore, 'the more upper-class and rural elements, which dominated the party hierarchy and produced two-thirds of the Scottish MPs, were pro-devolution, and the more urban and working-class elements were anti'.[78] Arnold Kemp identified no fewer than four groups: diehard opponents (Taylor, Iain Sproat and

Harvie Anderson), moderates (Rifkind et al.), 'maximalists' (those such as Russell Fairgrieve who favoured a more powerful Assembly) and finally a more radical group 'committed to a quasi-federal' settlement (which may have included Edward Heath).[79] Beyond the Parliamentary Conservative Party, most prospective candidates in Scotland were devolutionists, while both the Federation of Conservative Students in Scotland and the Scottish Young Conservatives were also keen supporters, although that would later change. In a pamphlet entitled *The Scottish Conservative Party: A New Model for a New Dimension*, Michael Forsyth and a young Edinburgh solicitor called David McLetchie even argued that 'internal reform' of the party had to 'prepare it for a future where a Scottish Assembly is a permanent feature of political life'.[80] Similarly, *The Scottish Conservatives: A Past and a Future*, written by Ian Lang and Barry Henderson (who the *Scottish Daily News* called 'the angry young men of a torn party'), declared: 'We must be seen as Scots who are Conservative rather than Conservatives who happen to be Scots.'[81]

Only when it came to Scottish constituency activists was there a clear majority against devolution. A vote on the subject at a special conference in January 1976 produced 103 for devolution, with 60 against and 40 abstentions.[82] This confirmed that the Scottish Conservative Party was split down the middle. While George Younger and Alick Buchanan-Smith – both Scottish spokesmen – had reluctantly accepted Rifkind's 'third chamber' compromise,[83] the diehards grew in confidence, forming a patriotic 'Keep Britain United' group – which included Teddy Taylor and Iain Sproat – just a week before the 1976 Scottish Conservative conference. Uncharacteristically, Younger hit out at the group during a speech in Wick. Describing it as a 'front' for all those opposed to devolution, he said its aim was 'to stampede the Conservatives into abandoning their long-standing belief in decentralisation and devolution on the basis of a short, sharp, scare campaign'. This, argued Younger, had to be resisted, because

the place to which they are leading us is the political wilderness. By various counts between 60% and 80% of Scots want some form of Devolution, and over half want some sort of Assembly.

Scottish Conservatives were first in the field eight years ago with a proposal for an Assembly and to go back on it now would quite simply be political suicide.[84]

At the 1976 Perth conference, Mrs Thatcher once again reiterated Conservative support for devolution and praised delegates for expressing 'understandable differences of opinion' over the policy without any 'personal rancour', which was ironic considering there had been a near riot when a show of hands endorsed the pro-Assembly line.

Thereafter the matter languished as MPs awaited publication of a Bill derived from the Labour government's white paper, which finally appeared in November 1976. A marathon Shadow Cabinet meeting the following month ended with a resolution to oppose completely the Scotland and Wales Bill on a three-line whip. 'I had no illusion that this could be done without some resignations,' recalled Thatcher in her memoirs. 'I wanted to minimize them, but not at the expense of failing to lance the devolution boil.' The next morning Rifkind, Younger, John Corrie (the Scottish Conservative Whip), Hector Monro, Hamish Gray and Russell Fairgrieve (the Scottish party chairman) demanded that Shadow Scottish Secretary Alick Buchanan-Smith be given special dispensation to abstain in the vote or they would all quit the front bench. Predictably, Mrs Thatcher refused, and five days later Buchanan-Smith as well as his deputy Malcolm Rifkind resigned.[85] The Shadow Cabinet explained that it opposed 'the *method* of devolution' in the Bill. 'Our belief in the *principle* of devolution and the need for a directly elected Assembly for Scotland', it added in a press statement, 'remains unaltered.'[86]

Mrs Thatcher tried to persuade her friend Betty Harvie Anderson to take over from Buchanan-Smith as Shadow Scottish Secretary, but she refused on the basis that she could not countenance even a residual commitment to devolution. Instead, the mantle fell upon Teddy Taylor, whose 'robust patriotism' Thatcher had long admired. The U-turn caused dismay among constituency associations in Scotland. John Bowis, a Central Office official from London, visited Scotland on 13 December 1976 and reported that he had 'met not one single person who understood the Shadow Cabinet's decision and approved it'. The only silver lining was a general feeling that whatever

Taylor's views on devolution, 'at least they will be vociferous in Scotland'.[87]

At the final Commons division, 42 Conservative MPs, including Edward Heath, Russell Fairgrieve and George Younger, either abstained or were paired under a 'conscience clause' finally sanctioned by Thatcher. Five – including Buchanan-Smith, Hamish Gray and Malcolm Rifkind – voted with the Labour government. The Bill passed with a majority of 45. Usefully for Mrs Thatcher, it later fell when the government lost a procedural division in February 1977. She then used the subsequent Scottish Conservative conference 'effectively to jettison the commitment to devolution'.[88] As Teddy Taylor recalled: 'No decision was ever made in the Shadow Cabinet to reject devolution. It just quietly slipped away.'[89]

Still absent was a robust case for the Union, be it Thatcherite or moderate. John Biffen, who was close to the anti-devolution Enoch Powell and would later serve as Thatcher's Leader of the House of Commons, even urged the party to exercise its characteristic pragmatism when it came to the future of the Union:

> The proper name of our Party is still 'Conservative and Unionist'. The word 'Unionist' means what it says. It presumes the maintenance of the Union is in the best interests of the four parts which it comprises. But the Union depends for its existence on consent, freely given. Therefore I make this one plea. If the experience of the next few years should reveal that there is an evident majority desiring self-government, then let separation be negotiated speedily and amicably. The Union may be valuable: it is not sacred. It is hollow if it binds people against their will.[90]

In 1976 Mrs Thatcher had established yet another committee of inquiry on Scottish party organisation. Its chairman was Russell Fairgrieve, the MP for West Aberdeenshire, whose remit was to compare the relationship between the National Union and Central Office in London with that between the Scottish Conservative and Unionist Association and the chairman's office in Edinburgh. Fairgrieve reported in April 1977 and proposed an even closer relationship with Smith Square. A new 'Scottish Director of Organisation' was to liaise closely with Central Office in London,[91] and while the Scottish party treasurer was preserved, finances were to be controlled by the UK party treasurer in London.

The SCUA, meanwhile, was to align its constitution with that of the National Union, paying affiliation fees direct to London and thereby allowing Scottish constituencies to send delegates to the UK conference for the first time. In time, this allowed Scottish activists to climb the UK party ladder: Geoff Campbell became chairman of the National Union in 1980 and Russell Sanderson its executive chairman in 1981, 'the most influential voluntary position in the Party'.[92] J. T. Ward judged that rather than the Scottish party becoming 'a mere satellite of London', the transition proved 'smooth and the reservations [from some activists] proved ill-founded', although Seawright more accurately viewed the Scottish party as having become 'an integral part of the London machine, in stark contrast to the degree of autonomy which had characterised Scottish Unionism'.[93]

There was tension between the moderate Scottish Conservative establishment and an impatient Mrs Thatcher on other fronts. When it came to 'dispersal', the policy of relocating London-based civil servants to the 'regions' (including Scotland), MPs such as George Younger came up against opposition from English MPs who represented 'commuter belt' constituencies. At a Shadow Cabinet meeting on 4 December 1978, Younger found himself battling hard

> to avoid them abandoning dispersal altogether. They were in a great panic about how many English marginals were 'in danger' (e.g. Bath, Gloucestershire and in London) because Defence workers from there did not want to go to Glasgow or Cardiff. A very anti-Scottish attitude was shown and no-one showed any sign of being sympathetic at first. I pointed out that work was well advanced at East Kilbride with the O[verseas].D[evelopment].M[inistry]. offices, and that St. Enoch site was also under preparation for the 4000-odd to go to Glasgow. This cooled them a bit and they eventually agreed not to abandon the principle but to say we would review the actual detail of which departments would go.

'Mrs. T.', added Younger, 'said that if Scotland rejects the Assembly we would have to try to be as helpful as possible. But if Scotland chose an Assembly they would get nothing. That just shows the attitude of hostility we now have to counter.'[94]

Younger had been deputising for Teddy Taylor, who had produced a typically idiosyncratic statement of 'aims and themes' for the Scottish Conservative Party ahead of the next election.

This was published in May 1978 as *Onward to Victory: A Statement of the Conservative Approach for Scotland* and advocated a second industrial revolution in Scotland, 'a fair and balanced regional policy' and the 'sensible' use of North Sea oil revenue. It also hinted at future controversies with its support for the 'Right to Buy' (housing) and the 'Right to Choose' (school places).[95]

Meanwhile, British politics was in flux. The so-called Lib/Lab pact (in which David Steel's Liberals propped up James Callaghan's government) was hanging by a thread, which meant every by-election was closely fought. Although the Scottish Conservatives did relatively well at the regional council elections of May 1978 (gaining more seats than any other party except Labour),[96] it failed to recapture, as it expected, Berwick and East Lothian in October 1978 (although its candidate did come a respectable second). Following the successful passage of the standalone *Scotland Act 1978*, meanwhile, Scotland looked ahead to a referendum on a unicameral Scottish Assembly in March 1979.

With the official Conservative line on devolution remaining a fuzzy 'no, but', in November 1978 George Younger dined with Russell Sanderson, the pro-devolution English MP Francis Pym (who had recently prepared four 'viable options' for the party[97]) and the SCUA vice-president Alistair Smith at the Caledonian Club:

> We talked round and round the problem of how to express a 'No' as 'no – but' to avoid being too negative. It is very difficult as there is only agreement between the various strands in the Party to be not too negative. There is no agreement at all about what alternative we could devise to the govt's Scotland Act ... Francis is still to make speeches on devolution and will try to keep a positive lead. We all expect a clear 'Yes' vote and only hope we may have a respectable 'No'. Only [Teddy Taylor] still thinks we might get the noes off the ground and win. I think the present scheme is very bad and dangerous, but we must have an end to this business and a 'Yes' is probably the best way.[98]

Like many in the party, Younger was concerned the referendum would reopen old devolutionary wounds and damage morale ahead of an imminent general election. Sure enough, as campaigning got under way the Scottish party split into various factions: the Federation of Conservative Students in Scotland launched the 'Student Campaign Against the Devolution Act', while Alick Buchanan-Smith and Malcolm Rifkind openly canvassed for a 'yes' vote. In a letter to constituency associations, Russell Sanderson made it clear that 'in campaigning for "No", the Party will not be campaigning against Devolution for Scotland but only against the type of devolution contained in the Act'. He also stressed that those supportive of devolution 'must feel free to pursue these views during the Referendum', for winning the general election was the party's 'prime objective'.[99]

'The referendum is to be fought constructively', wrote Younger in his diary, '& Mrs. T. will take part. She wants Alec D[ouglas]-H[ome] and Harold Macmillan to appear with her as those Scots ex-PM's cannot be matched by Labour.'[100] Home obliged with a speech at Edinburgh University, during which he urged Scots to vote 'No for a better bill'.[101] In response to the former Prime Minister's intervention, a 'Conservative Yes Campaign' led by students, and activists in Pollok and Cathcart was hastily established. Mrs Thatcher, meanwhile, argued that Conservatives advocated 'true devolution', not the 'bogus' sort 'which imposes yet more layers of government'.[102]

When the referendum finally took place on 1 March 1979 (St David's Day), a bare majority of those voting said 'yes' to devolution, but it was well below the required 40 per cent of the total electorate as stipulated in legislation. A brief statement could barely conceal Mrs Thatcher's glee. 'When only one-in-three Scots favour the Government's proposals for an Assembly,' it read, 'surely this is no basis for implementing the Scotland Act. This has been a good day for the United Kingdom.'[103] In her memoirs she was even blunter: 'Although I had not publicly campaigned for a "No" vote in the referenda in Scotland and Wales, that was the result I wanted.'[104]

Callaghan's government soon fell, and the Conservative Party manifesto merely included a bland commitment to hold 'discussions about the future government of Scotland'. On 4 May 1979, the SNP lost all but two of the 11 seats gained in October 1974, while the Scottish Conservatives did relatively well, coming second to Labour with 31.3 per cent of the vote (up from 24.7 in October 1974) and winning six more MPs (a total of 22), mainly at the expense of the SNP in rural constituencies like Moray and Nairn and Banffshire. Having recovered all its 1974 losses, the only black spot was the defeat of Teddy Taylor in Glasgow Cathcart, which left the party with just a single MP in Scotland's largest city.[105] Taylor believed the lesson of 1979, despite the loss of his seat, was that 'the SNP vote of 1974 was largely a protest vote and not a vote for independence, federalism, devolution or anything like that'.[106]

Contrary to subsequent mythology, many Scots voted Conservative for the first time in May 1979. 'Although she was on the "no" side in the devolution debate her opposition wasn't seen as dogmatic at that time,' recalled David McLetchie, who stood in Edinburgh Central and was soon to become a senior figure in the SCUA. 'There was also no sense that the 1976 U-turn was damaging in Scotland.'[107] As Charles Moore has argued, although some would later argue that 'by edging away from devolution' in 1976 Mrs Thatcher would eventually bring about 'the collapse of Scottish Conservatism', that was 'probably to impose later problems upon those of the period'.[108] As a turbulent decade drew to a close, the prospects for Scottish Conservatism looked relatively bright.

NOTES

1. SUA (1964), *The Year Book for Scotland 1964*, Edinburgh and Glasgow: Scottish Unionist Association, 7.
2. D. Seawright (1998), 'Scottish Unionism: An East–West divide?', *Scottish Affairs* 23, 55.
3. D. Seawright (1999), *An Important Matter of Principle: The Decline of the Scottish Conservative and Unionist Party*, Aldershot: Ashgate, 24–5.
4. M. Petrie (2022), *Politics and the People: Scotland, 1945–1979*, Edinburgh: Edinburgh University Press, 63.
5. D. W. Urwin (1966), 'Scottish Conservatism: A party organization in transition', *Political Studies* 14:2, 148.
6. The Highland and North-Eastern regions later became the 'Northern' area, while in 1972 the 'West of Scotland' swallowed up Glasgow and Paisley, leaving just three Area Councils. The substantial assets of the Eastern and Western Divisional Councils constituted the Scottish Unionist Association Trust, which thereafter dispersed financial support to Scottish Conservative candidates.
7. A. Kemp (1993), *The Hollow Drum: Scotland since the War*, Edinburgh: Mainstream, 110.

8. D. W. Urwin (1966), 160.
9. D. Seawright (1999), 81.
10. D. W. Urwin (1966), 161–2. For a full discussion of the 1965 organisational reforms, see D. Seawright (1999), 7–34.
11. SCUA (1966), *The Year Book for Scotland 1966*, Edinburgh: Scottish Conservative and Unionist Association, 7.
12. *Scotsman*, 12 May 1966.
13. *Scotsman*, 12 May 1966.
14. *Glasgow Herald*, 23 May 1966.
15. Ian McIntyre to George Younger, 1 May 1966, George Younger Papers, Acc 13116/21, Edinburgh: National Library of Scotland.
16. J. McMillan (1969), *Anatomy of Scotland*, London: Leslie Frewin, 93–7. The WDC's election post-mortem concurred that the candidate's 'name proved an electoral disadvantage'. See D. Seawright (1999), 90.
17. See I. Budge and D. W. Urwin (1966), *Scottish Political Behaviour: A Case Study in British Homogeneity*, London: Longmans. For a full discussion of religion and the Scottish Conservative Party, see D. Seawright (1999), 73–110.
18. Ian McIntyre to George Younger, 1 May 1966, Acc 13116/21.
19. Author's collection.
20. Opinion Research Centre: political attitudes in Scotland, March 1971, Conservative Party Archives, CCO 180/29/1/3, Oxford: Bodleian.
21. I. Budge and D. W. Urwin (1966), 112, 137.
22. 'Special attitudes in Scotland, Wales and the West Country': a survey conducted by the Opinion Research Centre for Conservative Central Office, November 1966, CPA, CCO 18/29/1/1.
23. E. Heath (1998), *The Course of My Life: My Autobiography*, London: Hodder & Stoughton, 294–5.
24. J. Campbell (2013), *Edward Heath: A Biography*, London: Pimlico, 216.
25. 'The Motivations behind Scottish Nationalism' (March 1968), CPA, CCO 500/50/1.
26. G. Pentland (2015), 'Edward Heath, the Declaration of Perth and the Scottish Conservative and Unionist Party, 1966–70', *Twentieth Century British History* 26:2, 260–1.
27. *Spectator*, 16 May 1968.
28. Robert Kernohan to Edward Heath, 6 May 1968, CPA, CRD 3/28/7.
29. G. Pentland (2015), 249–50.
30. A. Kemp (1993), 112.

31. D. Hurd (2003), *Memoirs*, London: Little, Brown, 174.
32. I. G. C. Hutchison (2001), *Scottish Politics in the Twentieth Century*, Basingstoke: Palgrave, 111–12. The Conservative New Towns campaign was wound up in the early 1970s.
33. M. Arnott and C. M. M. Macdonald (2012), 'More than a name: The Union and the un-doing of Scottish Conservatism in the twentieth century', in D. Torrance (ed.), *Whatever Happened to Tory Scotland?*, Edinburgh: Edinburgh University Press, 45.
34. J. Mitchell (2014), *The Scottish Question*, Oxford: Oxford University Press, 260.
35. D. Seawright (1999), 91.
36. M. Rifkind (2016), *Power and Pragmatism*, London: Biteback, 109.
37. Thistle Group (1967), *T. G. P. Number 1*, Edinburgh, 4–8.
38. Thistle Group (1968), *T. G. P. Number 2*, Edinburgh, 7–8.
39. *Glasgow Herald*, 31 March 1969.
40. *Scotsman*, 16 September 1968.
41. K. Dixon (2010), 'The Free Economy and the White State: Conservative student radicalism in St Andrews in the sixties and early seventies', *Scottish Affairs* 71, 27. See also C. Kidd (2012), 'Smithians, Thatcherites and the ironies of Scottish Conservative decline', in D. Torrance (ed.), *Whatever Happened to Tory Scotland?*, Edinburgh: Edinburgh University Press, 62–75.
42. I. G. C. Hutchison (2007), 'The Scottish Young Conservatives: A local case study – Central Ayrshire Constituency, 1950–c.1979', in A. Murdoch (ed.), *The Scottish Nation: Identity and History – Essays in Honour of William Ferguson*, Edinburgh: John Donald, 127, 135.
43. J. Mitchell (1990), *Conservatives and the Union: A Study of Conservative Party Attitudes to Scotland*, Edinburgh: Edinburgh University Press, 59–60.
44. SCCO (1970), *Tomorrow Scotland: Better with the Conservatives*, Edinburgh: Scottish Conservative Central Office.
45. E. Wright (1970), 'In defence of the United Kingdom', in N. MacCormick (ed.), *The Scottish Debate: Essays on Scottish Nationalism*, Oxford: Oxford University Press, 103.
46. Following a hunting accident in March 1971, the Earl of Dalkeith, the Unionist/Conservative MP for Edinburgh North since a 1960 by-election, became the first MP since the Second World War to enter the House of Commons in a wheelchair. He moved to the Lords in October on succeeding to his father's Dukedom.
47. The Edinburgh East Conservative association provided a microcosm of the party's declining fortunes: it had 2,425 members in 1953, rising to 3,325 in 1957, falling after a period of stability to

2,337 in 1963 and in 1970 1,696 (J. Ramsden, 1996, *A History of the Conservative Party: The Winds of Change: Macmillan to Heath, 1957–1975*, London: Longman, 104).

48. J. T. Ward (1982), *The First Century: A History of Scottish Tory Organisation, 1882–1982*, Edinburgh: SCUA, 41.
49. R. E. Dundas (1973), 'Why the Scottish Tories are in a mess', *The Crossbow*, August 1973.
50. M. Keating (1975), 'The Role of the Scottish MP in the Scottish Political System, in the UK Political System and in the Relationship Between the Two', PhD thesis, Glasgow College of Technology.
51. J. G. Kellas (1980), *Modern Scotland* (Second Edition), London: George Allen & Unwin, 137.
52. J. T. Ward (1982), 41.
53. See D. Torrance (2019), *Lord Clyde: The Orkney Judge*, Edinburgh: Birlinn, 46–51. For an account of Malcolm Rifkind's time as an Edinburgh councillor and his candidacies in Edinburgh Central and Edinburgh Pentlands, see M. Rifkind (2016), 107–20.
54. SCCO (1971), *Scotland and Europe: Seven Viewpoints*, Edinburgh: Scottish Conservative Central Office, 5, 8. Also contributing to the pamphlet were Hamish Gray MP, Barry Henderson and J. T. Ward.
55. M. Petrie (2022), 107. In 1968 Teddy Taylor had published a novel about a diligent but frustrated Scottish Conservative MP called *Hearts of Stone* (London: Johnson).
56. D. Hurd (2003), 210.
57. L. Bennie, J. Brand and J. Mitchell (1997), *How Scotland Votes: Scottish Parties and Elections*, Manchester: Manchester University Press, 223.
58. I. G. C. Hutchison (2001), 112.
59. M. Petrie (2022), 110.
60. D. Butler and D. Kavanagh (1974), *The British General Election of February 1974*, London: Macmillan, 247.
61. SCUA (1974), *Freedom for All the People – A Charter for Scotland*, Edinburgh: Scottish Conservative and Unionist Association, 1–6.
62. N. Fairbairn (1987), *A Life is Too Short: Autobiography: Volume One*, London: Quartet, 229. The second volume of Fairbairn's memoirs remains under lock and key, apparently on account of defamatory content.
63. *The Times*, 12 October 1974. Younger's Liberal opponent in October 1974 was a trainee teacher called Murray Tosh, who dramatically endorsed Younger on the eve of poll. He later became chairman of the Ayr constituency association and a Conservative MSP (see M. Tosh, 1992, *Keep Right On. The Story of the*

Conservative Party in Ayr Burghs and Ayr Constituencies, Ayr: Ayr Constituency Conservative Association).
64. Russell Sanderson to George Younger, 14 November 1974, Acc 13116/23.
65. D. Hurd (2003), 210.
66. Margaret Thatcher to George Younger, 16 February 1975, Acc 13116/28.
67. *Daily Record*, 22 February 1975.
68. Speech in Glasgow, 21 February 1975, Margaret Thatcher Foundation website.
69. Speech to Scottish Conservative conference, 10 May 1985, Margaret Thatcher Foundation website.
70. J. Campbell (2000), *Margaret Thatcher Volume One: The Grocer's Daughter*, London: Jonathan Cape, 397.
71. M. Thatcher (1995), *The Path to Power*, London: HarperCollins, 32.
72. John Davidson to George Younger, 27 October 1975, Acc 13116/23.
73. J. Mitchell (1990), 55.
74. R. Saunders (2018), *Yes to Europe! The 1975 Referendum and Seventies Britain*, Cambridge: Cambridge University Press, 349.
75. M. Petrie (2022), 110.
76. M. Petrie (2022), 178. For a similar analysis, see E. A. Cameron (2016), 'Unionism and nationalism: The historical context of Scottish politics', in D. McTavish (ed.), *Politics in Scotland*, London: Routledge, 15.
77. Memo dated 31 March 1976, CPA, CRD 4/15/10.
78. C. Moore (2013), *Margaret Thatcher The Authorized Biography – Volume One: Not For Turning*, London: Allen Lane, 375.
79. A. Kemp (1993), 133.
80. M. Forsyth and D. McLetchie (1975), *The Scottish Conservative Party: A New Model for a New Dimension*, Edinburgh: SCUA.
81. I. Lang (2002), *Blue Remembered Years*, London: Politico's, See also CPC (1975), *The Scottish Conservatives: A Past and a Future*, London: Conservative Political Centre.
82. C. Moore (2013), 375.
83. At a devolution conference sponsored by the Rowntree Foundation, Rifkind reiterated that a 'separate government for Scotland' would 'be the deathknell for the United Kingdom' (M. Rifkind, 1976, 'Scottish Conservative Party Devolution Committee Proposals', Rowntree Devolution Conference).
84. D. Torrance (2008), *George Younger: A Life Well Lived*, Edinburgh: Birlinn, 151.
85. M. Thatcher (1995), 325–6.

86. Shadow Cabinet statement dated 8 December 1976, CPA, CRD 4/15/8.
87. Memo dated 13 December 1976, CPA, CCO 20/11/82.
88. M. Thatcher (1995), 396.
89. C. Moore (2013), 375.
90. J. Biffen (1976), *A Nation in Doubt*, London: Conservative Political Centre, 12.
91. This was to be Graham Macmillan, the party's well-regarded agent in Yorkshire.
92. J. T. Ward (1982), 41.
93. D. Seawright (1998), 68.
94. Diary entry dated 4 December 1978, Acc 13116/221.
95. SCP (1978), *Onward to Victory: A Statement of the Conservative Approach for Scotland*, Edinburgh: Scottish Conservative Party, 16.
96. Grampian, Tayside and Lothian regions were all at some stage controlled by the Scottish Conservatives.
97. See F. Pym and L. Brittan (1978), *The Conservative Party and Devolution: Four Viable Options*, Edinburgh: SCUA. These were envisaged as Scottish Conservative proposals for submission to an all-party conference on devolution.
98. Diary entry dated 16 November 1978, Acc 13116/221.
99. J. Bochel, D. Denver and A. Macartney (eds) (1981), *The Referendum Experience: Scotland 1979*, Aberdeen: Aberdeen University Press, 22–3.
100. Diary entry dated 20 November 1978, Acc 13116/221.
101. D. R. Thorpe (1996), *Alec Douglas-Home*, London: Sinclair-Stevenson, 456. 'The Act as drafted was divisive,' Lord Home told *The Times* in 1995. 'I'm sure it was right to vote against it' (*The Times*, 10 October 1995). See also J. Mitchell (1990), 91–2.
102. Speech to Glasgow Conservatives, 19 January 1979, Margaret Thatcher Foundation website.
103. Statement dated 2 March 1979, CPA, CCOPR 315/79.
104. M. Thatcher (1995), 430.
105. See J. H. Young (1993), *A History of Cathcart Conservative and Unionist Association 1918 to 1993*, Glasgow: Cathcart Conservatives.
106. Opinion research file: general election, 1979, CPA, CCO 180/29/1/12.
107. Interview with David McLetchie, 6 October 2008.
108. C. Moore (2013), 378.

7

'We in Scotland':
1979–1997

Mrs Thatcher's first public speech as Prime Minister happened to be at the annual Scottish Conservative Party conference in Perth on 12 May 1979. 'We lost our standard bearer at the hour of victory,' she said, describing Teddy Taylor's defeat in Cathcart as a 'bitter blow'. 'It is a tribute indeed to his inspiration and his leadership that the army can march forward when its Captain has fallen.'[1] Instead, the Scottish Conservative army was to march forward under George Younger, who became Scottish Secretary. But he was not, as Chris Stevens observed, a 'populist Secretary of State who might redefine the Thatcherite creed in Scottish terms'.[2]

In her speech, the Prime Minister also explored why the Conservatives were still 14 short of a Scottish majority despite a UK-wide victory. 'Is it that our policies are not so popular in Scotland? Of course not. Every opinion survey … shows us that our main policies are overwhelmingly popular.' This was unsurprising, she added, as the 'Scots have always prided themselves on common sense politics'. Finally, Mrs Thatcher confirmed that her government would ask Parliament to repeal the *Scotland Act 1978*: 'But we have made it clear that we shall initiate all-party discussions aimed at bringing government closer to the people.'[3]

Although a few Scottish Conservatives kept the devolution flame burning over the ensuing decade, most were content to watch it flicker and dim. Instead, George Younger set about modifying fledgling Thatcherism for the Scottish electorate in three ways: first, he sought compromises over certain privatisations or threatened closures; second, he strove to protect historically high public spending levels in Scotland; and third, Younger presented it differently. 'Gentleman George', as he became known, never sounded harsh or dictatorial, but was instead smooth and reassuring.[4] James Mackay, who to his evident surprise was given a peerage so he could serve as Lord Advocate, was cut from similar cloth. More robustly Thatcherite was Nicholas Fairbairn, who became Solicitor General.[5]

Initially, things appeared to go relatively well. At the first direct elections to the European Parliament in June 1979, the Scottish Conservatives won five out of eight seats. Younger also won an early battle over the dispersal policy, organising a deputation of Scottish Tory MPs to Downing Street in order to win around a reluctant Prime Minister.[6] He was nevertheless conscious of the 'no mandate' charge that had attached itself to Gordon Campbell between 1970 and 1974, and 'tread the thin line between conceding in private and yet refusing to acknowledge in public the lameness of his own party's political mandate north of the Border'.[7] Although an argument that 'only made sense from a nationalist point of view' – a UK government only needed to command the confidence of Parliament rather than all its component parts – it nevertheless resonated.[8] One Labour MP even suggested the Prime Minister had 'no moral mandate' north of the border.[9]

Mrs Thatcher also had to contend with naked chauvinism, which in the late 1970s was practically baked into Scottish politics. The Labour MP Dennis Canavan, a strong proponent of that 'no mandate' argument, had warned his electors not to 'let that witch hang up her curtains in Downing Street!' This, judged Arnold Kemp, combined chauvinism 'with an appeal to female dislike of a woman who had got above herself'.[10] Indeed, references to 'that woman' were to fall easily from the lips of opponents, not just politicians but voters too. The party in Scotland could at least still rely on qualified support from the *Glasgow Herald* and *Scottish Daily Express* and, more regionally, the *Dundee Courier*. But after the constitutional excitement of the 1970s, the inter-party talks offered by the new government made comparatively dull copy. At their conclusion, the Select Committee on Scottish Affairs was revived and the Scottish Grand Committee reconstituted to meet at Edinburgh's old Royal High School (which had been fitted out to host the Scottish Assembly). At every opportunity, George Younger emphasised that 'Scotland, while fully part of the United

Kingdom, *is* governed from Edinburgh'.[11] There was not to be any greater Scottish control of Scottish affairs.

Instead, the Scottish Office made good on Noel Skelton's goal of a 'property-owning democracy' by introducing the Tenants' Rights etc (Scotland) Bill, the centrepiece of which was the 'Right to Buy', a policy first mooted by the Scottish Conservatives in 1974. At the 1980 Scottish party conference, the Prime Minister was positively evangelic:

> Let no-one say they do not want it. Since we published our proposals last summer, 1500 tenants in Scotland have bought their own homes, and at this moment another 12,000 applications to buy are being processed. But these are the lucky ones; they are tenants of local authorities – mostly Tory – which are willing to recognise their entitlement to become home-owners. There have been, to date, another 18,000 enquiries from would-be purchasers. Many of them will be frustrated in their ambitions until our Bill gives them the right which Labour councils are denying them. We shall not betray them.[12]

In 1979, 53 per cent of all household tenants in Scotland were in the public sector, compared with only 28 per cent in England, so the Conservatives believed the Right to Buy would reap electoral rewards. Take up was, however, initially slower in Scotland than in England (although this might have had something to do with opposition from Labour-led local authorities) and it soon became clear, to quote Neal Ascherson, 'that the upgrade from proletariat to property-owner had not changed their politics at all'.[13] At the 1983 conference, Mrs Thatcher lamented that only one in 20 Scottish council tenants had taken advantage of the policy, compared with about one in nine in England.[14] Beyond take-up, there was long-standing criticism of the impact on public sector house building, once a mainstay of Scottish Unionist policy.[15]

An unstated aim of the Right to Buy was a calculated erosion of local authority power. George Younger belied his gentlemanly demeanour by zealously pursuing Scottish councils which placed an increasing burden on ratepayers, who tended to be Tory-voting homeowners. Unless they reimbursed ratepayers, they faced a cut in the Rate Support Grant, something that made Scotland 'a test bed for the Government's offensive against local authority spending'.[16] This was not necessarily unpopular. In 1982 elections to Lothian Regional Council – the focus of recent spending battles – there was a tie between Labour and Brian Meek's Tory group with 22 seats each. An informal pact with the Liberal–SDP Alliance gave Meek control of the council.[17]

In other respects, the Scottish Conservative grassroots became restless. Alarmed at the effects of public spending cuts and a recession on Scottish industry (unemployment stood at 287,000), the 1981 Scottish party conference was a tense affair. One delegate, Arthur Bell, said he was running his business with little left over for himself or his workers. 'It was the cry of a Conservative whose patience was running out,' observed *The Times*.[18] In April 1981, Michael Ancram, the Scottish party chairman (and the first Catholic Conservative MP in Scotland) expressed concern that the party was polling just 17 per cent, with unemployment perceived as the most important problem facing the government in Scotland:

> We must continue to recognise the causes and demonstrate that Scotland is not losing out. The concept of George Younger as fighting for Scotland (almost 'troublesome') within the Government would be useful.[19]

Such posturing irritated the Prime Minister but contrived internal dissent was to become a feature of Scottish Conservatism, particularly when there was a Conservative government at Westminster.

Providing momentary distraction, meanwhile, were celebrations to mark the centenary of the party's voluntary wing (the National Union having been created in 1882). At a dinner in Edinburgh, 600 members of the Scottish Conservative and Unionist Association listened to speeches from the Prime Minister, Lord Home and George Younger, who paid tribute to the 'great guiding hands of the middle years such as Sir George Younger, my great grandfather, who first insisted on the paramount importance of organisation'.[20] Scottish Young Conservatives held a reception, barbecue and disco at Scone Palace (Lord Mansfield was Minister of State at the Scottish Office).[21]

The death in January 1982 of Commander Thomas Galbraith, first elected in Glasgow Hillhead shortly after the Second World War, had robbed the party of its last foothold in Scotland's largest city. At the resulting by-election, the SDP's Roy Jenkins stormed back to frontline politics, so it was not until the

Falklands War that Scottish Conservatives could look ahead to the next general election with anything other than apprehension. Mrs Thatcher delivered a rousing speech to the 1982 Scottish party conference following the recapture of South Georgia. 'It reminded me of the Nuremberg Rally,'[22] Younger told a friend after witnessing the delegates' enthusiastic response, a reminder of the gulf between many in the Scottish party establishment and its UK leader.

On polling day, the Scottish Conservatives retained 21 seats (down from 22 in 1979 because of Hillhead) and achieved a small swing of 1.7 per cent against Labour. But the party's Scottish vote share still fell, as it had in the rest of Great Britain. So while the so-called 'Falklands factor' had not added any support, it had most likely prevented further losses, two gains (Anna McCurley in Renfrew West and Inverclyde and Michael Hirst in Strathkelvin and Bearsden) having cancelled out two losses (Hamish Gray in Ross and Cromarty and Iain Sproat in Roxburgh and Berwickshire).[23] Michael Forsyth (Stirling) and Gerry Malone (Aberdeen South) also added two Thatcherites to the Scottish Conservative group in the House of Commons. Following past Unionist form, Mrs Thatcher elevated Gray to the Lords and retained his services as a minister. At her primary school in Paisley, meanwhile, Liz Truss had assumed the role of Mrs Thatcher in a mock election. 'I jumped at the hustings, but ended up with zero votes,' she later told the *Scotsman*. 'Even at that age, we knew it was simply unpopular to be a Tory in the West of Scotland.'[24]

In 1983 Mrs Thatcher replaced Edinburgh South MP Michael Ancram with James Goold of CBI Scotland as Scottish party chairman, an appointment which owed more to personal connections (Goold had been Betty Harvie Anderson's constituency chairman in East Renfrewshire) than any political skills on Goold's part.[25] Otherwise, the UK landslide created a certain complacency, even in Scotland, where, after all, 'the structural reasons for the weakness of political conservatism' remained.[26] Younger, who continued as Scottish Secretary, spent much of his time firefighting, chiefly two bitter strikes – miners' and teachers' – while he pushed for just one specifically Scottish policy initiative, the abolition of rates. David McLetchie, an unsuccessful candidate in 1979, believed that the teachers' strike in particular had a devastating effect on Scottish Conservative fortunes. 'We were constantly alienating the middle classes in certain sectors,' he recalled. 'It got to the stage when it would have taken a brave teacher or nurse to stand up and say "I support the Conservatives". We should naturally have been able to get professionals like teachers and doctors to support us, but instead there was a cumulative negative effect on them and their families.'[27]

And if the Scottish Conservative Party itself was what Michael Gove called 'a coalition of interests', most of them were by the mid-1980s 'diminishing':

> So the party's base became more and more elderly women, the Church of Scotland and the lairds. Once they diminished to a certain level then they started to talk only to themselves and become completely divorced from the reality of life in Scotland.[28]

'I remember going with her [Margaret Thatcher] to visit a local party chairman who lived in a laird-like castle in the Dee Valley,' recalled Andrew Turnbull, a future Cabinet Secretary but then a private secretary at Downing Street. 'It was completely removed from reality. There was this strange mix of lairds and people like Bill Walker and Teddy Taylor, and it didn't really hang together.'[29]

The Scottish party's right wing also received a lot of not necessarily helpful media attention. In January 1984, the Adam Smith Institute (founded in 1999 by St Andrews graduates) published its *Omega Report: Scottish Policy*, which recommended the 'abolition of automatic subsidies to Scotland'.[30] Another pamphlet published by the Federation of Conservative Students (FCS), *A Conservative Manifesto for Scotland*, advocated widespread privatisation, the legalisation of drugs and even incest between consenting adults.[31] The Lothian councillor Brian Meek was dismissive of what he called the 'crew-cropped specimens' of FCS, who in turn regarded the Scottish Young Conservatives as establishment wimps.[32]

At the 1985 Scottish Conservative conference, meanwhile, the Prime Minister tempted fate by quoting Disraeli – 'we are a national party or we are nothing' – adding that he had been 'referring not only to people in all parts of Great Britain, but to people from all walks of life'. Mrs Thatcher added:

> Scotland ought to be natural Tory territory. That's the way we want to see it. We did it in the 1950s and it is time that, together, we did

it again. Truly this is the way to One Nation, where all are different but all are equally important. Burns as always put it more colour-fully ...: 'The rank is but the guinea stamp; the man's the guid for a' that.' All different, all equally important. And he went on: 'Then let us pray that come it may, as come it will for a' that; that sense and worth, o'er all the earth may bear the prize and a' that'. I didn't expect to find so much pure Toryism in Burns. But there it is written long before we were here.[33]

Mrs Thatcher's challenge to reach 1955 levels of support was quixotic. At regional council elections in May 1986 the Scottish Conservatives managed just 16.9 per cent of the vote and 65 councillors, its poorest showing since the 1975 reorganisation of local government. Even rural Scotland, deferential and aristocratic still, was no longer loyal. Tayside and Grampian Regions fell to opposition parties (as had Lothian). A basic extrapolation of the results into parliamentary constituencies put the vast majority of Scottish Conservative MPs at risk. 'The problems facing Mrs Thatcher in her council of war with Sir James Goold and other grandees today', observed *The Times* of a post-election debriefing, 'is that despite the accommodations made with collectivism north of the border, Scottish Tories still lose elections.'[34]

One of those accommodations had been the closure of Gartcosh earlier that year, a quid pro quo for sustaining the even more totemic Ravenscraig steel plant. Iain Lawson, then a Conservative parliamentary candidate, quit the party (and later joined the SNP), while there were threats of disaffiliation from two constituency parties in the West of Scotland. When the vote was finally taken in the Commons on 24 January 1986, two Tories – Sir Hector Monro and Anna McCurley – voted against. Later that year, the Stirling MP Michael Forsyth helped oust Sir Hector as chairman of the Scottish Conservative Backbench Committee, replacing him with the stridently right-wing Tayside MP Bill Walker. Although Monro was hastily restored after the vote was rerun, this incident laid bare the Scottish party's internal ideological divisions.

But even Mrs Thatcher had taken care to say she was 'very much aware of the importance of Ravenscraig to Scotland ... to Scottish jobs':

In a way, it is more than to Scottish jobs; it is to Scottish morale. I know that. There is a Scottish dimension as well as a steel dimension. I will not forget what Ravenscraig did and the way it stood and the way it carried on during the coal-miners' strike ...[35]

During a subsequent reprieve for Ravenscraig, Ian Lang, then a junior minister at the Scottish Office, said it represented a long-standing 'dilemma over whether to play the Scottish card or the Unionist one':

> But this was not a Scottish card issue; nor was it a free market issue, since steel was still a state industry. Rather, it was an issue of good politics and common sense; and it challenged the unionism of our English government colleagues. We won the argument on this occasion, but only just.[36]

During 1985 the Scottish party also had to contend with a revaluation which increased the rateable values of Scottish households by about 260 per cent, industrial values by around 170 per cent and commercial values by somewhere between the two. Local Scottish Conservative associations were in uproar. 'I remember in my constituency [Eastwood] it was absolutely awful,' recalled Allan Stewart, 'people saying "why have we voted for a Conservative government when they raise our rates?"'[37] Sir James Goold, who believed revaluation was 'a huge vote loser' which meant that 'Scotland suffers, whilst England does not',[38] visited the Prime Minister in the middle of February 1985 'to describe the fury which had broken out north of the border when the new rateable values became known'.[39] Deputy Prime Minister Willie Whitelaw, shaken after repeatedly being heckled during a routine constituency engagement in Bearsden, also reported back to Downing Street that something had to be done.[40]

Douglas Mason's pamphlet, *Revising the Rating System*,[41] and another by Michael Forsyth, *The Case for a Poll Tax*, had helped popularise the idea that a radical response was necessary. 'Clear accountability is the outstanding virtue of a poll tax,' Forsyth's pamphlet argued. 'The lack of an alternative has been the excuse for inaction for far too long. There is an alternative. A poll tax is clearly feasible, fair and desirable. What is needed now is the political will to introduce it.'[42] That political will was to come from Mrs Thatcher. 'I know how commercial ratepayers feel,' she told Scottish Conservatives at their Perth conference in May 1985. 'I spent my early years living above the shop':

I think we have reached the stage when no amount of patching up the existing system can overcome its inherent unfairness ... Our aims are these. Any new scheme must be fairer than the existing scheme. The burden should fall, not heavily on the few, but fairly on the many. Councillors should always have to consider not only what they want to spend but also what it will cost their electors. Many Conservative councillors do this already – but many Labour councils do not.[43]

Even George Younger was booed as he made his keynote speech and Robin Harris, a close Thatcher aide who had been seconded to the Scottish party earlier that year, noticed 'what a mess our relations with the Scottish Party are'. 'The way in which the rates issue has been approached in a completely different manner North and South of the Border,' he elaborated, '[and] the Scottish Office's own attitude that it wins votes for the Conservatives in Scotland [by being] seen to oppose policies agreed by the UK Government.'[44]

Importantly given subsequent mythology, reforming the rates was never intended to make Scotland a 'guinea pig' but rather as 'a Scottish solution to a Scottish problem'. However, and as Jackson Carlaw has observed, the party responded much too hastily:

Supporters were outraged that the revaluation had 'people in Pollokshields paying higher rates than people in Knightsbridge' and in Strathclyde Region 'only 13% paying anything at all'. But there was no detailed consideration of the wider consequences because they [the Scottish party] believed this was a touchstone issue for Conservative voters. It proved the wisdom of those who argued from long experience not to tinker substantially with local government finance.[45]

The Abolition of Domestic Rates Etc (Scotland) Bill received its second reading in the House of Commons on 9 December 1986. By then the 'community charge' nomenclature was set in stone, as was its colloquial title of the Poll Tax. Malcolm Rifkind, who had replaced Younger as Scottish Secretary following the 'Westland Affair', hailed it as a 'radical reforming measure ... to abolish a discredited and unpopular local tax',[46] although like his predecessor he supported it for practical and political reasons rather than ideological. There was not a single dissenting Conservative voice at the Bill's second reading or committee stage and, on 11 February 1987, MPs voted on a guillotine motion to hasten its progress. It was to be introduced in Scotland on 1 April 1989.

Just four weeks before the 1987 general election, the Prime Minister told a delighted Scottish Conservative conference in Perth that the Queen had granted the Bill Royal Assent. 'Indeed, it was in response to your needs in Scotland', she explained, 'that we finally decided on the introduction of the community charge.'[47] But the decision to abolish rates in Scotland a year before England and Wales (a poll in late 1986 had found 80 per cent of Scots opposed) was to shape the Thatcherite legacy in Scotland and also informed a pre-election consensus – shared by Malcolm Rifkind – that the party in Scotland was about to be 'severely mauled'.

In a private memo written in January 1987, the Scottish Secretary also suggested to the Prime Minister that such an outcome would result in 'a major resurgence of the cry that the government had no mandate in Scotland':

> The [devolution] issue is not going to go away and another five years with the Scottish Office run by a minority party is certain to lead to very heavy pressure for proper democratic accountability. We may need to give further consideration whether the long-term interests of the Conservative and Unionist Party in Scotland will be best served by continued total opposition.[48]

The belief that the early introduction of the Poll Tax would help the Scottish Conservatives at the 1987 general election proved a colossal miscalculation, although there were doubtless other factors at play, not least the industrial strife of the mid-1980s.

While the Conservatives won another national landslide, in Scotland its share of the vote slumped to 24 per cent, down nearly five points on 1983 and only two points ahead of the SDP–Liberal Alliance (and 16 behind Labour).[49] Ten Scottish Conservative MPs lost their seats, not just backbenchers like Michael Hirst in Strathkelvin and Bearsden but Michael Ancram, the housing minister, Peter Fraser, the Solicitor-General, John Mackay, the education minister, Alex Fletcher, the former trade minister, and Gerry Malone, the Scottish Conservative whip. At one point it even looked as if George Younger, now Defence Secretary, might lose Ayr, although after several recounts he scraped home with a majority of 182. Ian Lang, who retained his Galloway constituency, remembered feeling 'like a survivor of the Battle of the Somme, disorientated and vaguely guilty'.[50] Teddy Taylor, who had been asked by Scottish Central Office to revisit his old stomping grounds during the campaign, later recounted his experience of speaking on behalf of a candidate:

> On looking round the vast audience of several hundred in the hall I had the feeling I was addressing something similar to a Tsarist rally of Russian emigres after the Revolution. It was a gathering of people who looked back with pride and joy at what they regarded as a happy history. None of those I spoke to (apart from the enthusiastic candidate) had the slightest hope of expectation that the old regime could possibly be restored ... The main change was simply that the Conservatives in Scotland now seemed to be regarded in their former heartland, in some unusual way as enemies of Scotland. And Labour, far from being the dangerous and crazy lunatics, as some regarded them in my new Southend East constituency, were seen as decent, respectable and patriotic chaps who could almost alone guarantee to be fighters for Scotland at Westminster.[51]

Taylor was not alone in having detected a profound shift. 'In Scotland a man can buy his council house and shares in privatised industries, and continues to vote Labour,' observed the journalist Allan Massie. 'The upwardly mobile still vote as their parents did, encouraged by newspapers and television stations which are almost unanimously hostile to the Tories ... Teachers, doctors and administrators see Mrs Thatcher as a threat to their way of life. As a result, the Tories have lost much of their tribal vote, while Labour has retained its.'[52] The only crumb of comfort was that militant Protestants, who had threatened to field candidates in opposition to the 1985 Anglo-Irish Agreement, failed to follow through.[53] Remarkably, even four years later the Conservative candidate for the Glasgow Central by-election was adopted on the basis of his 'outright opposition' to the Agreement.[54]

The election result naturally exacerbated tensions within the Scottish Conservative Party, which now polarised between two competing analyses of Thatcherism:

> Was it [the election result] poor because, as more upper-class and rural Scottish Tories tended to believe, the Conservatives had set their face against devolution and because free-market economics

were too strong meat for a deindustrializing Scotland? Or was it, as their lower-middle-class, pugnacious, reformist counterparts liked to argue, that Scotland had not yet been offered vigorous revived Unionism and a proper dose of Thatcherism?

Malcolm Rifkind, who remained Scottish Secretary, was in the first camp, and Michael Forsyth, who became one of Rifkind's junior ministers, was in the second. Although a strong Unionist, Thatcher found the nature of 'patriotism' in the non-English parts of the UK baffling, not least because in Scotland 'she could not play that card without being trumped by parties from the left'. According to her official biographer, Charles Moore, she discussed with colleagues how she and her party could be more successfully 'wrapped in tartan', but ultimately struggled with the idea – now mainstream in Scotland – that a party commanding the confidence of the House of Commons somehow lacked a 'mandate' (or legitimacy) in Scotland. On her first visit to Scotland after the election, the Prime Minister attempted some tartan wrapping by claiming that Thatcherism was merely a contemporary iteration of 'Adam Smithism' and thus thoroughly Scottish, but it did not resonate as intended.[55]

Having failed to identify a workable narrative, the Scottish Conservative Party instead indulged in another bout of reorganisation only a decade after the last. The defeated MP John Mackay took on the new post of 'chief executive' and the number of staff at the party's Chester Street headquarters in Edinburgh was to increase from 17 to 25. The party was also to keep all money raised in Scotland, while there was to be a new, more ostentatiously Scottish, party logo. In September 1987, a damning report by Michael Ancram, 'The Policies, Questions and Options: The Way Forward', was circulated to ministers and senior activists. Based on internal questionnaires, it concluded frankly 'that it is no use ignoring the perception that the Tories were seen as the English Party'.[56] It also suggested returning to the Unionist custom of making the Scottish Secretary party chairman, while allowing members to elect the SCUA president, the intention being to repair links between the voluntary and professional wings of the party. Sir James Goold also formed the Scottish Business Group (SBG), which came to include a number of well-known businessmen such as Bill Hughes of Grampian Holdings, Sir Hector Laing of United

Biscuits, Sir Ian MacGregor (formerly of British Steel and the National Coal Board), Lord Weir of Weir Pumps and Angus Grossart, a merchant banker.[57] The point of the group was not to formulate policy but to fundraise – a pressing concern given just £40,775 was raised by constituency associations in 1988 – and indeed by 1991 the SBG was much the most important source of party income.[58]

Reorganisation, meanwhile, was just one aspect of a three-pronged Conservative fightback north of the border. Not only was Malcolm Rifkind to rethink the relevance of Conservative policies to Scotland, but there was to be a charm offensive from the Lady herself. That Mrs Thatcher should pay more attention – or at least appear to pay more attention – to Scotland and to Scottish affairs was one of the central findings of Ancram's report and was to an extent backed up by a *Glasgow Herald* opinion poll in October 1987. This identified an undeniable 'Thatcher factor' inhibiting Scottish Conservative support. Eighty-four per cent of those polled said the Prime Minister was not very or not at all sympathetic to Scotland, but when asked if she should pay more attention and visit more often, most said yes. Furthermore, while 32 per cent regarded her as a good UK Prime Minister, only 9 per cent thought the same in a Scottish context.[59]

The academic A. D. R. Dickson attempted to probe Scottish attitudes a little more deeply in a 1988 study and identified specifically Scottish insecurities. 'We always seem to get the rough end of the stick in Scotland,' said one respondent. 'We always seem to be forgotten about.' All 'Maggie's interested in [is] ... the South-East of England', said another, while one respondent reckoned the Prime Minister did not worry 'about Ravenscraig because it's so far north and she's not relying, in all honesty, on the votes in Scotland'. 'These perceptions,' concluded Dickson, 'deriving from the historical development of Scottish society and its reflections in the cultural identity of Scots, are particularly focused on the personality of the Prime Minister':

> The public persona of Mrs Thatcher appears to many Scots to capture all the worst elements of their caricature of the detested English – uncaring, arrogant, always convinced of their own rightness ('there is no alternative'), possessed of an accent that grates on Scottish ears, and ... also associated with the conspicuously 'yuppie'/affluent South-East, and the City. These are bitter images for Scots, well aware of stark contrasts offered in Scotland by high

unemployment, pockets of appalling social deprivation in the major urban areas, and reared in a culture where Scottish Protestantism, while not denigrating the accumulation of wealth, has always emphasised its distaste for the flouting of its manifestations.[60]

Addressing her first Scottish Conservative conference since the election, the Prime Minister said she was 'sometimes told that the Scots don't like Thatcherism'. 'Well, I find that hard to believe,' she added with some more tartan wrapping, 'because the Scots invented Thatcherism, long before I was thought of':

> Scottish values are Tory values – and vice versa. The values of hard work, self-reliance, thrift, enterprise – the relishing of challenges, the seizing of opportunities. That's what the Tory Party stands for – that's what Scotland stands for. And that will be our message to the people.[61]

Although spirited, this attempt to tartanise Thatcherism had little effect when it came to the district council elections of May 1988. Already demoralised in Scotland's town halls, the Conservatives went from 189 councillors in 1984 to 162 four years later, trailing the SNP with just 19 per cent of the vote and retaining control of only three authorities in elections dominated by the imminent introduction of the Poll Tax.

There followed a trio of high-profile Scottish visits, two of which did not go according to plan. Immediately after the Perth conference, Mrs Thatcher attended the Scottish Cup Final at Hampden Park in Glasgow and was literally shown the red card (distributed by the SNP before the match) by thousands of booing football fans. Next was a speech to the annual General Assembly of the Church of Scotland, which the Prime Minister had first attended in 1981.[62] There, Mrs Thatcher was greeted with more red cards and a walkout from Kirk ministers opposed to her presence. The national Church of Scotland was no longer the Scottish Conservative Party at prayer: one survey suggested that only 34 per cent of Kirk members voted Conservative, although this was well above the party's Scottish share of the vote.

Subsequent accounts suggest the Prime Minister had put an enormous amount of work into her address, during which she acknowledged that the Church of Scotland had sprung 'from the independence of mind and rigour of thought that have always been such powerful characteristics of the Scottish people,' before adding as a joke, 'as I have occasion to know'. What followed was a sincere attempt to reconcile Conservatism with the Christian gospel, and indeed the applause at the end of Mrs Thatcher's address was sustained and enthusiastic, far from the 'stony silence' often depicted in historical accounts.[63] Yet the long afterlife of the so-called 'Sermon on the Mound' proved deeply negative.[64] As Malcolm Rifkind, whose idea the speech had been, later observed, it had got to the point where Scots would have objected had the Prime Minister recited excerpts from the telephone directory.

Another consequence of the election result was that pro-devolution voices within the party, never more than a few in number, grew louder. Michael Fry, Struan Stevenson and Brian Meek established the Conservative Constitutional Reform Forum (CCRF) in late 1987, and it planned a motion and fringe meeting at the 1988 Perth conference. Michael Forsyth and Bill Walker – aided by a group of Scottish Young Conservatives – interrupted the meeting by standing under a 'Devolution Sucks' banner and sporting 'Devolution NO; Thatcherism YES' badges. As Andrew Marr observed, Scottish party conferences now included such figures who formed 'a dark rectangle of waving, pin-striped conviction amid the dull moorlands of tolerant tweeds and the outcrops of pink-faced old ladies'.[65] Scottish Young Conservatives also involved themselves, alongside party veterans like Teddy Taylor, Nicholas Fairbairn and Bill Walker, in the John Buchan Club, which was established to proclaim the virtues of a free-market economy and the Union.[66] One SYC chairman, Brian Monteith, even taunted the anti-capital punishment Home Secretary Douglas Hurd with nooses and cries of 'hang the bastard' when he addressed their Peebles conference.[67]

More nuanced was Allan Stewart, who argued that a sudden U-turn on devolution would still result in Conservatives being perceived as less enthusiastic than their opponents. Putting forward 'some half-baked scheme', he added, 'would be the worst of all possible worlds. It would be derided by our opponents and would appall the business community who have thought very seriously about the implications.'[68] Inevitably, conference voted 300 to 11 against the CCRF motion (one delegate produced stickers which urged the party to 'Expel the 11'). 'We thought traditional Tory pragmatism would kick in at some point,' reflected Michael Fry. 'But we were all wrong.'[69]

'I am delighted that at this conference you resoundingly rejected the prospect of a second-class Scotland,' Mrs Thatcher declared in her conference speech shortly after the debate, 'cut-off from the rest of the United Kingdom by tax barriers that would destroy her economy.' 'As long as I am Leader of this Party,' she proclaimed, 'we shall defend the Union and reject legislative devolution unequivocally.' It was almost the Declaration of Perth in reverse, and took place exactly 20 years after Edward Heath had first committed the party to devolution.[70] 'It is because their patriotism is inborn, taken for granted and not paranoid or xenophobic', wrote Gerald Warner of late-1980s Scottish Conservatives, 'that they have the confidence to embrace a British identity that is wholly complementary to their Scottishness, rejecting a sterile and introverted separatism.'[71]

Malcolm Rifkind had attempted to square the circle between Thatcherite hostility and long-standing Scottish Unionist principles in a speech to the Aberdeen Chamber of Commerce:

> As Unionists, as well as Conservatives, we attach importance to Scots Law, to the national church, to our universities, to our Scottish banks and financial institutions, to our learned societies, to the contribution of Scottish regiments to the British Army, and to our ceremonial heritage. These express the Scottish identity and Scottish values, having stood the test of time and, for the most part, blossomed during the period of Union.

'The unity of the Kingdom', he added, 'is strengthened by diversity and ... neither requires nor would benefit from the Anglicisation of Scotland.'[72]

Rifkind was alluding to a then widespread view – one that appeared eccentric with the passage of time – that Scotland and Scottishness was somehow being extinguished. Scottish Television even broadcast a documentary entitled *The Englishing of Scotland*, while the Educational Institute for Scotland railed against the introduction of 'English' institutions such as school boards, a concern which ignored the existence of similar Scottish bodies in the 1920s.[73] In a lecture by the author William McIlvanney entitled 'Stands Scotland Where It Did?', he said:

> Margaret Thatcher is not just a perpetrator of bad policies. She is a cultural vandal. She takes the axe of her own simplicity to the complexities of Scottish life. She has no understanding of the hard-earned traditions she is destroying. And if we allow her to continue,

she will remove from the word 'Scottish' any meaning other than geographical.

Conscious of the retort that Scots were willing participants in many aspects of Thatcherism, Owen Dudley Edwards claimed:

> Thatcherism has done everything it can to bribe, bully and blackmail Scotland into bowing down before its gods of materialism and British chauvinism, self-enrichment and self-regard, community destruction and beggar-your-neighbour.

But to Gerry Hassan, this 'false collective memory syndrome' allowed 'part of Scotland to place the blame for our problems on one factor, to paint a black-and-white past ... and luxuriate in the power of victimhood'.[74] But elite narratives subsequently shaped (or perhaps reflected) mass opinion. An ICM poll found almost four-fifths of Scots agreeing that the Conservatives represented mainly an English party with little relevance to Scotland.[75]

The 1988 'Claim of Right' and subsequent Scottish Constitutional Convention were a response to this growing feeling of alienation between Scottish voters and its governing party, a feeling often expressed in pungently nationalistic terms. Malcolm Rifkind inevitably distanced himself from the cross-party gathering, choosing not to follow the more pragmatic approach of Scottish Unionists to the Scottish National Assembly of the late 1940s. Speaking in the Commons, the Scottish Secretary said that as it was 'not intended as a genuine debate on the merits and demerits of the constitutional changes which they have in mind', he did not consider it 'appropriate for the Government to be represented'.[76]

But while understandable, this put further distance between the apparently backward-looking Scottish Conservative party and a clear majority of Scottish voters, who were looking forward to some sort of change. With the Labour Party in Scotland now defining 'its own patriotism as an anti-Thatcher stance in which a devolved, collectivist Scotland could become a proud bulwark against the selfish individualism of Tory England',[77] the 'Scottish card' played by the Unionists in the late 1940s and early '50s was being dealt by a different hand. The centre-left Scottish political establishment – which included the media as well as political parties – now united in depicting Conservatism 'as being alien to the Scottish body politic'.[78]

That Scottish Conservatives were apparently intent upon dismantling the very totems of past regional policy – chiefly Ravenscraig – once championed by Scottish Unionists, allowed the narrative to build that Mrs Thatcher was deliberately engaged in the de-industrialisation of Scotland.[79] David McCrone has argued that the apparent failure of the Prime Minister's ideology was not merely due to the particular socio-economic structure of Scotland; rather it was that:

> In Scotland, the attack on state institutions – the nationalised industries, the education system, local government, the public sector generally, even the church, institutions which carried much of Scotland's identity – was easily perceived as an attack on 'Scotland' itself. Essential to current Conservative appeal south of the border was an appeal to 'the nation' on whose behalf politicians and the state act. But Scots had a nation of their own, and the vision of recreating bourgeois England was out of kilter not only with Scottish material interests, but with this alternative sense of national identity.[80]

To grandees like George Younger, however, this was primarily a PR problem: 'It's remarkable how good we are at doing the right thing economically but how incredibly bad we are at presenting it.'[81]

Only Scotland's business community remained unreconstructed in its support for the Scottish Conservative Party and its opposition to devolution. In a critique of the Scottish Constitutional Convention's emerging proposals, Lord Weir said they looked 'like a recipe for three evils – uncertainty, conflict and cost'.[82] In a slightly desperate move, a consortium of Scottish Conservatives, including the lawyer Ross Harper and former MP Iain Sproat, even embarked on a takeover bid for the *Glasgow Herald* with the endorsement of party chairman Sir James Goold. It came to nothing but demonstrated how keenly the party felt the loss of media support. While in the early 1950s Unionists had enjoyed 100 per cent editorial support from Scotland's four main newspapers, by the late 1980s this had fallen to around 13 per cent.[83]

Pamphlets, meanwhile, flowed thick and fast, just as they had in the mid-1970s during a similarly unhappy period for Scottish Conservatism. The Eastwood Conservative Association urged the party to stick to its principles locally and nationally,[84] while *Making Unionism Positive*, written by Liam Fox,

Alistair B. Cooke (of the Conservative Research Department) and Mark Mayall, not only strongly rejected legislative devolution but advocated a 'fundamental re-examination' of existing levels of administrative devolution. Their ideal destination was 'the assimilation of Scotland, sensibly and pragmatically, within the overall framework of Conservative policies, making proper allowance within it for the distinctive characteristics of Scottish life'.[85] This 'assimilationist' view was also expressed by the Edinburgh district councillor Kenneth Ferguson, who called it 'total Unionism'. Under this vision, the 'incompetent lot of officials in St Andrew's House' would be moved to London, where they would 'slowly integrate it into United Kingdom ministries'.[86]

Malcolm MacKenzie of the Scottish Tory Reform Group (STRG), which had been formed in 1978, took the opposite view in observing that to have equated the Scottish Conservative Party 'with all that Scots most dislike about "Englishness"' and root it in contemporary consciousness' had 'been a remarkable political achievement':

Scottish Toryism has somehow become displaced in Scottish consciousness. It has been afflicted by the near-lethal twin problems of being marginalized and of being perceived as inimical to Scottish culture ... The task facing Scottish Toryism is to change perception, to create a new reality, a task which will not be achieved by the endless repetition of statistics or reprimands on the subject of 'cultural dependence' by visiting English Ministers.[87]

Malcolm Rifkind, meanwhile, tried to soften the political tone at the 1989 Scottish Conservative conference by promising that he would be 'listening' throughout the coming parliamentary session. The implication was that after two years of controversial legislation there was to be a period of consolidation as the party reverted to more traditional 'One Nation' Conservatism. Prominent in this respect were the STRG's Arthur and Susan Bell, who 'rejected Thatcherism because they feared it would destroy the Conservative Party in Scotland and therefore the Union itself'.[88] Alarmed by the party's post-1987 lurch to the right, when the amiable solicitor James Highgate retired as president of the Scottish Conservative and Unionist Association, they took the unprecedented step of organising a 'slate' of moderate candidates. Their strategy worked. Not only did 'a wave of party energy' carry the popular Glaswegian lawyer Ross Harper 'past the Buggins' turn candidates and into the presidency', but the pro-devolution councillor Brian Meek became SCUA vice-president.[89] The membership nevertheless remained sleepy. Although a 1990 survey estimated there to be 43,000 members (35,000 seemed more likely), half that number were aged over 65 and belonged to generally moribund constituency associations.

But while moderates now controlled the party's voluntary wing, the opposite was true of its professional arm. When Lord Goold decided to retire as Scottish Conservative Party chairman in 1989, Mrs Thatcher spotted an opportunity to counterbalance a Scottish Secretary who had fallen back 'with a vengeance on the old counter-productive tactic of proving his Scottish virility by posturing as Scotland's defender against Thatcherism'. Having come to regard Michael Forsyth as the 'real powerhouse for Thatcherism at the Scottish Office', in July 1989 she 'overrode Malcolm Rifkind's objections and appointed Michael Chairman and Bill Hughes his Deputy'.[90]

Forsyth was a true believer. Assessing the first (for he was certain it was only the first) decade of Scotland under Thatcherism, he claimed that ten years 'of the Thatcher revolution have brought massive and sweeping improvements to Scotland'. 'With Thatcherism,' he enthused, 'harmony has replaced strife, and efficient order has taken over from shambling chaos.' He nevertheless acknowledged that the Prime Minister was not universally popular. 'Even some Scottish Tory MPs occasionally question her judgment,' Forsyth continued, 'believing that, if they push her hard enough, she will somehow bend to them. They are misguided. Mrs Thatcher, quite rightly, will not change her style. She knows it has served Scotland well.'[91]

Also unwilling to change his style was Forsyth. Within weeks of his appointment, out from the party's Chester Street headquarters

went senior departmental directors like Bob Balfour and Peter Smith and in came young right-wingers like chief of staff Russell Walters, and Simon Turner, the man who took over the role of chief agent. The attitudes and gung-ho approach of the discredited Federation of Conservative Students which had been Forsyth's political training ground came to be the accepted norm. John MacKay, the former Scottish Office Minister who had been chief executive, found himself sidelined.[92]

Even the American (and Republican) political strategist Grover Norquist, with funding from the Heritage Foundation, turned up in Edinburgh. 'You might be good for the States', he was told by Bill Hughes, 'but I doubt if you're applicable to Scotland.' Brian Monteith, a prominent Young Conservative, PR professional and friend of Forsyth's, also masterminded a glossy magazine called *Scottish Conservative*. In the first edition, its editor Sir Nicholas Fairbairn described the Scottish press as 'little Scotlanders ... yearning to return to those far-off days when Scotland was an independent oatmeal republic with a squabbling parliament presiding over abject poverty'.[93] Despite such deathless prose, the magazine ceased publication after just four issues and having cost the party around £200,000 (it was replaced by a cheaper newspaper format).[94]

Forsyth's appointment also blatantly undermined the authority of Malcolm Rifkind, who as Scottish Secretary was considered the party's de facto leader in Scotland. Not only did Forsyth remain a minister at the Scottish Office, but he now controlled party organisation and, most importantly of all, had a direct line to the Prime Minister. Unsurprisingly, Rifkind resented this enormously, a feeling compounded by growing attacks from certain newspapers. Kelvin Mackenzie, editor of the *Sun*, informed his Scottish editor, Jack Irvine, that following Forsyth's appointment as chairman it was now acceptable to 'put the boot in' to the Scottish Secretary.[95]

The appointment of a new party chairman coincided with a myriad of internal reports which sought Scottish solutions to what was increasingly acknowledged as a Thatcher-shaped problem. 'Canvassers uniformly reported that the Prime Minister is still perceived to be disinterested in Scotland,' the former Tory MP Michael Hirst informed members of the SCUA's Executive Committee. 'The Opposition parties have succeeded in whipping up the "hate factor" as fiercely as ever before, and disaffection is marked among public sector employees.'[96] Another internal memo, written by the future Scottish Conservative leader David McLetchie, also touched upon a much wider problem for the party. He argued:

I believe that the perception of the Conservatives as an English based and English run party is the biggest single factor in our current standing in Scotland. In my experience, all Scots are nationalists with a small 'n' at heart and we have ignored this at our peril. There is a far wider constituency of support for Conservative policies in Scotland than is currently reflected in Conservative votes.[97]

Forsyth was convinced that a change of style could tap into this latent Conservative support, although his small 'n' nationalist approach would only manifest itself several years later. 'The party organisation was stuffed with musty, amateurish old retainers who toodled around the place eating cake and were much happier discussing recipes than politics,' recalled Rae Stewart, a press officer who left just before Lord Goold retired as chairman. 'Then suddenly Forsyth brings in a bunch of young, impatient people who were into modern campaigning techniques. The old guard just found them too brash, too rude, too aggressively political.'[98] Anna McCurley, the former MP for Renfrew West and Inverclyde, simply called them 'weirdos',[99] although Seawright has concluded that the right of the party 'were in fact more in tune with the members' opinions on devolution, Europe and free market philosophy'.[100]

Nevertheless, anonymous letters began appearing in the letterboxes of constituency chairmen across Scotland. 'Appointed by the Prime Minister, he [Forsyth] was seen by many of us as the last chance for the Party in Scotland,' read one onslaught from 'A Chairman'. 'But we do not need the extremist riff-raff that Forsyth has brought into Chester Street … concerns now appear to be not those of the many former Tory voters we all meet on the doorsteps, but the concerns of an extreme and unpleasant minority of far-right troublemakers whose involvement brings nothing but shame on the Party.'[101]

Forsyth's followers, meanwhile, were apparently preparing to topple Malcolm Rifkind (his ally Ross Harper, by accident rather than design, had already resigned as SCUA president[102]). The resulting war of words often descended into petty squabbling rather than internal ideological debate. Arthur Bell, chairman of the STRG, spoke of 'blue trots' rampaging through Central Office, while Allan Stewart called Bell 'a pig-ignorant pipsqueak' (although that, he reflected later, was unfair to pigs). Forsyth even declared on BBC Radio Scotland that 'it was well known that Bell was the stupidest man in the Scottish Conservative Party'.[103] The media was briefed that Rifkind was not up to the job of Scottish Secretary. On this basis, a trio of right-wing

Scottish Conservative MPs (Nicholas Fairbairn, Bill Walker and Allan Stewart) even opposed the impeccably Thatcherite Law Reform (Miscellaneous Provisions) (Scotland) Bill, which sought to deregulate the legal profession in Scotland.[104]

At the Scottish Conservative conference in May 1990, held in Aberdeen rather than Perth for security reasons, matters reached a comic opera finale when the right-wing MP Bill Walker – nicknamed 'Biggles' – called publicly for Rifkind's replacement with Forsyth, arguing that the recent regional council elections had proved once and for all that he had to go. Rifkind, always quick off the mark with a witty riposte, brought down the house when he opened his keynote speech by looking at his watch and saying, 'Well, it's 12 o'clock and I'm still here'.[105]

Forsyth quashed the speculation in his chairman's address, saying he had 'quite enough on my plate at present'. He also launched a spirited defence of hardline Thatcherism. 'Radical policies do pay dividends,' he argued. 'Being weak-kneed will neither achieve our objectives nor win us support. Where we show we shall not waiver we reap the dividends.'[106] Nevertheless, it was at this conference that the counter-revolution finally got under way, ostensibly led by the Scottish Tory Reform Group. Its notables sought out the former Scottish Secretary George Younger, now chairman-designate of the Royal Bank of Scotland, and convinced him to persuade Mrs Thatcher to remove Forsyth. Many grandees had become convinced the Prime Minister simply was not aware of what was going on.

The Scottish Business Group, now chaired by James Gulliver of Argyll Foods, also warned that such 'public turbulence … was having a negative impact on donations'.[107] Forsyth bowed to the inevitable and resigned. 'It had been a brave attempt to bring the Scottish Tory Party into the latter half of the twentieth century and offer leadership and vision to people who had become all too used to losing or – even worse – winning on their opponents' terms,' recalled Mrs Thatcher bitterly in her memoirs. She added:

His [resignation] was taken as a sign that the attempt to extend Thatcherism to Scotland had come to an end. This combination of the Left and the traditional establishment of the Party to rebuff Thatcherism in Scotland was a prelude to the formation of the same alliance to oust me as leader of the Conservative Party a few weeks later – although I did not know it at the time.[108]

In a face-saving move suggested by Rifkind – who also viewed the affair as 'a microcosm of the growing fissure in the Conservative Party as a whole' – Forsyth stayed on at the Scottish Office but was promoted to Minister of State.[109]

And that, as Andrew Marr has written, 'was the beginning and the end of Scotto-Thatcherism in the Conservative Party'.[110] Lord Sanderson of Bowden succeeded Forsyth as chairman and promptly sacked all but one of his predecessor's appointments, 'calmly and steadily' rebuilding 'order at the centre and morale amongst the constituency associations'.[111] 'It was a terrible time for me,' reflected Lord Forsyth in 2008. 'I hated it.'

> I didn't want to do it. It was never going to work really because it put Malcolm Rifkind in a difficult position, and it put me in a difficult position as his junior minister. I was 36 and saw things in black and white so I'm sure there were faults on both sides. I was very driven by our political agenda, so I was probably not the best person to appoint as party chairman because schmoozing skills were not my thing. But what I was good at was campaigning, identifying weaknesses in my opponents and presenting policies in a way that attracted attention – that caused jealousies and resentments.

'If she had wanted me to run Scotland she should have appointed me Secretary of State,' concluded Forsyth, 'but in the end I did what she said because she was the boss.'[112]

A few months before these internal ructions reached their denouement, the 'Poll Tax' had become a reality in Scotland on 1 April 1989, and was met by a co-ordinated campaign of non-payment, militancy backed by the SNP if not the Scottish Labour Party. '[I]f, as the Scots subsequently claimed, they were guinea pigs for a great experiment in local government finance,' Mrs Thatcher reflected in her memoirs, 'they were the most vociferous and influential guinea pigs which the world has ever seen.'[113]

At elections to the European Parliament a couple of months later, Scotland became a Tory-free zone, with the party sinking to just more than a fifth of the popular vote, polling fewer votes than the SNP and losing their remaining two MEPs. 'You have always said that you didn't enter politics in order to be popular,' declared the broadcaster Kirsty Wark in a celebrated interview

with Mrs Thatcher, 'but why are you so unpopular in Scotland?'
A visibly taken aback Prime Minister responded:

> Well, I don't think I am necessarily the right person to answer that
> but I wouldn't entirely say it was true. What does please me is
> that Scotland is taking advantage of all the policies which is right,
> because I regard it as a very great honour to be Prime Minister of
> Scotland.

Although constitutionally correct, Mrs Thatcher's assertion that
she was 'Prime Minister of Scotland', together with frequent references in the same interview to 'we in Scotland',[114] ensured that
Wark versus Thatcher – broadcast on BBC Scotland in March
1990 – became one of the definitive expressions of an apparently
imperious Prime Minister's disconnection from her Scottish subjects. 'I said that I had often heard her say "You in Scotland",
when she was north of the Border,' recalled Sir Malcolm Rifkind
by way of an explanation for the curious phraseology:

> It made it sound as if she was visiting a foreign country. Try not
> to use that phrase, I suggested. She took the point and was in full
> agreement. She went in to record the interview and Michael Forsyth
> and I watched on the monitor. To our disbelief we heard her saying
> 'We in Scotland' not once, but several times. Not what I had had
> in mind![115]

Although in the regional council elections of May 1990 the
Conservative share of the vote actually increased by nearly 3
per cent compared with 1986, it was 'undoubtedly the case',
judged the SCUA vice-president Adrian Shinwell, 'that the perceived aggressive, hectoring attitude of the Prime Minister is
doing us enormous damage'. 'It matters not whether she is right
or wrong, it is her presidential style, her tone and her manner
which are creating the concern':

> If we are to pretend that the Prime Minister is other than an electoral
> liability in Scotland, then we are failing to recognise the deep-rooted
> concern that is expressed all around us ... Given her enormous
> energy, ability and commitment to the country in the past, it would
> be a tragedy if the Prime Minister were to be brought down by her
> own Party and yet I fear that this will happen if she does not see
> the writing on the wall and step down with her reputation intact.

'The fight is no longer for the minds of the Scottish people but
for their hearts,' concluded Shinwell. 'Without them, we shall

lose and we shall have failed our Party and our country.'[116] Shinwell's letter was unknowingly prescient. Just days later, Sir Geoffrey Howe's carefully calculated resignation speech precipitated a seismic series of events that resulted in Mrs Thatcher being brought down, as Shinwell had predicted, by her own party.[117] 'Thatcherism is dead,' rejoiced the STRG president Arthur Bell, 'long live Conservatism.'[118]

The election of John Major as UK Conservative leader (and, therefore, Prime Minister) offered the Scottish Conservative Party the chance of a reset following another turbulent decade. The new premier was also determined to take a 'completely different' approach to Scotland. Major moved quickly to vanquish the Poll Tax and chose Glasgow Cathedral as the location for a national thanksgiving service at the conclusion of the Gulf War (although there was criticism when an Anglican archbishop rather than the Kirk's Moderator led the proceedings). By April 1991, the Prime Minister had a 56 per cent satisfaction rating in Scotland, compared with 20 per cent for his predecessor a year earlier.[119] Scottish Election Study surveys also indicated that Major was regarded as more egalitarian, moderate and substantially more caring than the previous occupant of Downing Street. Indeed, he deliberately appointed the 'courteous, able and gentlemanly' Ian Lang to the Scottish Office, where 'his persuasive qualities were exactly what we needed to address the Scots' perception of the Tories as uncaring and extreme'.[120]

Rejecting the 'unwritten code' that Catholics 'were supposed to be Labour supporters ... whilst Protestants were Unionists', Lang made a point of meeting Cardinal Thomas Winning, the Archbishop of Glasgow, saying after one encounter that he was a man he could 'do business with' (the Free Presbyterian Church called it 'Fraternising with Antichrist'). Remarkably, Lang also became the first Secretary of State for Scotland to attend a Roman Catholic church service.[121] Scottish Conservatives remained sensitive to accusations of sectarianism. When its prospective candidate in the Western Isles said Catholics were 'non-Christians', he was swiftly replaced.[122]

Another Lang initiative was the publication of a public expenditure paper – something first done by Unionists in the 1930s and 1950s – in order to 'undermine the casual and wildly inaccurate claims being made by the SNP'.[123] This became GERS (Government Expenditure Revenue Scotland), which is still issued annually by the SNP-led Scottish Government. The figures were, of course, helpful given the continued growth of the Scottish economy to become the third wealthiest part of the UK after London and the South-East, although the political benefits of this were mitigated by the final demise of Ravenscraig in April 1992. Beyond Lanarkshire, however, the number of Scots who were out of work had been falling steadily since the late 1980s, and ultimately to below the UK average. While England and Wales entered recession in the early 1990s, Scotland did not. The Scottish economy was also now more diversified, the 'old and risky dependence on one or two exporting giants had been reduced and instead the industrial structure now resembled more closely that of the UK as a whole'.[124]

Translating economic success into votes, however, remained challenging. In November 1991, the Scottish Conservatives failed to hold Kincardine and Deeside in the by-election following the death of Sir Alick Buchanan-Smith, who had borne scars from the devolution splits of the mid-1970s. John Major looked ahead to a general election in 1992 and confessed in his memoirs to being 'deeply worried':

> Even if we won a majority across Britain, I did not know how we could continue to govern Scotland if we did not have sufficient Scottish MPs of good quality to man the Scottish Office. Devolution would have become inevitable, and I would have had to introduce it. The thought repelled me.[125]

The Prime Minister asked Ian Lang, Lord Mackay (the Scots-born Lord High Chancellor of Great Britain), Malcolm Rifkind and Douglas Hurd to prepare a 'line' should the Conservatives emerge (as generally expected) with no Scottish MPs. Rifkind suggested holding an immediate referendum on devolution.

Boldly, John Major instead turned the forthcoming election into a de facto referendum on the Union. Addressing a gathering of prospective parliamentary and district council candidates in February 1992, the Prime Minister said:

> We are a Unionist Party. We should fight for the Union. As we make that stand, we can do so firmly and clearly. For we do not do it for party political advantage ... And yet it is our Party that supports the Union. Not because it has always been good for us but because it has always seemed right to us. Not always in our political interest, but always in that of our Kingdom and the countries within it.[126]

Major's Unionist crusade also brought a new generation of London-based political advisers into contact with the Scottish party for the first time. While staying at Bute House, the Scottish Secretary's official residence, Jonathan Hill entered the dining room 'expecting to find the normal pre-press-conference panic going on'. Instead, there was:

> Silence – broken only by the rustle of newspapers and the industrious scrape of knife and fork. The Scottish Party top brass – with their wives – were at breakfast. And they clearly weren't going to interrupt their routine just for a general election. Jonathan's attempts to broach the subject of the press conference were rebuffed by a steady Protestant crunch of teeth on toast. No briefing.[127]

In more secular settings, Major 'could see tears streaming' down activists' faces during an election rally in Edinburgh on 26 March 1992, while at another (this time at Wembley) on 5 April he made 'the almost apocalyptic warning': 'If I could summon up all the authority of this office, I would put it into a single warning: the United Kingdom is in danger. Wake up, my fellow countrymen. Wake up now before it is too late.'[128] What was striking, observed Andrew Marr, 'was the nostalgic, post-imperial rhetoric this deadpan, unrhetorical politician chose to deploy'. But having decided to fight the election on this basis, Major and Ian Lang 'led their party with courage, humour and panache'.[129]

'Doomsday' – the loss of all Conservative seats in Scotland – was once again widely predicted. In Galloway and Upper Nithsdale, Lang was expected to lose ('It's no Lang noo', claimed SNP posters), while his final campaign poster urged Scots to 'Vote Conservative', the 'X' voting symbol provided by a billowing Saltire, the same symbol Lang had recently 'accused the separatists of wanting to tear out of the Union Flag'. 'We were determined to show ourselves as proud Scots,' he recalled in his memoirs, 'who far from being defensive over Scotland's place in the United Kingdom had the self-confidence to take pride in both our nation and our nation state.'[130]

Although Scots did not exactly 'wake up' to Major's call, on polling day it appeared that a certain number of Conservative abstainers had been persuaded to return to the fold. Not only did the party gain two Scottish MPs to reach a total of 11, but it modestly increased its share of the vote to 25.6 per cent on an equally modest swing of 2.5 per cent. Expectations had been so low, however, that the result looked like a triumph. It was also a blow for the opposition parties, in that it represented no major advance for Labour or the Liberal Democrats, although the SNP did significantly increase its share of the vote (by this point the *Scottish Sun* backed the SNP and independence; its English edition the Conservatives and the Union). Indeed, the Liberal Democrats even believed their support for devolution had lost them votes in Conservative-inclined seats.[131] The victory in Ayr of Phil Gallie – described by the *Guardian* as 'the thinking man's Rab C. Nesbitt' – 'stunned commentators and opponents alike'.[132] John Major's 'instinctive feeling' (one shared by many political analysts) was that his 'defence of the Union hardened support for the Conservative Party in Scotland during the election'.[133]

The result also put the Thatcher factor into some perspective. Rather than her unpopularity destroying the Scottish Conservative Party, in fact her impact was curiously neutral. At the October 1974 general election, held just months before she became leader, the Scottish party polled 24.7 per cent, while at the 1992 election, which took place more than a year after her resignation, the party polled slightly more at 25.6 per cent. Only the 1987 election result stood out as an undisputed black mark against Mrs Thatcher's electoral record. 'The 1992 election showed that the fall in Tory support had been halted,' she reflected in her memoirs, 'it had yet to be reversed'.[134]

In district council elections that followed the general election, Conservatives made another modest recovery, winning 23.2 per cent of the vote and overall control of four districts (Perth and Kinross, Berwickshire, Eastwood, and Kyle and Carrick). Nevertheless, even the Association of Scottish Conservative Councillors acknowledged a feeling among its members that the powers of local government had 'been very much eroded under the present Conservative Government'.[135] John Young, the acknowledged leader of Scottish Conservative councillors and a rare devolutionist, proposed that a referendum on Scotland's constitutional future form part of party policy.[136]

But what John Major had won was some much-needed breathing space, and instead of preparing for a referendum – by then a persistent demand of the SNP if not Labour and the Liberal Democrats – he promised to 'take stock' of Scotland's place in the Union.[137] The Scottish Conservative Party also took stock of its internal organisation a mere five years after the last such exercise. In an interim report, Adrian Shinwell frankly admitted that 'autonomy, while one of the strengths of the Party, is also one of its weaknesses', while a 'comprehensive membership scheme' was proposed in order to tackle parlous finances. 'To be frank,' observed Russell Sanderson, 'the Director and I are constrained in our endeavours by a lack of sufficient funds to do what has to be done to make our Party an effective political fighting machine.'[138] It was ever thus.

With the Glasgow Cathedral thanksgiving service of March 1991 in mind, John Major continued an old Unionist strategy of attempting to kill Home Rule sentiment with kindness. Edinburgh was chosen to host the European Summit of December 1992 (during which the Single Market was completed), Gleneagles for a meeting of EU environment ministers and Glasgow for a major statement on the Exchange Rate Mechanism (ERM). The last of those was overshadowed when sterling crashed out of the ERM a few days later. It was 'the Union', reflected Major in his memoirs, 'warts and all'.[139] The Prime Minister also met a carefully selected group of eminent Scots at Bute House, a bold if unsuccessful attempt to ingratiate himself and his party with Scottish intellectual life.

When *Scotland in the Union – A Partnership for Good* finally appeared in the spring of 1993, the press and political reaction was mixed but predominantly cynical. The Scottish Grand Committee (SGC) was to be beefed up and allowed to question Scottish Office ministers; the Scottish Affairs Select Committee (SASC, mothballed under Mrs Thatcher's final administration due to lack of personnel) was to be revived;[140] training development and control of the Scottish Arts Council were to be 'devolved' to the Scottish Office from the Department of Employment and National Heritage Department respectively; while civil servants dealing with North Sea oil regulation were to be 'dispersed' from London to Aberdeen.[141]

If this harked back to the 'Scottish Control of Scottish Affairs' agenda, what had appeared bold and in tune with Scottish sentiment in the late 1940s now looked weak and out of touch. James Kellas judged the party's continuing opposition to legislative devolution 'politically irrational',[142] and while Lang knew 'lots of people wanted it' (and that 'it was one of the reasons

why the media hated us'), there was never any prospect of a
mea culpa:

> Ultimately, for me it became an issue of irreducible principle … I
> could see the arguments, of heart and head, in favour of it. I sensed
> that sooner or later it would happen in some form, probably under a
> Labour government. But after I had thought about it long and hard,
> I could not bring myself to do anything other than stand firm over
> an issue that I could not believe to be in the best interests either of
> Scotland or of the United Kingdom.[143]

Lang also realised opposition to devolution was costing his
party support. At regional and European contests in 1994,
the Scottish Conservatives polled just 13.7 and 14.5 per cent
respectively, while in 1995 Scotland elected 32 new unitary
local authorities for the first time. Their boundaries had been
decided not by an independent commission but by the Scottish
Office, a blatant piece of gerrymandering which earned condem-
nation from opponents and the press. Lang had no doubt the
two-tier structure from 1975 was 'cumbersome, illogical and
wasteful', the 'mighty' Strathclyde Regional Council possessing
'no commonality of interest', but nevertheless the political intent
behind the reorganisation failed.[144] Having contested only half
the available seats, Scottish Conservatives won only 82 and
were left without control of a single local authority in Scotland.
    Petulantly, Michael Forsyth called the results 'unfair' while
Michael Hirst, now Scottish party chairman, suggested that
Scottish voters were 'ungrateful'.[145] Just weeks later a by-election
took place in Perth and Kinross, following the death of the
maverick MP Sir Nicholas Fairbairn. Privately progressive, he
had become almost a parody of a Tory knight of the shire after
resigning as Solicitor General in 1981, complete with castle, self-
designed tartan outfits and offensive views; John Calder called
him 'an anarchist of the right'.[146] But in one of Scotland's most
prosperous constituencies, the SNP's Roseanna Cunningham (a
republican) scored an impressive victory. As in Kincardine and
Deeside in 1991, voters proved 'willing to switch to the best-
placed challenger' in order to prevent a Conservative victory.[147]
James Douglas-Hamilton had even renounced an Earldom rather
than risk another by-election in Edinburgh West.[148] It did not
help that Scottish Conservative members were clearly demoti-
vated. One survey found that 77 per cent had never canvassed,

60 per cent had never delivered party leaflets and 73 per cent had never even displayed a poster.[149]

In June 1995, following John Major's re-election as Conservative Party leader, Michael Forsyth succeeded Ian Lang as Secretary of State for Scotland. Forsyth believed his predecessor's attempt at 'taking stock' had been a wasted opportunity to revitalise the Conservatives' Scottish appeal, especially given the unexpected reprieve provided by the 1992 general election. Although he still provoked party and media ire despite having, by his own admission, come to view politics in nuanced shades of grey rather than extremes of black and white, the new Scottish Secretary set about formulating 'Taking Stock Mark II'.[150]

Demonstrating that he had lost none of his late-1980s panache, Forsyth chose St Andrew's Day in 1995 to reveal his hand, the same day the Scottish Constitutional Convention was due to publish its detailed proposals for a Scottish Parliament. The Scottish Grand Committee was to become a 'parliament on wheels ... meeting in every sizeable town across Scotland', this time with powers to question ministers from other government departments with a remit in Scotland.[151] Local authorities were to be given more discretion over their budgets, while Forsyth reached into Scottish Unionist history by promising to repatriate the Stone of Destiny ahead of the 700th anniversary of its removal. 'It is our birthright to be Scottish,' he told the 1996 Scottish Conservative conference. 'It is our good fortune to be British. It is our duty to be Unionists.'[152]

While recognising Forsyth as 'a robust supporter for Thatcherite economic medicine', John Major also believed he had mellowed:

> Like Enoch Powell, he was a thinking man's populist. Privately quite liberal, and by conviction something of a libertarian, he possessed a sharp-toothed feel for the saleable parts of his Thatcherite inheritance, particularly those saleable in Scotland. But he suffered from the fact that he always looked as if he was plotting, even when he was not.[153]

Major's judgement, however, was perceptive. 'The old Thatcherite hardliner', observed even the STRG's Arthur Bell, 'had given way to a more emollient, more easy-going politician who promised to respond to the mood in Scotland.'[154]

Having built up a degree of media goodwill, Forsyth also began to attack vigorously the now fully formed blueprint for a Scottish Parliament, claiming the 'pygmy parliament' would cost £75 million to run, destroy the United Kingdom and diminish Scotland's standing at Westminster. In September 1996, the Scottish Secretary gathered his four Conservative predecessors in Perth to round off a summer campaign which asked Scots to sign a petition rejecting Labour's devolution plans. The SCC's proposals for tax-varying powers also came under particularly focused attack. The phrase 'tartan tax' had originally been mooted by Ian Lang, but Forsyth made it his own. Labour began to get cold feet and annoyed the Liberal Democrats, not to mention some of its own Scottish frontbenchers, by announcing that the parliament's fiscal powers would now form the basis of a second question in a proposed referendum.

But while spirited, Forsyth's energy could not disguise gloom about the forthcoming general election. Speaking in the House of Lords, Viscount Weir – perhaps the last of the Unionist industrialists who had once formed the bedrock of the party's business support – now lamented the reforms of 1965 and suggested the Scottish party 'would fare far better electorally if we now returned to our original and proper description' of 'Scottish Unionist'.[155] Rangers Football Club vice-chairman Donald Findlay later concurred that such a move would help the Conservatives speak with 'a Scottish accent': 'There is a lot to be said for having a Scottish party that is separate and independent, that will stand up for Scotland, but will be clearly allied to the UK party.'[156] Pre-election resignations, meanwhile, further sapped morale. Allan Stewart, who had already been compelled to resign from the Scottish Office after brandishing a pickaxe at anti-motorway demonstrators, quit as a candidate and Sir Michael Hirst as party chairman following lurid headlines concerning their respective private lives.[157] Hirst spoke darkly of a 'conspiracy' against him.[158]

At the general election in May 1997, the 'doomsday scenario' – averted in 1987 and 1992 – finally came to pass with the loss of every Conservative MP in Scotland, a grimly historic first. Michael Forsyth was one of seven Cabinet ministers to lose their seats, as were Malcolm Rifkind and Ian Lang. The Scottish political map had become a sea of Labour red and Liberal Democrat/SNP yellow. Analysis later revealed that the party

lost the constitutional 'argument' even among voters who generally considered themselves to be Conservative supporters.[159]
Support for the party had declined across all social groups and
classes, even with female voters among whom the party had
long enjoyed an advantage. While in 1979 35 per cent of those
aged over 55 and 25 per cent of those in the 18–34 age group
had supported the Conservatives, in 1997 those proportions
were 18 and 8 per cent respectively. As Lindsay Paterson concluded, this suggested the modern Scottish Conservative Party
had 'become alienated from Scottish society as a whole, not
just from some segments within it'.[160] The party had also lost
support across all religious groups, most significantly among
the Protestant working classes, once a key source of Scottish
Unionist strength. As Seawright concluded, the Conservatives
were still a Protestant party, 'simply not a very successful one'.[161]

To John Major, what really damaged his chances at the 1997
election 'was not the constitution, but the Conservative Party's
problems generally'. Not only when it came to 'sleaze' but on
Europe, where 'the party was as split in Scotland as it was in
England' – another significant shift since the 1970s.[162] Speaking
at a post-election press conference in Edinburgh, meanwhile,
the defeated Secretary of State and MP for Stirling explained
that he had been delayed due to traffic. 'So sorry for being late,'
Forsyth told the gathered media. 'The traffic was awful. Frankly,
I blame the government.'[163] This humour masked the fact that
the Conservative Party's elected representatives in Scotland now
numbered just 83 local councillors.

NOTES

1. Speech to Scottish Conservative conference, 12 May 1979,
   Margaret Thatcher Foundation website.
2. C. Stevens (1990), 'Scottish Conservatives – A failure of organization?', in A. Brown and R. Parry (eds), *Scottish Government
   Yearbook 1990*, University of Edinburgh, 85.
3. Speech to Scottish Conservative conference, 12 May 1979.
4. For a full analysis of Younger's period as Scottish Secretary,
   see D. Torrance (2008), *George Younger: A Life Well Lived*,
   Edinburgh: Birlinn.
5. *Independent*, 20 February 1995.
6. Diary entry dated 26 July 1979, George Younger Papers, Acc
   13116/221, Edinburgh: National Library of Scotland.

7. *Scotsman*, 30 November 1979.
8. E. A. Cameron (2016), 'Unionism and nationalism: The historical context of Scottish politics', in D. McTavish (ed.), *Politics in Scotland*, London: Routledge, 16.
9. *Glasgow Herald*, 12 September 1983.
10. A. Kemp (1993), *The Hollow Drum: Scotland since the War*, Edinburgh: Mainstream, 209.
11. D. Torrance (2008), 170.
12. Speech to Scottish Conservative conference, 9 May 1980, Margaret Thatcher Foundation website.
13. N. Ascherson (2002), *Stone Voices: The Search for Scotland*, London: Granta, 150.
14. Speech to Scottish Conservative conference, 13 May 1983, Margaret Thatcher Foundation website.
15. See I. Gilmour (1993), *Dancing With Dogma: Britain Under Thatcherism*, London: Pocket Books, 176.
16. J. Mitchell (1990), *Conservatives and the Union: A Study of Conservative Party Attitudes to Scotland*, Edinburgh: Edinburgh University Press, 116.
17. Meek's enthusiasm for devolution had lost him the nomination to succeed Betty Harvie Anderson in Renfrewshire East in 1979, the candidacy instead going to the devolution-sceptic Allan Stewart.
18. *The Times*, 11 May 1981.
19. J. Mitchell (2014), *The Scottish Question*, Oxford: Oxford University Press, 190.
20. D. Torrance (2008), 191. Donald Maclean became president of the Scottish Conservative and Unionist Association the following year. In 1984 his wife Muriel was among those murdered by the IRA during the Conservative Party conference in Brighton.
21. SCUA (1983), *Conference '83 Perth Thursday 12th–Saturday 14th May, 1983*, Edinburgh: Scottish Conservative and Unionist Association, 59–61.
22. H. Young (1991), *One of Us: A Biography of Margaret Thatcher*, London: Macmillan, 273.
23. Significantly, McCurley was a Catholic of Irish heritage. Sproat had embarked on an unsuccessful 'chicken run' from Aberdeen South, which the Conservatives held, to Roxburgh and Berwickshire, which it lost.
24. *Scotsman*, 27 September 2018.
25. P. Jones (1992), 'Politics', in M. Linklater and R. Denniston (eds), *Anatomy of Scotland: How Scotland Works*, Edinburgh: Chambers, 379.
26. W. J. Money (1982), 'Some causes and consequences of the failure

of Scottish Conservatism', in Z. Layton-Henry (ed.), *Conservative Politics in Western Europe*, London: Palgrave Macmillan, 55.

27. Interview with David McLetchie MSP, 6 October 2008.
28. Interview with Michael Gove MP, 28 July 2008.
29. Interview with Lord Turnbull, 3 June 2008.
30. ASI (1984), *Omega Report: Scottish Policy*, London: Adam Smith Institute, 3.
31. FCS (1984), *A Conservative Manifesto for Scotland*, Edinburgh: Federation of Conservative Students, 23.
32. Interview with Murdo Fraser MSP, 20 May 2008.
33. Speech to Scottish Conservative conference, 10 May 1985, Margaret Thatcher Foundation website.
34. *The Times*, 16 May 1986.
35. Interview with STV, 4 September 1985, Margaret Thatcher Foundation website.
36. I. Lang (2002), *Blue Remembered Years: A Political Memoir*, London: Politico's, 73.
37. Interview with Allan Stewart, 2 September 2008.
38. *Scotsman*, 6 April 1985.
39. Interview for *Aberdeen Press and Journal*, 30 April 1990, Margaret Thatcher Foundation website.
40. Whitelaw had contested Dunbartonshire East as a Unionist in 1950.
41. A St Andrews graduate, Douglas Mason led the Conservative group on Kirkcaldy District Council, where he chaired its Housing Committee and oversaw Scotland's first 'Right to Buy' council house sale. See C. Kidd (2012), 'Smithians, Thatcherites and the ironies of Scottish Conservative decline', in D. Torrance (ed.), *Whatever Happened to Tory Scotland?*, Edinburgh: Edinburgh University Press, 69.
42. M. Forsyth (1985), *The Case for a Poll Tax*, London: Conservative Political Centre, 8, 16.
43. Speech to Scottish Conservative conference, 10 May 1985, Margaret Thatcher Foundation website.
44. Memo dated 12 September 1985, Conservative Party Archive, CCO 20/11/96, Oxford: Bodleian.
45. Interview with Jackson Carlaw MSP, 3 April 2018.
46. HC Deb 9 December 1986 Vol. 107 c200.
47. Speech to Scottish Conservative conference, 15 May 1987, Margaret Thatcher Foundation website.
48. M. Rifkind (2016), *Power and Pragmatism: The Memoirs of Malcolm Rifkind*, London: Biteback, 232.
49. In Banff and Buchan, where Sir Albert McQuarrie lost to the future SNP leader Alex Salmond, there was evidence tactical

voting had eroded his majority (see Sir A. McQuarrie, 2013, *A Lifetime of Memories*, Durham: Memoir Club).

50. I. Lang (2002), 70.
51. *Guardian*, 22 June 1987.
52. *Sunday Times*, 14 June 1987.
53. M. Dyer (2003), 'The evolution of the Centre-right and the state of Scottish Conservatism', *Political Studies* 49:1, 44.
54. D. Seawright (1999), *An Important Matter of Principle: The Decline of the Scottish Conservative and Unionist Party*, Aldershot: Ashgate, 89.
55. C. Moore (2019), *Margaret Thatcher The Authorized Biography – Volume Three: Herself Alone*, London: Allen Lane, 17–19.
56. *Scotsman*, 10 September 1987.
57. A. Midwinter, M. Keating and J. Mitchell (1991), *Politics and Public Policy in Scotland*, Basingstoke: Palgrave Macmillan, 26.
58. J. Kellas (1994), 'The Party in Scotland', in A. Seldon and S. Ball (eds), *Conservative Century: The Conservative Party since 1900*, 689 and P. Jones (1992), 379.
59. *Glasgow Herald*, 1 October 1987.
60. A. D. R. Dickson (1988), 'The peculiarities of the Scottish: National culture and political action', *Political Quarterly* 59:3, 358–68.
61. Speech to Scottish Conservative conference, 13 May 1988, Margaret Thatcher Foundation website.
62. See D. Torrance (2009), *'We in Scotland': Thatcherism in a Cold Climate*, Edinburgh: Birlinn, 170.
63. R. Finlay (2008), 'Thatcherism and the Union', in T. M. Devine (ed.), *Scotland and the Union 1707–2007*, Edinburgh: Edinburgh University Press, 164.
64. Working to combat this was the Scottish Christian Conservative Forum, the chairman of which was R. D. Kernohan, a former employee at Scottish Conservative Central Office.
65. A. Marr (1992), *The Battle for Scotland*, London: Penguin, 170.
66. J. Kellas (1994), 686.
67. A. Kemp (1993), 197.
68. A. Stewart (1997), *The Long March of the Market Men*, Glendaruel: Argyll, 105. For a comprehensive survey of Conservative attitudes to devolution in the late 1980s, see J. R. Harper (1988), *Devolution: A Short Background Paper for Scottish Conservatives*, Glasgow: Society of Scottish Conservative Lawyers.
69. D. Torrance (2009), 184.
70. Speech to Scottish Conservative conference, 13 May 1988, Margaret Thatcher Foundation website.

71. G. Warner (1988), *The Scottish Tory Party: A History*, London: Weidenfeld & Nicolson, 226.
72. CRD (1989), *The Campaign Guide 1989*, London: Conservative and Unionist Central Office, 455–6.
73. J. Kellas (1994), 692. See also M. Arnott (1993), 'Thatcherism in Scotland: An Exploration of Education Policy in the Secondary Sector', PhD thesis, University of Strathclyde.
74. G. Hassan (2012), '"It's only a Northern Song": The constant smirr of Anti-Thatcherism and Anti-Toryism', in D. Torrance (ed.), *Whatever Happened to Tory Scotland?*, Edinburgh: Edinburgh University Press, 80–1, 87.
75. D. Seawright and J. Curtice (1995), 'The decline of the Scottish Conservative and Unionist Party 1950–92: Religion, ideology or economics?', *Contemporary British History* 9:2, 334.
76. HC Deb 21 December 1988 Vol. 144 c428.
77. C. Moore (2019), 18–19.
78. D. Seawright (2010), *The British Conservative Party and One Nation Politics*, London: Continuum, 135.
79. See S. Kendrick and D. McCrone (1989), 'Political studies in a cold climate: The Conservative decline in Scotland', *Political Studies* 37:4.
80. D. McCrone (1991), *Understanding Scotland: The Sociology of a Stateless Nation*, Edinburgh: Edinburgh University Press, 172.
81. K. Roy (1989), *Conversations in a Small Country: Scottish Conversations*, Ayr: Carrick, 181.
82. Viscount Weir, D. MacKay and A. Stewart (1990), *Scottish Assembly: We're Better Off Without It*, Edinburgh: Scottish Conservative Political Centre.
83. D. Seawright (1999), 181.
84. ECA (1987), *Apostles Not Apologists: The Eastwood View*, Paisley: Eastwood Conservative Association.
85. L. Fox, M. Mayall and A. B. Cooke (1988), *Making Unionism Positive*, London: Centre for Policy Studies, 15.
86. J. Mitchell (1990), 111.
87. M. L. MacKenzie (1988), *Scottish Toryism, Identity and Consciousness*, London: Tory Reform Group, 225.
88. A. Kemp (1993), 199–200.
89. P. Jones (1992), 379–80. See also R. Harper (2016), *Beyond Reasonable Doubt: A Memoir*, Edinburgh: Black & White, although it includes curiously little about Harper's political career.
90. M. Thatcher (1993), *The Downing Street Years*, London: HarperCollins, 620–1.
91. *Sunday Express*, c. January 1990.

92. *Glasgow Herald*, 7 September 1990.
93. D. Torrance (2009), 223.
94. A. Kemp (1993), 194–7.
95. A. Kemp (1993), 193.
96. 'Report on the 1989 Euro-Election Campaign', Scottish Conservative and Unionist Association Papers (SCUA), Acc 12514/2, Edinburgh: National Library of Scotland.
97. 'SCUA – 1989 and beyond: Observations of David McLetchie', Acc 12514/2.
98. Interview with Rae Stewart, 6 August 2008.
99. *Glasgow Herald*, 2 August 1990.
100. D. Seawright (1999), 45.
101. Letter to constituency chairmen, November 1989, SCUA Papers, Acc 12514/3.
102. On the morning of Mrs Thatcher's July 1989 visit to Scotland, the *Sun* ran a front-page story falsely accusing Harper of having been involved with a prostitute.
103. A. Kemp (1993), 204.
104. See D. Torrance (2009), 224–6.
105. *Scotsman*, 13 May 1990.
106. *Glasgow Herald*, 13 May 1990.
107. A. Kemp (1993), 207.
108. M. Thatcher (1993), 623.
109. M. Rifkind (2016), 246.
110. A. Marr (1992), 171.
111. I. Lang (2002), 186–7.
112. Interview with Lord Forsyth, 22 April 2008.
113. M. Thatcher (1993), 653.
114. *The Margaret Thatcher Interview* (BBC Scotland), 9 March 1990, Margaret Thatcher Foundation website.
115. Sir Malcolm Rifkind to the author, 6 December 2008.
116. Adrian Shinwell to Sir Michael Hirst, 6 November 1990, SCUA Papers, Acc 12514/4.
117. George Younger was in nominal charge of both of Thatcher's leadership election campaigns (see D. Torrance, 2008, 243–59). In the late 1980s he joined the board of the Royal Bank of Scotland and became chairman in 1992, an indication of how much Edinburgh's financial services sector had grown during the Thatcher era.
118. *Sunday Times*, 25 November 1990.
119. *The Economist*, 6 April 1991.
120. J. Major (1999), *John Major: The Autobiography*, London: HarperCollins, 417.
121. I. Lang (2002), 129.

122. *Glasgow Herald*, 15 February 1992.
123. I. Lang (2002), 184.
124. T. Devine (1999), *The Scottish Nation 1700–2000*, London: Allen Lane, 597–8.
125. J. Major (1999), 417.
126. J. Major (1992), *Scotland in the United Kingdom*, London: Conservative Political Centre, 7–8.
127. S. Hogg and J. Hill (1996), *Too Close To Call: Power and Politics – John Major in No. 10*, London: Warner, 244.
128. J. Major (1999), 424.
129. A. Marr (1992), 225–6.
130. I. Lang (2002), 187.
131. See D. Torrance (2022), *A History of the Scottish Liberals and Liberal Democrats*, Edinburgh: Edinburgh University Press, 154–5.
132. A. Stewart (1997), 157.
133. J. Major (1999), 424.
134. M. Thatcher (1993), 623–4.
135. D. McCrone, L. Paterson and A. Brown (1993), 'Reforming local government in Scotland', *Local Government Studies* 19:1, 12.
136. A. Marr (1992), 224.
137. See I. Macwhirter (1992), 'The disaster that never was: The failure of Scottish opposition after the 1992 general election', *Scottish Affairs* 1, 3–8.
138. SCUA (1992), *Shaping Up For The Future: Interim Recommendations of the Review Committee*, Edinburgh: Scottish Conservative and Unionist Association.
139. J. Major (1999), 422. Major complained that 'whenever there was a grievance to be found, the Scottish media and the opposition parties seized on it and turned it into evidence of the lack of understanding by the English for the Scots'.
140. See A. McConnell and R. Pyper (1994), 'A committee again: The first year of the revived Select Committee on Scottish Affairs', *Scottish Affairs* 7, 15–31.
141. See Scottish Office (1993), *Scotland in the Union: A Partnership for Good*, Cmnd 2225, Edinburgh: HMSO.
142. J. Kellas (1994), 679–80.
143. I. Lang (2002), 165–6. Devolution, wrote Lang, 'was a hovering presence throughout my time in Scottish politics. Often muted, occasionally dominant, but always there casting its shadow over every passing political issue, it was like the bass drone of the bagpipes.'
144. I. Lang (2002), 152.
145. D. Denver and H. Bochel (1995), 'Catastrophe for the

Conservatives: The council elections of 1995', *Scottish Affairs* 13, 27–41.

146. *Independent*, 20 February 1995.
147. A. Brown, D. McCrone and L. Paterson (1998), *Politics and Society in Scotland* (Second Edition), London: Macmillan, 153.
148. J. Douglas-Hamilton (2009), *After You, Prime Minister*, London: Stacey International, 182–92. Douglas-Hamilton was later given a life peerage.
149. D. Seawright (1999), 33.
150. See I. Macwhirter (1995), 'Doomsday two: The return of Forsyth', *Scottish Affairs* 13, 15–26.
151. Forsyth also argued for votes in the Scottish Grand Committee to be binding, 'which meant losing our majority in Scottish votes. We tried to find a way of moving it in that direction but at that time there was no real will in the party to concede the principle of votes in Scotland deciding Scottish issues' (Interview with Lord Forsyth).
152. *The Times*, 10 May 1996.
153. J. Major (1999), 425.
154. *Scotsman*, 4 July 1996.
155. HL Deb 4 July 1995 Vol. 565 cc1003-65. 'I speak as a Unionist who supports Conservative policies', added Viscount Weir, 'rather than as a Conservative.'
156. *Herald*, 24 February 1997.
157. 'Hirst Blames Tories For His Downfall', BBC politics 97 website: https://www.bbc.co.uk/news/special/politics97/news/05/0507/scot.shtml
158. *Scotsman*, 7 May 1997.
159. A. Brown, D. McCrone, L. Paterson and P. Surridge (1998), *The Scottish Electorate: The 1997 General Election and Beyond*, Basingstoke: Palgrave Macmillan, 137.
160. A. Brown, D. McCrone and L. Paterson (1998), 155-7.
161. D. Seawright (1999), 197.
162. J. Major (1999), 428. Survey data appeared to show that Scottish Conservative supporters were more Eurosceptic than those in England. See D. Seawright (1999), 45.
163. D. Torrance (2006), *The Scottish Secretaries*, Edinburgh: Birlinn, 335.

8

The Wilderness Years:
1997–2011

Michael Dyer likened the general election of 1997 to 'a creeping nemesis' that had 'surreptitiously debilitated' the Scottish Conservative Party's 'vital organs over a generation'. 'Unable to stabilise its support,' he added, 'it lacks a secure geographical base, an identifiable social constituency of any size and loyalty, and has a weak ideological purchase on the political debate.[1] All this was true, and would remain so for another often painful couple of decades in the Scottish political wilderness.

The party's response to the overwhelming defeat also followed a familiar pattern: two reviews – organisational and policy – together with a range of suggestions to change the party's name, break its link with the party in London and even embracing devolution now it was about to become a reality. 'We have been perceived, wrongly in many cases, as an English party with a branch office in Scotland,' explained Arthur Bell of the Scottish Tory Reform Group (STRG). 'I think that has got to go. There are fundamental changes coming in Scotland which will not allow us to survive at all if that perception is maintained.'[2] Jackson Carlaw, the party's deputy chairman, called for 'a complete redefinition of the party' which, in a nod to Tony Blair, he called 'New Tories, New Scotland'.[3]

Peter Lynch identified three 'fundamental' challenges for the Scottish Conservatives: first, adjusting to devolution 'in terms of party organisation, policy, autonomy and campaigning' to 'reverse its image as an anti-Scottish party'; second, rebuilding electoral support ahead of the first devolved elections in 1999; and third, developing a coherent relationship between the Scottish and UK parties.[4] None of those three challenges, however, would be addressed as quickly as they might have been.

The Scottish Conservative conference that followed the election wipeout amounted to a post-mortem on the election result. The new UK Conservative Party leader William Hague (reports suggested most Scottish Conservatives had supported Kenneth Clarke) attacked what he called a 'flawed referendum' but conceded that, if established, a Scottish Parliament would exist 'for quite a long time to come'.[5] When delegates debated a motion condemning devolution, only two speakers challenged the party line. Paul Burns, a former office-bearer, spoke for the majority when he declared: 'If we were right in May we remain right now.' Only 12 delegates voted against the motion, an indication that the mood of the party was as it had been a decade earlier. Lloyd Beat, of the Scottish Conservative Political Centre, compared the STRG with Militant's infiltration of the Labour Party and called for Arthur Bell to be expelled. Having remained within the party for a surprisingly long time, Bell and his wife Susan eventually joined the Liberal Democrats,[6] as did the former Scottish Conservative MP Anna McCurley.

At Westminster, the still anti-devolution Liam Fox (a Scot representing an English constituency) became opposition Scottish Affairs spokesman, while a 'no, no' referendum campaign took shape ahead of the two-question referendum due in September 1997. The director of 'Think Twice' was Michael Forsyth's friend Brian Monteith, who had also led the Student Campaign Against the Devolution Act in 1979. Peter Fraser, the former MP and Lord Advocate, became campaign director, while the former Scottish Conservative treasurer Sir Matthew Goodwin filled the same role at Think Twice. Of its 13 vice-chairmen, four were or had been Church of Scotland ministers. It spent £275,000 during the campaign, £5,000 more than 'Scotland Forward', the umbrella 'Yes' group comprising Labour, the Liberal Democrats and SNP.[7] Forsyth made no public comment, although an unrelated visit from Baroness Thatcher (who was due to address a conference of American travel agents in Glasgow) during the last week of campaigning proved a godsend for pro-devolution campaigners and journalists. The *Daily Record* professed itself to be:

DELIGHTED she is here. Why? Because she's the best possible reason yet why Scots should vote YES YES on Thursday.

186 SCOTTISH CONSERVATIVE AND UNIONIST PARTIES

Thatcher ruled Scotland from London for more than a decade and caused untold misery. We didn't vote for her. Again and again the Scottish voters rejected her cynical brand of greed and callousness. But we could not escape her malign influence VOTE YES, YES – FOR NO MORE MAGGIES.[8]

On 11 September 1997, the Scottish Conservatives suffered another heavy defeat when Scottish voters overwhelmingly endorsed a Scottish Parliament (74.3 per cent) with tax-varying powers (63.5 per cent), albeit on a surprisingly low turnout of 60.4 per cent. The Belfast/Good Friday Agreement signed a few months later further recalibrated the British–Irish Union which had once been so important to Scottish Unionism. With Northern Ireland's constitutional status in the hands of its 'people', the 'Unionist' portion of the Scottish Conservative Party's full title now almost exclusively referred to the Anglo-Scottish Union.

Seeking to get ahead of the curve, Michael Fry urged the party to support fiscal autonomy for the new Scottish Parliament, arguing that the 'obvious field for radicalism is the fiscal one, of taxing and spending'.[9] A year later, Fry co-authored a Tuesday Club pamphlet entitled *Full Fiscal Freedom for the Scottish Parliament* with Peter Smaill and the future MSP Murdo Fraser. This was the first mention of a concept that would increasingly dominate the political discourse of a devolved Scotland and, significantly, it started life as a Scottish Conservative idea.

The Strathclyde Commission, however, avoided recommending anything so bold and instead urged a merger of the party's voluntary (SCUA) and professional wings to form the 'Scottish Conservative and Unionist Party'. Lord Strathclyde had rejected changing the name of the party, joking that whatever it chose to call itself, 'to a large section of the population it would forever remain the ******* Tories!'[10] A single Scottish Executive was to run the party with a chairman appointed jointly by that Executive and the UK party leader, together with a deputy chairman elected by Scottish party members.[11] They were consulted ahead of a special party conference in Dundee on 7 March 1998, at which Sir Malcolm Rifkind – the SCUA's final president – promised a root-and-branch review of Scottish Conservative policies, adding that the party should 'dare to differ' from those in England and Wales.[12]

Rifkind's report, *Scotland's Future*, made an interesting effort to embrace devolution via recommendations which were a clever mix of style and substance. He suggested the first meeting of the new legislature take place in Parliament House ('to symbolise continuity with our past') and that its opening 'be treated with full dignity including the presence of the Sovereign and the use of the Scottish Regalia' (as indeed it was in July 1999). It should, added Rifkind, 'have a Government not an Executive', a change in nomenclature later given effect by an SNP government, and a 'Premier' rather than a First Minister. Other proposals would be implemented by future Conservative governments, i.e. 'a binding commitment that the devolution legislation could never be abrogated without the consent of the Scottish Parliament', while others, such as direct representation for the devolved nations in a reformed House of Lords, became fixtures of broader programmes of reform promoted by other parties.[13] The 'prime challenge' for Scottish Conservatives in 'the New Scotland', wrote Rifkind elsewhere, was 'accepting the need to craft a new language of unionism for a reborn United Kingdom'.[14]

Two candidates, meanwhile, competed for the leadership of the party: the former Ayr MP Phil Gallie and former SCUA president David McLetchie, the latter an Edinburgh lawyer with a working-class background. From a curious electorate of prospective candidates and constituency association chairmen (174 in all), McLetchie won by 91 votes to 83. Although he identified with the right of the party (he too was close to Michael Forsyth), his election was nonetheless welcomed by pro-devolutionists such as Cllr Christine Richard – now the party's most senior elected representative – and the Scottish Tory Reform Group. 'We stand', declared McLetchie in an attempt to define his Conservative philosophy, 'for the folk that take their turn at cleaning the stair.'[15]

The party did its best to emphasise its 'Scottishness' ahead of elections to the Scottish Parliament in May 1999, the manifesto for which was entitled 'Scotland First', an echo of the SNP's former slogan, 'Put Scotland First'. William Hague declared 'you are truly a Scottish party' at a Hampden Park rally,[16] while McLetchie extended the footballing analogy by claiming the election gave his party 'an opportunity to get back on the pitch' and away from the 'side lines'.[17] Scottish Central Office presented

Tasmina Ahmed-Sheikh, its candidate in Glasgow Govan, as 'typical of the new breed of Scottish Tory, young, talented and determined'. 'She certainly makes a change', observed the journalist Murray Ritchie, 'from tweedy old colonels.'[18] A year later she defected to the SNP, citing the 'rightward switch in Tory policy' under Hague's leadership.[19]

Based on 1997 voting figures, the Scottish Conservatives ought to have won 22 MSPs, although opinion polls suggested the total might be as low as 12. In the event, the party managed 18, while it came third in terms of vote share.[20] Ironically, an electoral system opposed by Conservatives had ensured their survival in an institution most of its members did not want. 'For the first time in a generation, there are Conservatives representing every region in Scotland,' said McLetchie, putting a positive spin on the outcome. 'We will be the Unionist Opposition at Holyrood.'[21] At European Parliament elections the same year, the party secured two MEPs, again due to PR. Yet McLetchie remained conscious that his party had contrived to lose a whole generation of potential supporters:

> This lost generation sees itself as Scottish and British, not British and Scottish, and we must see it that way too. From now on, in Scotland's first and oldest political party, we will be putting Scotland first. That will be at the heart of new Unionism. Labour tries to label the SNP as Tartan Tories as a badge of shame. But we must claim it as a badge of pride. We are the Tartan Tories – Scotland's other national party.[22]

An important factor aiding the party's new lease of life was the financial backing of the Monte Carlo-based businessman Irvine Laidlaw. As well as providing the party with more than £250,000 before the first Scottish Parliament elections, Laidlaw (later Lord Laidlaw) facilitated a new HQ on Princes Street for a peppercorn rent. Significant amounts of money, for example, were spent on high-profile advertising designed by the Yellow M agency, which included a controversial poster depicting SNP leader Alex Salmond as a Teletubby living in 'Scot-laa-laa-land'.

In the new Parliament itself, McLetchie quickly found his feet as a confident and credible performer, despite having the least political experience of the four main party leaders. He essentially pursued a 'core vote' strategy, highlighting the new Parliament's failings – not least a growing row about the cost of a new building at Holyrood – and appealing to social conservatives by arguing that Scottish Executive priorities, such as the repeal of Section 28, were out of kilter with those of most Scots. But although McLetchie's attacks on the Scottish Executive were often effective, this hardly amounted to a positive Conservative vision for a devolved Scotland.

Nevertheless, the Scottish Conservative candidate John Scott won the first by-election to the new Parliament in Ayr on 16 March 2000 with a majority of more than 3,000. This provided a valuable psychological boost to a party keen to detect any signs of an electoral recovery, although an internal election for the post of deputy chairman was less helpful. The former Tayside North MP Bill Walker (an unreconstructed antidevolutionist) won a convincing victory, even though 10 MSPs had signed nomination papers for Kim Donald. The result was overshadowed by a spate of resignations – Sir Adrian Shinwell as chairman of the candidates' board as well as Jacqui Low and Gordon McIntosh (husband of Lyndsay, a Tory MSP) from the party's executive, all a result of discontent with (former MP) Raymond Robertson's performance as party chairman.[23]

At around this time, the Scottish Conservative Party also initiated an ideological shift, although one motivated more by electoral considerations than political economy. Sir Stewart Sutherland's report on long-term care for the elderly had recommended making the 'personal care' aspect of support for elderly Scots free, and the party's health spokespeople, Mary Scanlon and Ben Wallace, wrote to Sir Stewart in support of this finding.[24] Scanlon confirmed this apparently statist slant by indicating that 'as a general principle' the party did not want the private sector to play a bigger role in healthcare provision north of the border.[25] In June 2001, meanwhile, David McLetchie sent a message of support to the organisers of Scotland's Gay Pride festival, a surprising gesture given the party's recent stance on the repeal of Section 28. The centrist Conservatism of the interwar years had made a comeback, even though social attitudes surveys suggested Scotland was becoming a *more* conservative country during this period.[26]

Those in the party who wanted to see less state spending on welfare rather than more were perturbed by the long-term care for the elderly pledge, and when Scanlon suggested banning sweet cigarettes, one 'prominent activist' said: 'That's not a

Conservative policy. We're the party of individual freedom – we don't go around banning things.'[27] But with half an eye on the next UK general election, party chairman Raymond Robertson said the Scottish Conservatives had 'listened and learned ... and welcomes the chance to show the people of Scotland just how much we have changed'.[28] Indeed, several figures involved in the party during this period remembered a 'desperate desire [among MSPs] to cease being pariahs and be liked; accepted within the Scottish political mainstream, which was dominated by broadly social democratic attitudes.'[29] But attempts to reposition – or indeed 'detoxify' – the party were confused and sporadic: there was no co-ordinated or ideologically consistent strategy.

It also had little effect in electoral terms. At the 2001 UK general election, the Scottish Conservative Party's apparently 'rock-bottom' vote share of 1997 – 17.5 per cent – fell even further to 15.6 per cent. The only silver lining came in the form of Peter Duncan, the Scottish party's sole victor in Galloway and Upper Nithsdale (Sir Malcolm Rifkind had failed to regain Edinburgh Pentlands). In the wake of William Hague's resignation as Leader of the Opposition, the twin refrains of changing the party's name and fiscal autonomy resurfaced once again.

David Davis, one of those bidding to succeed Hague, advocated not only fiscal autonomy for Scotland but devolution for England. Former Chancellor Kenneth Clarke (who won support from centrist MSPs like Murray Tosh and David Mundell) also sought to address Scottish issues, although not entirely successfully, while Iain Duncan Smith (who was backed by right-wing MSPs Brian Monteith and Phil Gallie) suggested the Scottish leader join his Shadow Cabinet at Westminster. The 2001 Scottish Conservative conference was supposed to provide a platform for the leadership contest, but instead it was 'overshadowed by internal conflict and instability which [further?] damaged the party's image in Scotland'. 'Blood on the agenda at Perth' was one newspaper headline, while another read: 'Backstabbing and blood-letting ... it's party time for the Tories.'[30]

The latter half of the Scottish Parliament's first term played witness to further division and disruption. Not only did the Mid-Scotland and Fife MSP Nick Johnston resign, alleging by way of a parting shot that David McLetchie had 'no idea how to lead',[31] but the spring of 2002 was dominated by another row about candidate selection, the party's Scottish executive (which did not want to give members a vote) seemingly at odds with most of the 19-strong MSP group (who wanted a one-member-one-vote system for the selection process). All this from a party that, as one source told a journalist in late 2001, found 'politics rather vulgar and ungentlemanly'. The Scottish Conservatives, observed Douglas Fraser, were simply 'struggling to find a role in the new terrain of Scottish devolution and Tony Blair's occupancy of a wide swathe of the political centre ground'.[32]

Iain Duncan Smith, meanwhile, drew inspiration from a visit to Easterhouse in February 2002, which later germinated into some genuinely interesting ideas concerning welfare and poverty. McLetchie's attempt a few months later to develop this strategy was less successful, merely linking intergenerational poverty to a long-standing Conservative interest in family values.[33] The high-profile scalp claimed by the Scottish Conservative leader at the end of 2001 did at least offer some respite. McLetchie's relentless attacks on Henry McLeish over the 'Officegate' affair finally provoked the Labour First Minister's resignation. The trouble came in converting such 'opposition' into electoral support, particularly in the absence of a clear message about what the party stood for in Scotland. As the party's sole Scottish MP Peter Duncan admitted in the run-up to the 2003 Scottish Parliamentary elections: 'Our failure is that we haven't yet tapped into that [Centre-Right] market. We haven't yet made ourselves the obvious home for that [potential] 35% support.'[34]

That campaign brought new troubles when two sitting Conservative MSPs (Keith Harding and Lyndsay McIntosh), who had both been ranked too low on their respective lists to win re-election, defected to the fledgling Scottish People's Alliance, a populist but well-funded vehicle which proved a damp squib. In a personal triumph for David McLetchie, he won Edinburgh Pentlands from Labour, while the party also held Ayr and took Galloway and Upper Nithsdale from the SNP, giving the party a trio of first-past-the-post seats. Its 16.6 and 15.5 per cent of the vote in the constituency and list votes respectively, however, represented only modest progress compared with its 1999 result. There was also a slight increase in concurrent local government elections, but the party's 15.1 per cent vote share represented a 'slow death' given the 28.6 per cent it had gained in 1974.[35]

As Alexander Smith argued in his study of the Dumfries and Galloway Conservative Association during the 2003 election, post-devolution Scottish Tories had buried themselves in 'banal activism' to avoid facing up to the deeper and more difficult questions over their future.[36] Convery called it 'banal parliamentarianism'.[37] This malaise was mirrored at Central Office in Edinburgh. 'We said we accepted devolution but appeared very grudging about it,' recalled a key figure. 'We'd simply demonised it too much, talking about the "tartan tax" and all that. So at some point we needed a big, bold statement to show people we had changed as a party, but we kept putting it off.'[38] Some Conservative MSPs worried that if they appeared too enthusiastic about the Scottish Parliament then it would put off their core voters. The 2003 manifesto even proposed cutting the number of MSPs to 108. 'This was not', judged Alan Convery, 'a party at ease with devolution.'[39] Indeed, when asked if he would now endorse devolution should there be another referendum, McLetchie not only said he would not but acknowledged that he was still largely unpersuaded as to its merits.[40]

Faced with two paths in 1999 – embracing or merely tolerating devolution – Convery concluded that the Scottish party

> chose to follow neither. Instead, they sought a middle road which avoided party conflict, wholeheartedly embraced the Parliament at a procedural level, and left them after 2007 being compared unfavourably to their Welsh colleagues whose attitude and election results suggested they might be dealing rather better with the regional/national dilemma.

Scottish Conservatives had not managed (unlike the Welsh party) to 'absorb the Scottish Parliament at a philosophical level'. Rather they behaved as if the advent was a 'traumatic experience', striking at the heart of its 'conception of unionism'.[41] And it would take Scottish Conservatives quite a lot longer to fully process that trauma.

Conservative MSPs such as Brian Monteith and Murdo Fraser continued to press David McLetchie to view fiscal autonomy as the necessary 'big, bold statement', and in May 2004 the possibility was at least discussed at an MSP awayday at the Huntingtower Hotel in Perth. McLetchie, however, said he remained 'utterly opposed' to the idea of giving the Scottish Parliament full fiscal powers, but conceded that it was 'unhealthy' for the Parliament and Scottish Executive to be seen 'wholly as a spending institution with limited financial responsibility'.[42]

In October 2004, Peter Duncan, the sole Scottish Conservative MP and thus Shadow Scottish Secretary in Michael Howard's Shadow Cabinet, also succeeded David Mitchell as party chairman in Scotland. Despite being the Scottish party's 'link' with London, tension remained between unreconstructed elements at Westminster and those trying to make devolution 'work' on the Mound. Speaking in the House of Lords, for example, Michael Forsyth suggested getting rid of all 129 MSPs and instead having Scottish MPs inhabit the Scottish Parliament on specified days. When James Gray, the Scots-born MP for North Wiltshire, made the same suggestion a week after being appointed Shadow Scottish Secretary following the 2005 general election, he was compelled to resign by furious MSPs. Relations between Central Office in Edinburgh and the MSP group were also poor, each viewing the other as politically ineffective.[43]

That election (2005), in which the party's share of the vote rose slightly (0.2 per cent) to 15.8 per cent, also produced just one Scottish Conservative MP, although not the same one as in 2001. Peter Duncan lost the newly redrawn constituency of Dumfries and Galloway, while in the new seat of Dumfriesshire, Clydesdale and Tweeddale, the South of Scotland MSP David Mundell overturned a notional Labour majority. He would be the first of several Conservative MSPs to swap the Scottish Parliament for Westminster – the North-East list MSP Ben Wallace also became the MP for Lancaster and Wyre – something political opponents said demonstrated the party's lack of commitment to devolution.

Once again, the election result highlighted the party's failure to recover any ground in Scotland. In Wales, by contrast, Conservatives gained three MPs, having won none in 1997 and 2001. Murdo Fraser now called openly for the party to emulate the German CDU/CSU model, supporters of which Peter Lynch called 'the Bavarian wing'. 'It would entail a separate party, separately funded, with separate responsibility for policy,' explained Fraser. 'There would be two parties united by conservatism.'[44] Although swiftly dismissed by David McLetchie and other senior party figures, this was essentially the prospectus on which Fraser would fight the 2011 leadership contest.

After improperly claiming more than £5,000 for taxi expenses, McLetchie resigned as Scottish Conservative leader in November 2005. Annabel Goldie, his deputy, took over as interim leader and, within a matter of days, was confirmed as leader in a 'coronation' arranged by party managers to avoid a prolonged leadership contest. Murdo Fraser withdrew from the non-race in return for the deputy's post and kept the fiscal autonomy flame burning, although less ostentatiously than before. The new UK Conservative leader David Cameron said he 'certainly did not rule out' full fiscal autonomy should the Scottish party choose to follow that path,[45] an early indication he was more willing than most to contemplate new strategies. Even so, Conservatives in London continued to view the party in Scotland with incomprehension. 'I'm not really sure we know what to make of them, really,' said one senior London Conservative.[46] 'The organisation up there was completely ramshackle,' recalled George Bridges:

> They didn't understand what we [the UK party] were trying to do at all, and I had absolutely no control up there as Director of Campaigns. It was a complete struggle, so they employed an extra person [John Read] for us to liaise with, but it didn't make much of a difference.[47]

There was much criticism of Annabel Goldie in her first six months as leader, although she was in many respects McLetchie Mark II. Both were good performers and more interested in tactics than grand ideological exercises (i.e. fiscal autonomy), while both were also cautious and diligent when it came to internal party management. In June 2006, Goldie appointed Douglas Osler, a former civil servant, to lead a nine-strong policy advisory group charged with developing ideas for the next Holyrood manifesto. This recommended fiscal autonomy, but the Conservative MSP group quickly ruled it out. Just 'as Scotland has changed', was Goldie's paradoxical refrain, 'the Scottish Conservative party has changed and is changing'.[48]

Despite several forays north of the border, David Cameron failed to make much of a connection with Scottish voters, his perceived 'poshness' one of several barriers. 'I'm a Cameron,' he declared in an effort to break through, 'there is quite a lot of Scottish blood flowing through these veins.'[49] When Cameron asked David Mundell, his Shadow Scottish Secretary since late 2005, for his thoughts, he said in a memo leaked to coincide with the party's May 2006 conference that there was a 'simple lack of thinkers' among Scottish Conservative MSPs at Holyrood, and that while Goldie had made a reasonable start as leader she possessed a 'lack of activity and strategic thought'. The Scottish party, meanwhile, simply did not 'get' the new moderation of the UK party.[50]

At some point during 2006, therefore, Cameron authorised party grandee Francis Maude to draw up plans for what the *Spectator* called a 'velvet divorce' between the Scottish and UK Conservative parties. Several senior Conservatives – including Shadow Chancellor George Osborne – saw the logic of this position, while it attracted grassroots support via the influential ConservativeHome website. 'With independence, a new name, and new personnel, the Scottish Conservatives can break free in one leap,' judged Tim Montgomerie. 'They will no longer be seen as stooges of a London establishment.'[51] It would provide, in summary, a win-win situation for Cameron: if it worked, he would enjoy greater Scottish support; if it did not, then he would not be tainted by its continuing electoral failure. 'There is no divorce,' responded Annabel Goldie. 'It's just not going to happen.'[52] Conservative Central Office in London also felt compelled to issue a denial.

Goldie at least demonstrated a flair for publicity on the campaign trail for the 2007 Holyrood elections, riding quad bikes, going ten-pin bowling and delivering fruity one-liners. David Cameron even called her his 'Scottish Auntie':[53] She 'appeared unmanaged ... as if she did not pay any attention to image makers and party handlers, running her own campaign the way she wanted, and it worked'.[54] On polling day the result was not quite as bad as some in London clearly expected, the party's constituency vote holding steady at 16.6 per cent but the list vote shrinking to 13.9 per cent. The Scottish Conservatives lost one of its 18 MSPs. Concurrent local government elections, conducted using the single transferable vote for the first time, produced an increased vote share (15.6 per cent) and yielded 20 additional councillors.[55]

If one moment in the Scottish Parliament's eight-year existence required a strong Conservative and Unionist Party it was the point at which the SNP formed its first, albeit minority, Holyrood administration. Initially, however, the Scottish Conservatives – in common with the defeated Labour and Liberal Democrat coalition partners – floundered, unsure of how to respond. Murdo Fraser was the only senior figure to articulate a coherent solution to what he characterised as a constitutional 'mess'. 'Perhaps the end point will be a federal, or quasi-federal, United Kingdom,' he wrote in October 2007. 'A reformed House of Lords might act as a pan-UK "senate" binding the UK together.'[56]

Instead, Conservative MSPs formed part of a cross-party commission suggested by the new Scottish Labour leader Wendy Alexander. Goldie used a debate on this to reaffirm that Conservatives are 'positive participants in devolution', while her predecessor David McLetchie sketched out the 'fundamental characteristics' of the Union, thus demarcating what he called 'red, white and blue lines':

> [A] constitutional monarchy; a united, democratically elected Government and Parliament; common defence and security arrangements; a common citizenship; a common currency; a UK central bank; a UK single market; common taxes to fund the responsibilities of national Government; and social security and welfare programmes that promote cohesion and unity and ensure equitable treatment across the nation as a whole.[57]

Others, such as Tory MSP Margaret Mitchell, described the Calman Commission as 'a knee-jerk reaction' to the election of a minority SNP government.[58] Most Scottish Conservative members reacted much as they had to Edward Heath's Declaration of Perth in 1968, with a mixture of muted enthusiasm and scepticism.

Derek Brownlee, the Scottish Conservative finance spokesman, had urged Annabel Goldie to take advantage of the SNP's minority status while doing something to demonstrate the party's political 'relevance'. Goldie allowed Brownlee to establish a working relationship with SNP Finance Secretary John Swinney, which paid dividends early the following year when the Conservatives secured three concessions from the SNP's first budget: 500 new police officers, more money for drug rehabilitation and an accelerated scheme of tax relief for small businesses.

There were obvious risks in a Unionist party keeping the SNP afloat, but the party was playing the long game, judging that by the next devolved election in 2011 they would be able to say: 'Look, this is what we achieved in Opposition; if you give us more power and more MSPs we will achieve even more.'

After the budget deal, one Conservative MSP even claimed the party had achieved more in one vote than during the previous eight years.[59] Reflecting on these events a few years later, Derek Brownlee said:

> What we got out of that budget was credibility; it was the first time we'd led the news in ages, and it was seen as quite a coup. Yes, John Swinney was using us for numbers, but we were using him to get stuff we could punt at an election. What better way to decontaminate than to align ourselves with the SNP?[60]

David Cameron, meanwhile, promoted the so-called 'respect agenda' (the brainchild of David Mundell, his Shadow Scottish Secretary), promising that, as Prime Minister, he would 'govern the whole of the United Kingdom, including Scotland, with respect'.[61]

The Calman Commission reported in June 2009, prompting a mini-crisis in the Scottish Conservative Party as Annabel Goldie appeared to distance herself from its recommendations to extend some financial and welfare powers to Holyrood, thus crossing McLetchie's red-white-and-blue lines. Her problem, as ever, came in attempting to reconcile several factions of the party: those uncomfortable with greater devolution, those anxious to go much further and those in between who did not much care either way. 'There is nothing in our manifesto that says we have to back Calman,' complained one sceptical Tory MSP. 'We must be very careful. A lot of our people do not like the way the party is travelling.'[62] Eventually, Goldie endorsed Calman's findings but, as with everything concerning devolution, it appeared grudging.

There were high hopes as Scottish Conservatives prepared for the 2010 UK general election, with some predicting gains of around 10 seats. These proved wide of the mark. Although the party's vote share increased by a modest 0.9 per cent, it still emerged with just one seat despite spending significant sums of money in around a dozen target constituencies, falling victim to anti-Conservative tactical voting and the effective weaponisation of Mrs Thatcher's legacy by Labour.

As far as David Cameron (now Prime Minister in a Conservative-Liberal Democrat coalition) was concerned, Scotland was a Liberal Democrat responsibility, David Mundell (who held on in Dumfriesshire, Clydesdale and Tweeddale) having been compelled to deputise for a Scottish Secretary (briefly Danny Alexander, then Michael Moore) drawn from the coalition's junior party. Reports suggested Cameron had 'given up' on the Scottish party, which later relocated to a more modest headquarters when Lord Laidlaw withdrew funding. The Prime Minister was happier with the situation in Wales, where the Conservatives had pursued a 'three Rs' remedy: engaging in a 'rainbow' alliance with Plaid Cymru, supporting a referendum on law-making powers and party reform.[63] It appeared to be working, for at the 2010 general election eight Welsh Conservative MPs were elected (an increase of five on 2005) with 26.1 per cent of the vote.

Back in Scotland, there was the usual post-election commission to review party organisation. This, chaired by the former SCUA president and party chairman Lord Sanderson (the *News of the World* unkindly depicted him as 'Torysaurus'), reported later in 2010. *Building for Scotland: Strengthening the Scottish Conservatives* painted a bleak picture of 'moribund' local associations at the bottom and 'weak' leadership structures at the top. A party that could boast 40,000 members in 1992 now had only 10,000 (although even that figure was probably optimistic). More widely, the review admitted that Scots remained unclear as to 'what the Scottish Conservatives stand for', except that the party was still considered to be 'anti-Scottish'.

Sanderson considered but ruled out a change of name or in the Scottish party's relationship with Central Office in London. He noted that Scottish Conservatives 'obtain numerous benefits from being part of the UK party, including [the] opportunity to access resources, training and expertise and for members to vote for the UK leader'. Therefore, 'given the Conservative commitment to Scotland remaining within the United Kingdom, it is both appropriate and beneficial that there should be an integrated relationship between the Scottish Conservatives and the UK party'.

Although Sanderson's remit – like Lord Strathclyde's in 1997/8 – had not included policy matters, his report chose not to 'ignore the quantity of submissions on whether or not Scotland should have greater fiscal accountability' and recommended it be 'discussed fully between both the Scottish Conservatives and the UK party, as well as forming the basis of a fully informed debate within the party membership'. Sanderson's key recommendation, however, was that a 'distinctly Scottish leader' ought to command the whole Scottish party rather than just its MSPs.[64]

This put Annabel Goldie in a difficult position, forced to counter speculation that she would not survive re-election following the 2011 Holyrood election (a timetable stipulated by Sanderson). Ironically, polling suggested Goldie was a popular and respected figure on the Scottish political scene; it was just that she – and her party – struggled to turn this personal appeal into votes.[65] Ahead of that election, Goldie said there was 'going to be no bullshitting'. 'Give me more and we will deliver more for Scotland,' she added, reminding voters that her party had delivered more police officers, help with business rates and a town centre regeneration fund.[66] But there remained little in the way of original thinking. The Thatcher-era policy of school vouchers was still the centrepiece of its educational agenda 21 years after the Iron Lady had left office. The Holyrood manifesto, meanwhile, promised to reintroduce prescription charges, introduce a variable university graduate fee and replace community service with short prison sentences.[67]

Visiting Inverness during the 2011 Holyrood election campaign, David Cameron did his best to remain upbeat about Scottish Conservative prospects. 'We have to emphasise three things,' he told journalists:

First, the Scottish Conservative Party is a party of the United Kingdom, that we – head, heart and soul – would never put at risk. We're always the real, true believers in strengthening our union.

Second, that the Scottish Conservative party is Conservative, yes, but it's Scottish, run by Scots, for Scots. It makes decisions for Scotland. It does not take orders from Westminster ... It is, if you like, more Unionist but also more Scottish.

The third thing, absolutely crucially, and it will take some time to get to 50 per cent [of the vote] ... Classic Conservative, Centre-Right, strong, patriotic, family, pro-enterprise values are the values that millions of people in Scotland share. And if we can get people to link their values with their voting behaviour, seeing a party that is both absolutely for the United Kingdom but fundamentally Scottish, that to me is the long-term answer to getting back to that magic number.[68]

This suggested a greater degree of engagement from the UK leadership than had existed for some time, but on polling day the Scottish Conservative and Unionist Party – which in 1955 had secured a majority of both votes and MPs – registered its worst ever result, 13.9 and 12.4 per cent of the constituency and list votes respectively, enough to elect just 15 MSPs (five fewer than anticipated following boundary changes). The SNP won an unprecedented single-party majority, albeit on a low turnout. As John Curtice concluded, the Conservatives continued to hold 'little appeal' for the vast majority of Scots, who believed Scotland's devolved institutions 'should constitute the pre-eminent layer of government in Scotland'.[69] In other words, the Scottish party's representatives still looked as if they would rather Holyrood simply disappeared.

NOTES

1. M. Dyer (2001), 'The evolution of the Centre-right and the state of Scottish Conservatism', *Political Studies* 49:1, 48.
2. *Scotsman*, 19 May 1997. Arthur Bell later quit the party, accusing it of 'blindness to reality' over the devolution issue (*Herald*, 7 July 1997).
3. *Scotsman*, 8 May 1997.
4. P. Lynch (2003), 'The Scottish Conservatives, 1997–2001: From disaster to devolution and beyond', in M. Garnett and P. Lynch (eds), *The Conservatives in Crisis: The Tories after 1997*, Manchester: Manchester University Press, 164.
5. Conference report, BBC Scotland, 27 June 1997.
6. *Scotsman* and *Herald*, 26–28 June 1997.
7. D. Denver, J. Mitchell, C. Pattie and H. Bochel (2000), *Scotland Decides: The Devolution Issue and the 1997 Referendum*, London: Routledge, 58–70.
8. *Daily Record*, 9 September 1997.
9. *Herald*, 24 September 1997.
10. *Scotland on Sunday*, 5 October 1997.
11. SCUA (1998), Strathclyde Commission, *Made in Scotland – The Final Report*, Edinburgh: Scottish Conservative and Unionist Association. The party's Glasgow office had closed in October 1997. The Commission also considered rebranding as the Scottish Unionist Party, the Scottish New Unionist Party (proposed by Malcolm Rifkind), the Scottish Conservative Party, the Progressive Conservative Party, the Scottish Tory Party and even the Scottish Democratic Conservative Party.
12. Press Association, 7 March 1998.
13. M. Rifkind (1998), *Scotland's Future: The Report of the Scottish Conservative Policy Commission*, Edinburgh: Scottish Conservative and Unionist Party, 6–11.
14. *Scotsman*, 20 March 1999.

15. B. Taylor (2002), *Scotland's Parliament: Triumph and Disaster*, Edinburgh: Edinburgh University Press, 183.
16. *Scottish Daily Mail*, 29 January 1999. This was published as *The Hampden Declaration*, Edinburgh: Scottish Conservative and Unionist Party.
17. *Sunday Times*, 4 April 1999.
18. M. Ritchie (2000), *Scotland Reclaimed: The Inside Story of Scotland's First Democratic Parliamentary Election*, Edinburgh: Saltire Society, 35.
19. *Scottish Daily Mail*, 15 June 2000. Ahmed-Sheikh later became an SNP MP.
20. See P. Jones (1999), 'The 1999 Scottish Parliament elections: From anti-Tory to anti-Nationalist politics', *Scottish Affairs* 28, 1–9.
21. *Scotsman*, 8 May 1999.
22. B. Taylor (2002), 192.
23. B. Taylor (2002), 195.
24. *Herald*, 30 June 2000.
25. *Health Service Journal*, 17 August 2000.
26. D. Torrance (2012), 'The wilderness years', in D. Torrance (ed.), *Whatever Happened to Tory Scotland?*, Edinburgh: Edinburgh University Press, 111.
27. *Sunday Herald*, 18 March 2011.
28. *Scotsman*, 27 September 2000.
29. D. Torrance (2012), 99.
30. See P. Lynch (2003), 178.
31. *Scotsman*, 11 August 2001.
32. *Sunday Herald*, 2 September 2001.
33. B. Taylor (2002), 197–9.
34. *Herald*, 3 February 2003.
35. A. McConnell (2004), *Scottish Local Government*, Edinburgh: Edinburgh University Press, 142.
36. A. Smith (2011), *Devolution and the Scottish Conservatives*, Manchester: Manchester University Press.
37. A. Convery (2016), *The Territorial Conservative Party: Devolution and Party Change in Scotland and Wales*, Manchester: Manchester University Press, 45.
38. D. Torrance (2012), 101.
39. A. Convery (2020), 'The Scottish Conservative Party', in M. Keating (ed.), *The Oxford Handbook of Scottish Politics*, Oxford: Oxford University Press, 247.
40. B. Taylor (2002), 192.
41. A. Convery (2016), 72–3.
42. *Scotland on Sunday*, 9 March 2004.
43. A. Convery (2016), 58–9.

44. *Scotsman*, 23 May 2005.
45. *Scotsman*, 21 December 2005.
46. *Scotsman*, 12 July 2006.
47. P. Snowdon (2010), *Back from the Brink*, London: Harper Press, 247.
48. *Daily Express*, 28 October 2006.
49. D. Torrance (2012), 104.
50. *Daily Record*, 8 March 2007. See also H. Macdonell (2009), *Uncharted Territory: The Story of Scottish Devolution 1999–2009*, London: Politico's, 188.
51. *Spectator*, 7 April 2007.
52. *Scotsman*, 6 April 2007.
53. See A. Bednarek (2012), '"Handbagging" the Feminisation Thesis? Reflections on women in the Scottish Conservative and Unionist Party', in D. Torrance (ed.), *Whatever Happened to Tory Scotland?*, Edinburgh: Edinburgh University Press, 149–69.
54. H. Macdonell, 196.
55. See D. Denver and H. Bochel (2007), 'A quiet revolution: STV and the Scottish council elections of 2007', *Scottish Affairs* 61, 1–17.
56. *Scotsman*, 31 October 2007.
57. Scottish Parliament Official Report, 6 December 2007.
58. Scottish Parliament Official Report, 25 June 2009.
59. *Scotsman*, 7 February 2008.
60. Interview with Derek Brownlee, 1 December 2011.
61. *Daily Express*, 13 February 2010.
62. *Daily Telegraph*, 19 June 2009.
63. D. Melding (2012), 'Refashioning Welsh Conservatism – A lesson for Scotland?', in D. Torrance (ed.), *Whatever Happened to Tory Scotland?*, Edinburgh: Edinburgh University Press, 136–7.
64. Lord Sanderson (2010), *Building for Scotland: Strengthening the Scottish Conservatives*, Edinburgh: Scottish Conservative and Unionist Party. See also A. Convery (2016), 59–61.
65. R. Johns, D. Denver, J. Mitchell and C. Pattie (2010), *Voting for a Scottish Government: The Scottish Parliament Election of 2007*, Manchester: Manchester University Press, 49.
66. *Scotland on Sunday*, 2 January 2011.
67. C. Carman, R. Johns and J. Mitchell (2014), *More Scottish than British: The 2011 Scottish Parliament Election*, Basingstoke: Palgrave Macmillan, 17.
68. Press Association Scotland, 20 April 2011.
69. J. Curtice (2012), 'Why no Tory revival in Scotland?', in D. Torrance (ed.), *Whatever Happened to Tory Scotland?*, Edinburgh: Edinburgh University Press, 124.

9

Out of the Wilderness?
2011–2023

'The Scottish Conservative Party has not produced a leader of stature', judged Chris Stevens in 1990, 'identifiable by his or her Scottishness.'[1] After yet another disappointing election result in May 2011, that was about to change. The impact of Ruth Davidson's leadership, however, would prove to be a slow burner, but when it finally ignited in 2015–16, Scottish Conservatism – or more accurately Unionism – finally attracted significant new support for the first time since the 1950s.

Reflecting on her election seven years after the event, Davidson said she had had 'no intention' of succeeding Annabel Goldie, who announced her resignation a few days after the election. 'I was the youngest member of our parliamentary group and the only new face,' Davidson wrote in 2018. 'I needed to learn my trade before I could even think about taking on any sort of leadership role.' But then, by Davidson's account, Murdo Fraser announced his plan to create a completely new centre-right party in Scotland. 'The idea that a new party with a new name – but essentially the same people and policies – would suddenly succeed where the current model had failed struck me as illogical,' said Davidson:

> After a long talk with a senior member of the Scottish party, I was persuaded to stand for the leadership ... I [became] the youngest party leader of a major political party anywhere in the UK, as well as the least experienced. I had no idea how to lead, and on the horizon I had the single biggest and most important vote in my lifetime – on the very existence of the United Kingdom.[2]

There was a degree of post-hoc analysis in this account, not least because Davidson's path to the leadership had been more premeditated than a spontaneous response to Fraser's candidacy.[3]

The party leadership election of 2011 generated a lot of media interest, particularly Murdo Fraser's declaration that there was 'no future for the Scottish Conservative and Unionist Party in its current form'.[4] His proposal for a completely new party won support from a majority of Scottish Conservative MSPs and party grandee Sir Malcolm Rifkind.[5] Fraser presciently pitched a possible independence referendum 'not as a threat, but as an opportunity':

> Just as our opposition to devolution throughout the 1980s and 1990s defined us then. So, our approach to Scotland's constitutional future in the 2010s will define us now. Our early opposition to the Scottish Parliament has led to us being portrayed as anti-Scottish. And, whether we like it or not, that is still the perception of much of the Scottish electorate. To counter it, we need both an admission and a reality-check. Painful as it may be for us to admit, our analysis of the impact of devolution was overstated. The idea that devolution is inevitably a slippery slope to separation. And that any power devolved is a step closer to independence. Such a message was too simplistic.

Fraser included a *mea culpa* on his previous support for 'Full Fiscal Freedom', something he now saw as 'independence in disguise'. But he still 'strongly' supported the 'principles of financial devolution, where the Scottish Parliament is more responsible for the money it spends'. It was time for the party, he concluded, 'to be enthusiastic about the evolution of devolution'.[6]

Lacking a competing vision beyond the post-Calman Commission status quo (given legislative effect by the *Scotland Act 2012*), Ruth Davidson ended up being the 'continuity' candidate, her five-point plan to revitalise the party (including comprehensive policy reviews) winning support from two MSPs and another party grandee, Lord Forsyth. As Alan Convery has observed, in the absence of any major ideological or policy differences beyond the constitution, issues of personality became more prominent: 'Who would most likely lead the Scottish Conservatives to electoral success?'[7]

Davidson won the contest by 2,983 votes to second-placed Fraser's 2,417 but began her tenure in a position similar to that later experienced by UK Labour leader Jeremy Corbyn, sustained by a party membership mandate but lacking significant support among parliamentary colleagues. An early initiative was a rebranding exercise, with a new Scottish party logo to replace David Cameron's doodled tree. This was unveiled towards the end of 2012, an eight-pronged cross Davidson said was 'distinctly Scottish but with colours which clearly reflect our pride in the United Kingdom'.[8] Davidson herself represented the biggest image change for a party long associated with social conservatism and Section 28. Working class, young and gay, she defied standard Conservative stereotypes, although her involvement with the Church of Scotland and Territorial Army were more traditionally Tory.

Davidson was deemed to have performed well enough at the weekly First Minister's Questions, although without landing too many blows on (admittedly more experienced) SNP First Minister Alex Salmond. At local government elections in May 2012, her party continued its electoral decline, losing 28 councillors compared with 2007. Davidson appeared unable to set out, as promised, a precise strategy for a Conservative revival north of the border, prompting 'internal muttering' about her leadership and even talk that Murdo Fraser would 'launch a coup'.[9]

When it came to domestic policy, Ruth Davidson also failed to innovate, instead observing during the 2012 UK Conservative Party conference that a 'corrosive sense of entitlement' in Scotland meant that only 12 per cent of Scottish households paid more in taxes than they received via public services. There were noises about freeing schools from local authority control (and 'vouchers', a policy from the late 1980s), halting wind farms and strengthening non-custodial sentences, but as one journalist commented, 'it was traditional Tory fare and entirely predictable'.[10] Writing in a published diary, *Telegraph* columnist Alan Cochrane declared Davidson 'absolutely awful':

She is totally and utterly useless and so are her team. They haven't a bloody clue but she is the problem – big problem. Not up to the job ... and I suspect that some hacks will start asking questions. [David] Mundell said he knew she wasn't cutting the mustard ... but he claims they've got someone lined up to help her. Christ, they need it.[11]

'When I was elected leader of the party', Davidson told one journalist, 'I was pretty clear about the fact that things were going to have to change and you didn't reverse 19 years of stagnation and decline overnight.'[12]

When Ruth Davidson became leader of the Scottish Conservative Party, its unionism remained 'prisoned in marble', a reluctance to concede any ground to the SNP – even an extension of devolution as in Wales – having prevented it from thinking imaginatively about the future of the Union.[13]

On becoming Leader of the Opposition, however, David Cameron and his Shadow Chancellor George Osborne had become attracted to the idea of proactively initiating a referendum on Scotland's place in the UK, the goal being to 'seize the initiative north of the border, and put a lid on the nationalist clamour'. Although the idea floundered due to likely opposition from Prime Minister Gordon Brown (his party's Scottish leader, Wendy Alexander, made a similar proposal in late 2007), their 'cogitations' had given 'them an appetite for radical thinking'.[14] Also thinking radically was Sir John Major, who in July 2011 abandoned his instinctive unionism and proposed devolving 'all responsibilities except foreign policy, defence and management of the economy' as a *quid pro quo* for reducing Scottish representation at Westminster and abolishing the block grant.[15] As 2011 drew to a close, a trio of Scottish grandees – the Lords Strathclyde, Lang and Forsyth – visited Cameron at Downing Street with bold advice to hold 'a referendum within the next three months' but without yielding 'on the question, the timing or franchise'. The Prime Minister was not convinced. 'Once we concede a referendum,' he is said to have replied, 'how do we stop conceding it again and again?'[16]

By early 2012, Cameron had warmed to the idea, realising that the 'sense of grievance against a distant, out-of-touch Westminster government would only grow'. He chose the *Andrew Marr Show* to announce plans for a 'fair, legal and decisive' referendum via a Section 30 Order under the *Scotland Act 1998* (a temporary transfer of legislative authority). Momentarily wrong-footed, the Scottish Government held to the line that Westminster authority was unnecessary, although it later agreed to negotiate terms. Cameron hired 'two brilliant characters' to advise him, the former Scottish Conservative spin doctor Ramsay Jones ('a golf-loving, politics-loving wheeler-dealer') and the 'meticulous, clever and universally respected' Andrew Dunlop, a former special adviser to George Younger and Margaret Thatcher he had first encountered in the 1990s.[17]

The 'Edinburgh Agreement' was signed in October 2012 and at the first cross-party meeting of 'Better Together', a remarkable alliance of Conservative, Labour and Liberal Democrat figures, it was agreed that the Conservatives would provide the cash, Labour the campaigning machine and Liberal Democrats a concentration on their 11 Scottish constituencies.[18] David Cameron predicted that the forthcoming battle for the Union would imbue the Scottish Conservatives with renewed vigour, just as resistance to Irish Home Rule had a century before. Indeed, the referendum came to act as a focal point for several Scottish party strategies: organisational, leadership and constitutional.[19]

Although used to campaigning against devolution and, indirectly, against independence, Scottish Conservative activists were not used to making arguments *for* the Union or, in the context of their leader's post-2013 strategy, for greater powers (especially when few of them agreed with that goal). This was the corollary of Michael Billig's 'banal nationalism', an unthinking and 'banal unionism' which saw no need to justify itself. The party's 'Conservative Friends of the Union' campaign, however, indicated the existence of 'unionist' support beyond that for the Scottish Conservatives. By November 2012, this had attracted 50,000 offers of support and money.[20]

But there was a strategic problem when it came to reforming that Union. During the leadership election, Davidson had declared that the Calman Commission's recommendations for the partial devolution of fiscal and welfare powers to Holyrood were to be a 'line in the sand'. This, however, was washed away by the Prime Minister in February 2012. 'When the referendum is over,' Cameron told business leaders, 'I am open to looking at how the devolution settlement can be improved further.'[21] Alan Convery has been critical of such 'ad hoc' constitutional policymaking,[22] although the Prime Minister's pledge compelled Davidson to respond. In a March 2013 speech, she argued that:

> With the benefit of hindsight, I believe we found ourselves on the wrong side of history in 1997. We fought on against the idea of a Scottish Parliament long after it became clear it was the settled will of the Scottish people. Our decision not to take part in the Scottish

Constitutional Convention gave the impression that Scotland's constitutional future was not a matter of interest to us, beyond keeping Scotland in the UK. For many, the fact we were a lone voice saying 'no' in the referendum campaign simply underlined the impression we had no real faith in our own country. It made us look as if we lacked ambition for Scotland.

'We can talk to ourselves, as perhaps we have too often in the past,' she added. 'We can hold to the old ways and follow a path of slow decline. Or we can choose to do something about it.'[23]

A key part of Davidson's leadership strategy thus became establishing distance between *her* party on the periphery and David Cameron's party at the centre, which she did by gently criticising the UK leader or differing on policies like immigration, something tolerated by party HQ in London. 'Ruth and I were immediate political soulmates,' recalled Cameron in his memoirs. She 'came to embody the pro-devolution, anti-independence, modern, compassionate Conservative Party'.[24] The Prime Minister channelled John Major in 1992 by stressing what John P. Mackintosh had called 'dual identity'. 'Not only can you love Scotland and love the United Kingdom,' said Cameron, 'not only can you drape yourself in the Saltire and the Union Jack, but you can be even prouder of your Scottish heritage than your British heritage – as many in Scotland are – and still believe that Scotland is better off in Britain.' He and Davidson even repeatedly acknowledged the possibility of independence if not its desirability. Cameron said he would never suggest 'Scotland could not make a go of being on its own'. 'Of course Scotland could govern itself,' he said. 'So could England. My point is that we do it so much better together.'[25]

And while obviously Scottish, Ruth Davidson took care to emphasise her 'nationalist unionism'. 'I am a Scot, and I am proud of my country,' she declared, but 'no political party – and no side in the constitutional debate – has a monopoly on patriotism.'[26] Elsewhere Davidson said Conservatives shared the SNP's 'faith in Scotland's future', although their 'faith' was 'not blind to the facts'.[27] She established a working group to make good on the Prime Minister's promise of further powers, which was chaired by party grandee Lord Strathclyde.[28] Murdo Fraser, who had proposed greater fiscal accountability as well as a new party in 2011, was quick to note the irony, although he concluded it was 'still too early to herald a new dawn', a reminder that Davidson did not enjoy unequivocal support from her Holyrood colleagues. Even Lord Forsyth, an early backer of Davidson's leadership, said her plan for greater fiscal devolution was 'a bit like a suicide mission' that would hit Conservative supporters 'extremely hard in the pocket',[29] a line that evoked his 1990s campaign against Labour's 'tartan tax'.

Davidson's biographer viewed the 2013 Scottish Conservative spring conference as 'the point at which she tackled internal critics and delivered a fundamental change to the party that would make it electable again'.[30] Scottish Government legislation to legalise same-sex marriage later that year also helped the Scottish Conservatives to 'modernise' in the same way Cameron had with similar legislation in England and Wales. Initially reluctant to talk about her private life (she had broken up with a long-term partner in March 2013), it increasingly came to the fore. Davidson's speech in that debate was widely praised:

> I believe that marriage is a good thing. I saw the evidence of that every day growing up in a house that was full of love. My family had the stresses and strains that are common to all, but there was never any doubt, question or fear in my mind that our togetherness was in any way insecure ... I do not want the next generation of young gay people to grow up as I did, believing that marriage is something that they can never have.[31]

Although an unthinkable speech for a Scottish Conservative to have made even a decade earlier, Davidson's stance on same-sex marriage and other aspects of gender politics 'remained situated within conservative understandings of family life and social and political change'. 'Her gender and sexuality were, in this sense, not aberrations', judged Jennifer Thomson, 'but rather continuations of a conservative political projection her party had promoted for some time.'[32]

Lord Ashcroft, meanwhile, analysed Scottish Conservative prospects in a report, *Cameron's Caledonian Conundrum*, published in October 2013. Based on a 10,000-sample poll, focus groups and follow-up surveys, it found what many Scottish Conservatives had long believed, that there were 'potential Tories at large in Scotland'. Ashcroft identified three drawbacks for the potential Conservative vote in Scotland: first, they doubted the Conservatives were 'on their side'; second, they did not feel the party cared much for Scotland or for devolution;

and third, they considered the Conservatives to be irrelevant in Scottish elections. At the same time, he found swing voters had 'a generally positive view' of Ruth Davidson, remembering, for example, that she had been asked for proof-of-age identification while trying to buy beer at a concert at Glasgow's Hampden Park. When it came to policy, Ashcroft's findings suggested greater fiscal responsibility could be to the party's 'political advantage'. 'As long as voters think the Scottish Parliament exists to sign the cheques,' concluded Ashcroft, 'while the fiscal prudence happens elsewhere, the Conservatives will seem redundant.'[33]

Indeed, even before Lord Strathclyde published his recommendations, David Cameron told the 2014 Scottish Conservative conference that giving Holyrood 'greater responsibility for raising more of the money it spends' was 'what Ruth believes – and I believe it too'. In a Q&A session with members of the Strathclyde Commission, only one questioner was (politely) opposed to the idea of devolving more powers, an indication – according to party strategists – that most Scottish Conservatives had learned to stop worrying and love legislative devolution.[34] Having been, as Convery put it, 'anti-devolutionists' (until 1999), 'willing participants' (1999–2009) and then 'half-hearted supporters of further powers' (2009–14), the party was finally working its way towards a 'definitive answer'.[35] At European Parliament elections held in June 2014, meanwhile, the Scottish Conservative vote increased (albeit on a low turnout). But given UKIP's vote had doubled in Scotland (enough to elect one of five MEPs), this was considered a good result.

The *Commission on the Future Governance of Scotland* reported in May 2014 and recommended, as expected, the full devolution of income tax and some additional welfare powers. Notably, it made no mention of reforming or abolishing the Barnett Formula, which Davidson had earlier declared to be 'in its death throes'.[36] Nevertheless, Alan Convery viewed the Strathclyde Commission as significant in two ways: first, the Scottish Conservatives appeared to have 'found a path through the competing ideological demands of their Conservatism and Unionism' and, second, for the first time since the 1970s they had 'something authentically Tory and positive to say about devolution'. Even more strikingly, the party had managed to 'outbid' Scottish Labour when it came to further devolution,[37] something which had not happened since the 'Scottish Control of Scottish Affairs' agenda of the late 1940s. Convery called it 'a Conservative philosophy of devolution'. As Lord Strathclyde put it:

> When these actions are taken within the context of Conservative policies on empowering individuals and decentralising power throughout the rest of the UK, it is clear that empowering the Scottish people to shape their own nation within the security of a United Kingdom is not just something we are willing only to grudgingly accept, it is something that sits at the very heart of what it means to be a modern Scottish Conservative.[38]

Davidson said she relished the opportunity to 'marry these vital Conservative instincts' of responsibility and accountability, Holyrood's ability to spend but not (necessarily) tax having proved 'a licence to avoid difficult decisions and blame others'.[39] The Strathclyde Commission recommendations were published just months before the independence referendum and eventually dovetailed with similar commitments from Davidson's 'Better Together' colleagues in Labour and the Liberal Democrats. Although the Scottish Conservative leader was initially a rather marginal figure in that long campaign, she had gained in prominence as she grew more confident, performing particularly well (she was, after all, a former journalist) in televised debates.[40] The party was, for once, remarkably disciplined, with only a tiny fringe of Conservatives pledging support for independence.[41]

It later emerged that Davidson had been unhappy with her UK party colleagues in the later stages of the referendum campaign (or at least wanted that to be the perception). She thought the Prime Minister, Ed Miliband and Nick Clegg deciding to 'chuck PMQs and dash to Scotland' was a 'gimmick', while she was reportedly 'f***ing furious' with Cameron over the so-called 'Vow', which formalised the three parties' plans to extend devolution should there be a majority 'no' vote. 'I wish', Davidson remembered saying, 'people would just hold their effing nerve.'[42] After the result, David Cameron held his, although it resulted in a needless own goal. Ignoring warnings not to crowbar 'English Votes for English Laws' into what his coalition partners would have preferred to have been a low-key speech the morning after, he told Nick Clegg: 'I just don't care. We've only got one Conservative MP north of the border. Let Labour sort it out. It's now their problem.'[43] This attitude persisted at the following year's general election when the UK Conservative Party weaponised the idea that Alex Salmond and Nicola Sturgeon would control a minority Labour government. But according to Joe Pike, Davidson had no objection to this, having herself referred to 'Alex Salmond pulling the strings in Westminster'.[44]

Two days before the Smith Commission (formed after the referendum to make good on the Vow) published its report, Ruth Davidson apparently told Andrew Dunlop, Cameron's adviser on Scotland, that the UK Government would 'have to suck it up' and deliver whatever Lord Smith recommended.[45] This it did, and indeed the Strathclyde Commission's recommendations on the specifics of tax devolution (income tax, VAT and air passenger duty) were largely implemented via the *Scotland Act 2016*. It was quite a turnaround for a party which had once railed against tax devolution and, given 'the political dynamics in Scotland', a 'remarkable' fiscal achievement for an opposition party.[46] 'We were at our lowest ebb, we had our least number of political representatives, least amount of money, the least amount of direction,' Ruth Davidson later reflected of the pre-2014 Scottish Conservative Party, 'we were considered a joke, and actually the referendum helped us pull together as a party.'[47]

With the Union apparently secure, Ruth Davidson next made an audacious bid to occupy 'the centre-ground of Scottish politics'. She also framed Nicola Sturgeon, who was about to succeed Alex Salmond, as, rather improbably, the 'most Left-wing First Minister Scotland has ever known', as well as a referendum 'denier' determined to 'put the country back through what we've just finished'.[48] When Salmond formally resigned as First Minister in November 2014, the Scottish Conservative leader nominated herself as his successor, feeling the need to offer 'an alternative vision of Scotland'. This hinted at a developing strategy of framing the Scottish political arena as Sturgeon vs Davidson.

Scottish Conservatives hoped the referendum result might help them capture 'No' voters from other unionist parties, but over the next six months the polls did not budge, although the psephologist John Curtice had detected a modest rise in Scottish Conservative support between 2012 and 2014.[49] Undeterred, Davidson predicted that thousands of so-called 'Tartan Tories' were 'coming back home', attracted by what she called the 'best-regimented, best-organised, best-resourced and best-recruited' campaign in 20 years.[50]

It was at this stage that Davidson began to attract a small group of media cheerleaders, although what Tim Bale has called a Conservative Party 'in the media' did not exist to anything like the same degree as in England.[51] 'Fearless, fiery and funny ... Ruth's the poster girl for a Tory revival' proclaimed the *Scottish Daily Mail*, although the article's author, Chris Deerin, noted a weak 'talent pool' beyond Davidson, Murdo Fraser and Eddie Barnes, her 'canny, street-smart' director of strategy and communications. Deerin also attempted to extract a political philosophy from the Scottish Conservative leader. 'The reason I'm a Tory is because I believe people make better decisions about their lives than the state,' she told him:

> I believe hard work should be rewarded, that aspiration and opportunity shouldn't be dirty words, that a pound in the pocket is better spent by the person who earned it rather than by some nameless, faceless government official ... It doesn't matter where you're from, it's what you do and where you're going that counts. Responsibility, hard work, just reward, helping those at the bottom and clearing a path for others to explore even greater horizons.[52]

This was an orthodox blend of Thatcherite and Cameronian tropes, and indeed, beyond setting herself against SNP-style universalism (on, for example, prescription charges and tuition fees), the Scottish Conservatives remained policy-lite almost four years into Davidson's leadership.

A Sri Lankan pollster called James Kanagasooriam then entered the scene. On applying a specially developed psephological model to Scotland he found that areas which looked Conservative in England and Wales were, in Scotland, divided between the SNP, Labour, Liberal Democrats and the Conservatives. Although this meant the Scottish Conservative vote was scattered, it also represented an opportunity. When he analysed the 2014 referendum vote, Kanagasooriam realised that temperamentally Conservative voters in Scotland overlapped with those who had voted 'No'. As Tim Shipman has written:

> The logical conclusion was that rather than run on bread-and-butter political issues, Davidson should perform 'political arbitrage' by attempting to reconstitute the Tories as 'the Unionist party', and effectively refight the referendum in order to bring all the potential Tory supporters back under one roof.[53]

Furthermore, Ruth Davidson's background and personality – gay and Christian, Army reservist and pro-Europe – meant she was 'political alchemy', perfectly placed 'to demographically hold different groups together'.[54]

At the 2015 UK general election, however, Davidson worried that her sole MP in Scotland, David Mundell, would be swept away by a SNP tsunami. Mundell held on, but the party garnered its lowest-ever share of the vote. 'The persistence of an anti-Conservative mood amongst a significant part of the Scottish electorate', concluded James Mitchell, 'remains important.'[55] Davidson put a brave face on the result, arguing that hers was the only pro-UK party to increase its vote, although the SNP made much of it being the worst Conservative performance (14.9 per cent) in Scotland in more than 150 years.[56]

The party's strategy of trying to 'cleave away' unionist voters from other unionist parties in places like Perthshire had failed. 'It was clear from focus groups they [electors] were still voting for the SNP on the basis of competence,' said one senior Scottish Conservative official. 'And in that election, the SNP suddenly became relevant.' At the same time, it had become clear there existed 'a clear unionist feeling, a desire to stop the SNP', something the party was conscious it had to 'harness'. After the election, therefore, the party 'modelled' 'no' voters in parts of Scotland with growing numbers of Conservative voters. They identified 'fashionable followers', those (generally younger) voters attracted by Davidson, and 'credibility voters', strong unionists who wanted to vote Conservative but did not think there was any point. 'Both were latent voters,' noted the party official, 'and we had to motivate them'.[57]

When attempts to present the Scottish Conservatives as the 'real alternative' to the SNP fell flat,[58] party strategists instead began to adopt a more 'realistic' analysis of what they might hope to achieve in May 2016, and 'that was coming in second place'. A YouGov poll in February 2016 put the party at nearly 20 per cent on the regional list vote, while instead of canvassing in the traditional fashion, activists asked voters 'who would best stand up to Nicola Sturgeon'. They were surprised when people volunteered 'Ruth Davidson', even echoing party messaging in expressing the need for a 'strong opposition'.[59] In early 2016, the Scottish Conservatives also began to push a line about Labour and the Liberal Democrats being 'soft' on independence, and indeed the constitutional question began to drown out everything else. 'We didn't go on policy,' recalled the source, 'because we didn't need to.'[60] A Scottish Conservative tax commission had reported in January 2016, which proposed a new 'middle band' of income tax.[61]

In preparation for the 2016 Holyrood election, Ruth Davidson also oversaw what was depicted as a gentle 'changing of the guard' but was, in reality, more like 'Murder on the Orient Express'.[62] In all, seven of the party's 15 MSPs were intending to stand down, which allowed the party to bring forward some new faces, most prominent of which was the constitutional academic Adam Tomkins, formerly a left-wing republican.[63] The Scottish Conservatives then kicked off the campaign by conceding defeat to the SNP. Davidson declared herself 'ready to serve' as opposition leader in the Scottish Parliament, while the backdrop at her party's pre-election conference declared in large blue letters: 'Ruth Davidson for a Strong Opposition.' For the next 62 days, declared David Cameron at the same gathering, 'we're going to fight to become the official opposition'.[64] This novel pitch was calibrated to make voting Conservative feel like less of a commitment while portraying the Scottish party as the only reliably Unionist option, Labour having made noises about supporting independence.

For once, electoral reality matched expectations. On polling day, the Scottish Conservatives pushed Kezia Dugdale's Scottish Labour Party into second place at Holyrood, winning 31 MSPs (24 of them new), including Ruth Davidson in Edinburgh Central, a significant urban (and constituency) gain. She was, however, 'under no illusion that everybody who voted for me in that seat is a true-blue, dyed-in-the-wool Tory',[65] an acknowledgement that unionist votes were not the same as Conservative. Nevertheless, the Scottish Conservative leader's stock rose inexorably; David Cameron tweeted his congratulations and Ladbrokes cut the odds on Davidson succeeding him as UK Conservative leader from 50/1 to 33/1.[66] The SNP, deprived of an overall majority, attempted to play down the Scottish Conservative result, arguing that the party's vote share was still lower than that in 1987.

Thereafter Davidson ditched the colourful photocalls with which she had become associated during the election campaign, conscious of the need to adopt a more 'serious' demeanour now she was leader of Scotland's largest opposition party. She also continued to claim the political centre ground, declaring herself 'a John Major Conservative', while acknowledging that the Scottish Conservatives were still 'on probation'. 'These are very mobile votes and they can be taken elsewhere pretty quickly,' she told the *Telegraph*. 'One good election doesn't make a revival.' Local government elections in 2017, she added, would ensure the revival was 'built on stone and not sand'.[67] As Diffley has observed, the party's recovery was sudden rather than gradual, and could not be traced (as many later argued) to the immediate aftermath of the independence referendum.[68]

The sense of elation did not last long, not least because of an imminent referendum on the UK's membership of the European Union. Even before it took place on 23 June 2016, journalists were briefed that should Boris Johnson become UK Conservative leader (as looked likely in the event of a 'Leave' vote) then the Scottish Conservatives would 'break away ... under a new name', a variation on an old theme (although it was later rebutted by Davidson). She went head-to-head with Johnson during one of the EU campaign's highest-profile debates at Wembley Stadium, comparing his 'brazen chauvinistic style' to that of Alex Salmond, 'this time repeated for a UK audience'.[69] A curious feature of the campaign, meanwhile, was a clandestine donation to the pro-Brexit Democratic Unionist Party (DUP) brokered by a former vice chairman of the Scottish Conservatives, around £200,000 of which was used to fund a two-page 'Vote Leave' advert in the *Metro* newspaper (which did not circulate in Northern Ireland).[70]

Initially, the majority Leave vote looked as if it might cause serious damage to Davidson's standing. 'We thought, after all these years [the party's recovery has] lasted six weeks; it was never meant to be, the misery will continue,' recalled a senior party official. A 'crisis' meeting was quickly convened, at which it was assumed support for independence would 'go way ahead, that we were in for a bumpy ride'. With two words, however, Nicola Sturgeon – who said another independence referendum was 'highly likely' – provided a 'shot in the arm for unionism ... it meant we had something to say; it gave us something to get through the rest of 2016 and into 2017.'[71] 'The 1.6 million votes cast in this referendum in favour of Remain', cautioned Davidson, 'do not wipe away the two million votes that we cast [in favour of the Union] less than two years ago.'[72]

But as Alan Convery has observed, the UK's decision to leave the EU 'exposed wider constitutional tensions'. Having played a prominent role in the official UK-wide 'Stronger In' campaign, Davidson had to 'very quickly change her position after the result in order not to open up a wide division between the UK and Scottish Conservative parties'.[73] She called Theresa May, who succeeded Cameron as UK party leader and thus Prime Minister, a 'proper grown up ... best placed to navigate the stormy waters ahead'.[74] In turn, May highlighted that the 'full title' of her party was 'the Conservative and *Unionist* Party', which meant it believed 'in the Union: the precious, precious bond between England, Scotland, Wales and Northern Ireland.'[75]

Davidson spoke of the UK remaining part of the EU Single Market and Customs Union and thus retaining reciprocal freedom of movement, telling the 2016 UK Conservative Party conference that 'immigrants should be made to feel welcome in the UK'.[76] This pragmatic Brexit stance would prove unsustainable, but in the wake of the Holyrood elections and EU referendum, Davidson had 'arrived on the UK's political stage',[77] experiencing the sort of limelight experienced by Nicola Sturgeon a year earlier. News of her engagement to partner Jennifer Wilson made UK front pages while, visiting London on 13 July, she was sworn of the Privy Council and entertained members of the Commons Lobby ('Labour's still fumbling with its flies' was one memorable line, 'while the Tories are enjoying a post-coital cigarette after withdrawing our massive Johnson'), all of which fuelled speculation of a move to Westminster and a bid for the UK party leadership.[78]

By September 2016, Ipsos MORI found Davidson's 'satisfaction' rating with voters at +31 per cent, 17 points ahead of Nicola Sturgeon (whose rating was +14 per cent).[79] Policy development, however, continued to take a back seat. In October 2016, Davidson expressed opposition to grammar schools in Scotland and joined UK colleagues in urging a general extension of the franchise to 16- and 17-year-olds, but otherwise the resurgent Scottish Conservative Party did not seem terribly interested in ideas. Alan Convery believed this was due to the dominance of the constitutional question, meaning the Scottish party had not experienced the same 'difficult debates about modernisation' experienced by the UK party, instead preferring 'familiar and comfortable themes'.[80] 'Like so many politicians who have emerged from the world of media, she is stronger on presentation than substance,' was James Mitchell's view. 'It is clear what the Tories oppose but not what they support.'[81] In Davidson's own words, she was attempting to get 'back to proper, old-fashioned, blue-collar Toryism that somehow, somewhere, half our party forgot'.[82]

The 2017 Scottish Conservative Party spring conference – the first since 1998 to be held in Glasgow – found Ruth Davidson on pugilistic form. She spoke of her party as a 'government in waiting', ready to 'demand a politics that no longer obsesses over the colour of a flag, but rather focuses on the content of our lives'. But the main message was clear. 'This party – the Scottish Conservative and Unionist Party – will never waver in our determination to stand up for the decision we made as a country. We will fight you every step of the way. We said no. We meant it. Are you listening, Nicola? No. Second. Referendum.'[83]

At First Minister's Questions, Davidson bellowed 'sit down!' at the First Minister during a highly charged debate on the prospect of a second referendum, but she refused to say if the UK Government should block a Section 30 Order, a legal necessity (as in 2014) for the Scottish Parliament to legislate. In 2015 she had conceded a 'mandate to hold one' should the SNP win 'an outright majority' with a clear pledge, as in 2011. 'In the longer term, Westminster saying "No you cannae" will not play well in Scotland,' Davidson observed, 'and I think that it would damage the unionist cause.'[84] This condition – a single-party SNP overall majority – had not been met in 2016, so when Nicola Sturgeon asked for a Section 30 Order at the end of March 2017, Theresa May's 'now is not the time' response (devised by Davidson and May adviser Fiona Hill) was deliberately nuanced, 'oscillating between flexibility and principle'.[85]

The Scottish Conservatives soon launched a financial appeal and online petition against a second independence referendum. 'We got 120,000 signatures in 24 hours and money like we'd never had before,' recalled a senior party official. 'We could feel the momentum.' At the same time, the party's local government candidates and councillors were unhappy about the campaign 'being all about Ruth and the constitution'.[86] Nevertheless, the First Minister's s30 Order request gave the Scottish Conservative local government campaign a boost, as did the Prime Minister's decision on 18 April (backed by two-thirds of MPs) to hold a 'snap' general election on 8 June 2017.

A row over the so-called 'rape clause' highlighted ongoing tensions between the Scottish and UK parties. As Ailsa Henderson and James Mitchell have observed, Davidson's 'communication skills failed her when she was forced to defend Conservative policies'.[87] But such issues were eclipsed by the rolling of two separate election campaigns – local and general – into one, with the pithy and consistently uttered line 'we said no, we meant it', as used in Davidson's March 2017 conference speech. Whereas in the rest of the UK elections were fought on the basis of Brexit, in Scotland discourse was framed by the yes/no cleavage of 2014. As James Mitchell observed, they had 'essentially become a single-issue party', with independence being as important to the Conservatives as it was to the SNP.[88] Although reductive, this anti-independence messaging appealed to 'unionist' voters who would not otherwise countenance voting for the 'effing Tories'. On 6 May 2017, almost 20 years since the Scottish Conservative Party lost all its MPs in Scotland, it gained 164 additional councillors, even in parts of Glasgow and Paisley hitherto considered 'no-go' areas.[89] The media made much of a Conservative win in Ravenscraig, 25 years after its eponymous steelworks had shut down.

The party had already decided to target 12 Scottish constituencies in the forthcoming UK general election, something the pollster John Curtice believed could credibly 'threaten the SNP's vice-like grip on Scottish representation in Westminster'.[90] Davidson spoke of a 'titanic battle' to oust Angus Robertson, the SNP's Westminster leader,[91] whose Moray constituency had come within a whisker of voting 'Leave' in June 2016. Lending further credibility to such ambitions was the ferocity of the SNP's response. 'The more Tory MPs there are, the heavier the price Scotland will pay,' warned Nicola Sturgeon darkly. 'The bigger the Tory majority, the more they will think they can do anything to Scotland and get away with it.'[92]

Scottish Conservative strategists, meanwhile, targeted two groups of voters, middle-class unionists who had stopped supporting the party because of the 'stigma' and perceived wastefulness, and also 'Yes-Leavers', small 'c' Conservatives who had voted 'Yes' in 2014 but 'Leave' in 2016. 'People didn't change their vote because of Ruth personally,' recalled a senior party official, 'but she made the journey easier for them – she was the key that opened the door.'[93] For her campaign team,

Davidson was a 'gateway' drug to voting Tory.[94] Signalling that another long-standing trope was weakening, focus groups also recognised Davidson as 'more of a Scottish Conservative, as opposed to an English Conservative in Scotland'.[95] Not only that, but 'Davidson's verve and enthusiasm' served to highlight 'the incompetence of the broader Conservative campaign'.[96]

The Scottish Conservative leadership resisted 'significant' efforts by Downing Street to 'make the election in Scotland all about Theresa May' and her mantra 'strong and stable'.[97] Davidson was summoned to London when she began departing from this script, but on showing Lynton Crosby Scottish polling he replied: 'I completely understand. Crack on.'[98] Campaign material featured Davidson rather than the Prime Minister, successfully creating 'a distinct agenda from that of the party south of the border', a combination of 'Scottish distinctiveness' and 'staunch unionism'.[99]

On polling day, the Scottish Conservative Party managed to win 13 MPs, a dozen more than it had managed in any UK general election since 2001, and in parts of Scotland it had last represented in 1992.[100] There could be no more jokes about there being more pandas in Edinburgh Zoo than Scottish Conservatives in the House of Commons. There was almost a 14th, the Scottish Conservative MEP Ian Duncan narrowly failing to unseat the SNP's Pete Wishart in Perth and North Perthshire. He was soon made a peer and a minister, something strongly condemned by the SNP.

Davidson later hailed the MPs as 'Scotland's champions', a 'team' who would 'aim to stand up for Scotland's interests – and to show that those interests are best served by being part of the UK'.[101] There was even talk of the group acting as 'a party within a party', willing 'to defy Theresa May' in favour of Ruth Davidson.[102] But it soon became clear the Scottish MPs saw themselves as primarily accountable to the London leadership, something encouraged by the Westminster party whips.[103] Although not quite the Scottish Unionist Members Committee of the 1950s, the group did elect John Lamont (Berwickshire, Roxburgh and Selkirk) convener and Douglas Ross (Moray) his deputy.

The 2017 election, concluded Henderson and Mitchell, represented an opportunity for the Scottish Conservatives to build support by 'translating unionist votes into Conservative votes'.

At the same time, they warned presciently, 'their base is fragile and might easily fall away at the next election'.[104] With Theresa May now dependent upon the anti-same-sex marriage DUP to maintain 'confidence' in the House of Commons, Ruth Davidson emphasised the Scottish party's new 'progressive' persona. 'I am a practising Christian,' Davidson had declared in 2016. 'I am a Protestant. I am a Unionist. I am Scottish and British. I am engaged to a Catholic Irishwoman from county Wexford who was educated by nuns. For me, equal marriage isn't about one religion or county or community.'[105]

Still rumours circulated of plans for Davidson to swap Holyrood for Westminster, either as an MP or as a peer. The *Guardian* later revealed a 2016 plan for Davidson to 'do a[n Alec] Douglas-Home', moving from the House of Lords to a safe Commons seat, 'the best bet to stop Johnson, and all with [David] Cameron's backing'.[106] This had been far-fetched, but Davidson told the *Spectator* she had not 'ruled it out. If devolution is going to work, then actually there has to be the ability to move between chambers and parliaments.'[107] But by early 2018 there were already signs of fragility in the Scottish Conservative revival. Perhaps with this in mind, Davidson reportedly banned 'toxic Tories' such as Boris Johnson, Liam Fox and Michael Gove (the latter two Scottish) from her party's spring gathering, a source explaining that she did not 'want folk from the party down south dominating the conference'.[108] In any case, it did not take place due to bad weather. Boxes of a well-produced but rather lightweight pamphlet entitled *Scottish Conservative Unionist* went undistributed. This spoke of setting out 'a positive agenda on social policy' by making Scottish education, once again, 'the best in the world', 'tackling the underlying causes of social injustice' and creating 'a genuine meritocracy'.[109] But all in all, the party played it safe, repeatedly 'emphasising its unionism rather than seek to convert unionists who had voted for the party into Conservatives'.[110]

There was also trouble at Westminster. The Scottish Conservative group of MPs was divided over Brexit, their views ranging from 'a clean break' (i.e. no deal) to the softest possible deal. The East Renfrewshire MP Paul Masterton was among those named and shamed by the *Telegraph* as a 'mutineer'; he said he would not support legislation which undermined 'devolution and does not respect the integrity of the

Union'.[111] Other Scottish MPs felt misled by their own whips as to negotiations between the Scottish and UK governments.[112] And when it emerged the Withdrawal Agreement would bind the UK to the Common Fisheries Policy until December 2020, the Moray MP Douglas Ross said it 'would be easier to get someone to drink a pint of cold sick than try to sell this as a success'.[113]

Davidson insisted that any deal had to be the same throughout the UK (a curious stance given Unionism had long tolerated divergence) and argued against special provisions for Northern Ireland, fearing it would strengthen Scottish Government demands. In October 2018 she and Scottish Secretary David Mundell even threatened to quit if the Northern Ireland point was ceded.[114] Conservative MSPs were also compelled to support the UK Government when it ignored the Sewel Convention and overruled the Scottish Parliament for the first time since 1999. UK ministers argued that Brexit was not a 'normal' situation, while Downing Street attempted to draw Scottish Conservative MPs closer 'to show the administration cared about the Union'. There was bemusement at the relative distance of Davidson, who had never held a scheduled meeting with her MPs on frequent visits to London. They now held group meetings at Dover House (rather than the Commons) and no longer had a permanent convener.[115]

Towards the end of April 2018, meanwhile, Davidson had surprised the Scottish (and UK) political world by being the first incumbent leader of a political party to become pregnant, having undergone IVF treatment with her fiancée Jennifer Wilson. Davidson had recently published a book entitled *Yes She Can: Why Women Own the Future*, just as speculation she might see her own future at Westminster reached its height. But in an intensely personal interview for the *Sunday Times*, a heavily pregnant Davidson danced 'unselfconsciously' for a photographer before saying:

> No, I do not want to go and be a junior minister in the Lords. I'm coming back to do my job and beat Nicola Sturgeon. And on a human level, the idea that I would have a child in Edinburgh and then immediately go down to London four days a week and leave it up here is offensive … You have to want it. And I don't want to be prime minister … I value my relationship and my mental health too much for it. I will not be a candidate.[116]

There was widespread praise from political opponents and allies, Theresa May saying she thought it had been 'incredibly brave' for a senior politician to be 'so open and so honest about her own mental health and what she's been through'.[117] Davidson arrived at the subsequent UK Conservative Party conference hand-in-hand with her fiancée, pitching herself as the 'pro-Union conscience of the party' in a keynote speech.[118] Jackson Carlaw, a former party deputy chairman, became acting leader of the Scottish Conservative Party.

Davidson had intended to return from maternity leave in May 2019, just a few weeks after the UK was supposed to 'exit' the EU at the end of March. Instead, she returned to the helm as what she had once called the UK Conservative Party's 'psychodrama' reached its final, dramatic scenes. Talk of a long extension to 'Brexit day' was deemed 'catastrophic' for the Scottish Conservative revival. 'A lot of our voters are leave', a shadow cabinet minister explained, 'and they just want us to get out.'[119] As the former Prime Minister Tony Blair had observed, 'the vulnerability of Ruth Davidson's Conservatives is that they are tied to Theresa May'.[120]

But having been, as one senior party official put it, 'protected, insulated to some degree from Brexit by the Scottish constitutional factor',[121] that 'buffer' became worn as the battles of 2014 receded further into the past. During one particularly fierce exchange at First Minister's Questions, Nicola Sturgeon – whose party had spent the last three years depicting Ruth Davidson as a hard-line Thatcherite – attacked the Scottish Conservative leader in personal as well as political terms:

> Perhaps the difference between Ruth Davidson and me is that I have principles, and I stick to my principles. Ruth Davidson would not recognise a principle. She used passionately to oppose Brexit; now she supports Brexit. She used to demand that we stay in the single market; now she wants us to be taken out of the single market. Of course, Ruth Davidson also used to call Boris Johnson names that I cannot repeat in the chamber. Now, she is cosying up to Boris Johnson – the arch-Brexiteer. I cannot help but think that it is a pity that flip-flopping is not an Olympic sport, because if it was, Ruth Davidson would be a guaranteed gold-medal winner.[122]

Some of this was pre-election rhetoric, for European Parliament elections took place the following day. Davidson's relative personal popularity did not prevent her party polling just 12 per cent of the vote, better than in any other part of the UK but still six points down on 2014. Other critics targeted the hitherto obscure Scottish Unionist Association Trust – the 'historic proceeds', as trustee Peter Duncan put it, 'of raffles and tombolas' – which was charged with channelling 'dark money' to Conservative parliamentary candidates,[123] spurious claims the party struggled effectively to rebut.

Davidson began to tell close associates that 'she really did feel as if she wanted to go' as party leader,[124] an inclination compounded when Boris Johnson bid to succeed Theresa May as UK Conservative leader and Prime Minister. Long anticipated due to Brexit instability, there had been reports of something called 'Operation Arse', an attempt by Scottish Conservatives to prevent a Johnson premiership, fearful of its likely impact on both the party in Scotland and, more broadly, the Union.[125] Half the Scottish voters who had backed the Conservatives in 2017 claimed they would abandon the party if he became leader. Although three Scottish Conservative MPs argued that Johnson's 'moderate and modern conservatism' would complement that of Davidson,[126] most Scottish Conservatives found the leadership contest traumatic, particularly after three relatively harmonious and successful years. 'Looking at this sh*t show,' one senior figure told the *Daily Record*, 'I'm not sure I could vote for us. I don't know how anyone else is expected to be able to.'[127] The SNP, meanwhile, had revived its pre-devolution rallying cry of 'no mandate', stressing that since 2010 the Conservatives led a government Scotland had not 'voted for'.

It did not help that a YouGov survey of Conservative members found 63 per cent would back Brexit even if it meant Scotland leaving the UK (a figure that would rise in the months ahead). Davidson wearily told party members to 'take a long, hard look at themselves', arguing that the 2016 referendum result ought to be delivered, just 'not at the expense of breaking up the UK'.[128] As the commentator Andy McIver put it: 'In England, it's Conservative first, Unionist second; in Scotland, it's Unionist first, Conservative second, and that is manifesting itself in a very difficult way for the Scottish Tory Party.'[129] A series of parliamentary votes on Brexit had seen the 13 Scottish Conservative MPs move towards a harder line than Davidson had promoted. In the first 'meaningful vote', two had been among 118 rebels voting against the government; by the second this was reduced to one; and by the third vote no Scottish Tory MP was opposed.[130]

Luke Graham, one of the 2017 Scottish MP intake, believed the 'paucity of Scottish Conservatives pre-2017' had rendered Westminster 'complicit' in a Scottish nationalist 'agenda', 'rushing to devolve more and more powers to Scotland and Wales without considering the full economic, social and cultural impact'.[131] Even Theresa May had spoken of a tendency to 'devolve and forget'. Graham and others particularly resented the Scottish Government's perceived incursion into 'reserved' territory, i.e. international affairs. This informed what might be called the 'New Unionism', a multi-point agenda articulated by several Scottish Conservatives at Westminster. The Stirling MP Stephen Kerr proposed primary legislation to enable 'direct UK government spending in devolved areas in partnership with devolved administrations'; an 'urgent review' of English Votes for English Laws; and 'detailed proposals to replace EU regional funding' with 'a UK-level fund',[132] all of which ultimately came to pass.[133]

Towards the end of his term as Scottish Secretary, meanwhile, David Mundell announced that a new UK Government 'hub' in Edinburgh would be called 'Queen Elizabeth House', complete with 'dedicated Cabinet room, the first of its kind outside of London'. He viewed this as a 'focal point' to boost awareness of the UK Government's work in Scotland. 'The UK Government needs to make the case every day for what it does in Scotland,' he said after leaving the Cabinet, 'the way the Scottish Government makes the case every day for independence.'[134] Mike Kenny and Jack Sheldon identified 'a new ethos of unionist activism' involving 'the central state making and showing the case for Union, seeking to do much more to wean people away from nationalist politics by demonstrating the tangible benefits it can supply'.[135] All this suggested a move away from what Alan Convery identified as 'devo-pragmatism' (typified by Ruth Davidson after 2012) towards 'ultra-unionism', there being only a few 'radical reformers', quasi-federalists such as Murdo Fraser.[136] Boris Johnson, meanwhile, praised the 'awesome foursome' (the UK) and made himself 'Minister for the Union', a piece of symbolism borrowed from Canadian federalists.[137]

Davidson was reportedly 'livid' at the sacking of her ally David Mundell as Secretary of State for Scotland. Alister Jack succeeded him, although the appointment of Robin Walker, an

MP with an English constituency, as one of his junior ministers (the first since A. J. Balfour in 1886) provoked such a backlash that Gordon MP Colin Clark, an early backer of Johnson, was later added to the team.[138] Davidson used a newspaper column to assert that her 'position exists independently of government. I don't have to sign a no-deal pledge to continue to serve.'[139] A Commons vote in July 2019 on legalising abortion and same-sex marriage in Northern Ireland also highlighted that social liberalism had not fully permeated the Scottish Conservative group of MPs. Six voted against abortion and five against same-sex marriage.[140]

Then, on 29 August 2019, Ruth Davidson announced her immediate resignation. 'You all know – and I have never sought to hide – the conflict I have felt over Brexit,' she said in a statement, which avoided any criticism of the Prime Minister or his controversial move to prorogue Parliament. She later admitted her departure had 'been a long time coming', that the 'fire that had kept me slugging it out for all these years … had somehow become dimmed'.[141] Nevertheless, Davidson took care to leave open the prospect of 'a second act'.[142] There was a general consensus that Jackson Carlaw, who once again became acting leader, should take over without a contest, but instead he faced a challenge from right-wing MSP Michelle Ballantyne.

As the journalist Alex Massie observed, Davidson had been 'the beneficiary of a great realignment of Scottish politics in which the dividing lines ceased to be between left and right and were instead between nationalist and Unionist', and thus her resignation deprived 'her party and, more importantly, Unionism of its most compelling champion',[143] an unequivocally Scottish 'leader of stature', as Chris Stevens had put it in 1990. As the BBC's Sarah Smith commented, Davidson's unique selling point had always been that 'she doesn't look like and doesn't sound like a Tory'.[144] Even Murdo Fraser admitted he had underestimated his opponent in 2011, but with 'a combination of energy, charisma, and a great deal of effort, she took the Scottish Conservatives from political irrelevance to being the second force in Scottish politics': 'By making the Conservatives the party of the Union, we were able to garner the votes of many of those who would not in the past have considered supporting us.'[145]

Indeed, this remained the dividing line as voters elected a new House of Commons for the third time in four years.

Analysis suggested almost half the Scots electorate believed the UK's departure from the EU to be the most important issue in terms of how they voted.[146] Ailsa Henderson has observed that by 2019, Scottish voters had become divided into four 'tribes': Yes Remainers, Yes Leavers, No Remainers and No Leavers. 'The SNP's hunt for votes was mostly confined to the two Yes tribes, and the transformation of the Scottish Conservatives from a Remain-supporting to a hard Brexit party meant that it was likely to fare best with "No Leavers".'[147] As the Brexit deadline (later extended) of 31 October 2019 approached, the Scottish party continued to stress the need for a deal, that is until shortly before the Conservative Party autumn conference when Jackson Carlaw signalled a U-turn:

> Another extension, another three months, with nobody really agreeing on what they would do during that [time] or what the outcome would be, is far more damaging for Scotland, for the United Kingdom and for business, for everybody, than finally getting to a point where we resolve this issue and move on.[148]

Reports suggested Carlaw had failed to inform the Scottish Conservative shadow cabinet, provoking 'cold fury' among some colleagues.[149]

'Where the message in the rest of the UK is "Get Brexit Done",' wrote now former Scottish Conservative leader Ruth Davidson shortly before polling day, 'in Scotland it is "No to Indyref 2". They are two sides of the same coin.'[150] A focus group conducted in Dunblane found that voters believed 'an overall Tory majority would stop the SNP'. Ruth Davidson, despite no longer being leader, featured heavily on party literature, while Jackson Carlaw faced the election unconfirmed as party leader and with a relatively low profile, not least because his party had been built around Davidson since the independence referendum. SNP posters, meanwhile, featured the top of Boris Johnson's head with the declaration: 'It's time to decide.'

As the campaign progressed, however, Scottish Conservatives became increasingly confident they would not only hold but indeed gain seats. But given the volatility of the past few months and the fact they were defending several highly marginal seats, polling day represented the first setback the party had experienced since 2015. It went from 13 to six MPs although its share of the vote remained steady at 25 per cent. A 3.5 per cent swing away from the Conservatives had been enough to lose them Aberdeen South, Angus, Ayr, Carrick and Cumnock, East Renfrewshire, Gordon, Ochil and South Perthshire and Stirling. 'The party came out of the 2019 election depressed,' recalled an adviser. 'Our six MPs were irrelevant given Boris's majority.'[151]

Jackson Carlaw was confirmed as Scottish Conservative leader on 14 February 2020, comfortably defeating Michelle Ballantyne, who had not won public backing from any MPs or MSPs, by 4,917 votes to 1,581. She had criticised Carlaw's single-issue focus on independence during the general election, something generally acknowledged as having been a mistake. Carlaw promised a policy review to offer 'a fresh narrative for the union', while indicating that he had 'already said to Boris Johnson that, as leader, when I think Scotland's interests require me to speak out, I will'.[152]

This was an attempt to maintain necessary distance between the Scottish and UK parties, but that was to become increasingly difficult. When Carlaw (as acting leader) had visited the Prime Minister at Downing Street in October 2019, 'Boris was of the view that "muscular unionism" was the way to go'.[153] This was the most ubiquitous of the phrases scholars had used since 2018 to describe a shift in the Conservative Party's approach to the UK's 'territorial code', among them 'hyper-unionism', 'know-your-place unionism' and 'Anglo-centric British nationalism'.[154] The central planks of 'muscular unionism' were largely those identified by Scottish Conservative MPs between 2017 and 2019. 'English Votes for English Laws' was suspended in April 2020 and abolished the following year, but the *Internal Market Act 2020*, which received Royal Assent towards the end of that year, was its main legislative manifestation. Vehemently opposed by the Scottish and Welsh Governments, who alleged a 'power grab', this laid claim to state aid as a reserved matter and equipped the UK Government with the ability to spend money in devolved areas. Without much enthusiasm, the Scottish Conservative Party acquiesced.

But before all this came Covid-19, a seismic event which, among other things, led to Jackson Carlaw's downfall after only a few months as leader. According to a senior party strategist, he 'overcompensated, doing the statesmanlike thing and backing Nicola Sturgeon' in her efforts to combat the pandemic. 'It meant we [the party] couldn't then criticise her. That bred discontent in the MP and MSP group.'[155] By this point, the former MP Luke Graham was also running Downing Street's 'Union Unit' and pushing for a more aggressive response to the SNP. Compounding matters was the fact that even Scottish Conservative voters 'thought Nicola was amazing and doing a good job ... they viewed her as a maternal figure'. Jackson Carlaw, however, 'was not Nicola Sturgeon'.[156] Polls also indicated that support for independence was rising, leading many in the party to fear losing its 2016 gains at the next Holyrood election in May 2021.

In May 2020, the Moray MP Douglas Ross, who had been appointed a Scotland Office minister in December 2019, resigned over prime ministerial adviser Dominic Cummings having broken lockdown rules. And when the part-time football referee made an effective speech in the Commons attacking the SNP, momentum gathered for him to replace Carlaw as leader. Ross was initially reluctant, given he was not an MSP, but when Carlaw resigned on 30 July 2020 to make way for a 'younger and fresher voice', he announced his candidacy the following day. Ross was elected unopposed on 5 August, with Ruth Davidson – still an MSP despite having been nominated for a peerage – agreeing to handle the weekly First Minister's Questions at Holyrood. Ross said he would contest the North-East Scotland list in 2021.[157] Ross's only policy departure was to end his party's opposition to 'free' tuition fees in October 2020, thus bringing the Scottish Conservatives into line with every other party at Holyrood.[158]

The 2021 Scottish Parliament election campaign was aided by donations from Robin MacGeachy and his wife, former Labour voters in Eastwood who had backed Brexit and ended up supporting the Scottish Conservatives because of Ruth Davidson's leadership.[159] This meant the Conservatives could outspend the other unionist parties while repeating its well-worn message from the 2017 and 2019 UK general elections: 'You helped us stop a referendum in 2019, let's stop it again in 2021.'[160] The party's biggest concern, ironically, was former Labour MP George Galloway's 'Alliance for Union', although in the event his brand of 'radicalised Unionism' proved a damp squib.

On polling day the Scottish Conservatives lost two constituency seats, Ayr and Edinburgh Central (which had been gained by Ruth Davidson in 2016), although its constituency vote only dipped by 0.1 per cent, while it gained its highest-ever share on the regional list with 23.5 per cent. The outcome – 31 MSPs – defied expectations but confirmed that unionist votes remained more important than ideologically Conservative support. 'Our biggest increase was in the east end of Glasgow,' recalled a party strategist. 'It was the first time I was conscious that the Orange Order had mobilised behind us via their Unionist Clubs. We took their votes but didn't engage with them.'[161] Such a connection had also been alleged in 2016–17, even though the Orange Lodge of Scotland protested that most of its members were Labour supporters, including six who had been elected as councillors.[162] More broadly, Professor Sir John Curtice believed tactical voting had benefited Conservatives in the same way it had once worked against them.[163]

The election result deprived the SNP of an overall majority and thus got Boris Johnson out of a tight spot in terms of pressure to concede a second independence referendum. The Prime Minister had been unusually engaged during the campaign, calling Scottish party strategists daily to keep across the polling and expectations. At this point, Ruth Davidson finally joined the House of Lords while Luke Graham left Downing Street's Union Unit. He was briefly succeeded by Oliver Lewis (known as 'Sonic'), but when he also departed, Lord McInnes, the longstanding director of the Scottish Conservative Party, took on the job in September 2021 to general acclaim.

The previous month, the Prime Minister had demonstrated what many saw as his toxicity by joking that 'thanks to Margaret Thatcher' closing 'so many coal mines across the country', the UK had 'had a big early start' on tackling climate change. According to BBC Scotland, Johnson then laughed and told reporters: 'I thought that would get you going.' It certainly did that, with Nicola Sturgeon condemning his remarks as 'crass and deeply insensitive'.[164] Scottish Conservatives had long expressed concerns about the impact of a Johnson premiership and in January 2022 Douglas Ross called on the Prime Minister to resign over the long-running 'Partygate' scandal. Asked to respond on the BBC's *Newsnight*, Jacob Rees-Mogg, the Leader of the House of Commons, said the Scottish Conservative leader had 'always been quite a lightweight figure'.[165] Muscular unionism would not even spare its own. But after Russia invaded Ukraine, Ross changed his mind: the Prime Minister, he said, should now remain in post to lead the UK's response.

When the Scottish Conservatives lost 63 seats and 5.6 per cent of the vote at the 2022 local government elections, Ross was quick to blame Partygate for the poor performance, although others suggest his unclear stance on Johnson's future was the real explanation. Some of the party's heaviest losses were in Glasgow, where it went from eight to two councillors, and in Perth and Kinross, where it lost control of the council to the SNP. The Scottish Labour Party, now led by Anas Sarwar, had beaten the Conservatives into second place, an important psychological victory for one of the other parties of the Union. After the local government elections, Craig Hoy MSP replaced Rab Forman as Scottish party chairman, while Ross appointed Meghan Gallacher MSP his deputy. The product of a Lanarkshire steel town and independence-supporting parents, Gallacher's university dissertation had focused on the decline of the Scottish Conservatives.[166]

Life for Douglas Ross did not get any easier. In September, the *Scottish Sun* reported that two groups of Conservative MSPs were plotting moves to oust him as leader following a series of 'gaffes'. Ross's chief of staff, head of digital and director of communications had all recently departed, while an offer of employment to Craig Paterson, who claimed to have worked for ex-Scottish Labour leader Jim Murphy, was withdrawn after the media discovered that claim was false. Others complained that Ross was trying to do too much as an MP, MSP and party leader. He risked, claimed anonymous briefings, 'being continually buffeted by events at Westminster'. Polling, meanwhile, suggested the party would face another 1997-style wipeout at the UK general election.[167]

Interviewed in October 2022, Ross acknowledged 'challenges' but pointed to the 2021 Holyrood result as 'the best-ever election result we've had in Scotland since devolution'. Asked if he remained confident of winning a £50 bet he had made with Nicola Sturgeon as to who would quit first, Ross replied in the affirmative.[168] The Scottish Conservative leader remained neutral in the UK leadership race that followed Boris Johnson's resignation as Prime Minister. Although Rishi Sunak had enjoyed positive approval ratings in Scotland as Chancellor, others recalled him arguing that 'England should break away' from a Union which did not 'make financial sense'.[169] While Liz Truss had purposefully ignored Nicola Sturgeon during her brief premiership, Sunak made a point of calling the First Minister on his first day in office. Taking the long view, Iain McLean said the new Prime Minister 'would be wise to choose vanilla over muscular unionism', respecting the Sewel Convention and respecting 'the entrenchment of devolution'.[170]

When in November 2022 the Supreme Court unequivocally ruled that the Scottish Parliament did not have the legislative authority to hold a second independence referendum, the response of Conservatives – both in Scotland and at Westminster – was studiously understated. A prolonged row over Scottish plans for the reform of gender recognition laws also found Alister Jack, the Conservative Secretary of State for Scotland, confident enough to 'veto' devolved legislation via section 35 of the *Scotland Act 1998*. This was a calculated risk, although opinion polling later found majority support for the move – even among a sizeable minority of SNP supporters.[171]

The UK Conservative Party was also privately jubilant when Nicola Sturgeon announced her resignation as SNP leader and First Minister in February 2023, although Scottish Conservatives were conscious it might provide space for a Labour recovery in Scotland. 'As a unionist, I'm delighted,' one Scottish Conservative MP told the *Spectator*. 'But as a Conservative, it's a nightmare.'[172] Douglas Ross, however, found himself £50 better off. As the SNP entered a turbulent period, polling indeed revealed an increase in those intending to vote Labour at the UK general election due by the end of 2024. When the former Brexit negotiator Lord Frost suggested that the SNP's 'implosion' was 'a chance to put failing devolution into reverse', senior Scottish Conservatives reacted angrily. Murdo Fraser said devolution had allowed his party 'to shine a light on SNP failures … Conservatives will not be rolling it back', while the Central Scotland MSP Stephen Kerr tweeted: 'Devolution works. It's the SNP that are failing.'[173] A quarter of a century after the 1998 devolution referendum, Conservatives in Scotland still found themselves attempting to navigate complicated political and constitutional terrain.

NOTES

1. C. P. Stevens (1990), 'Scottish Conservatism – A failure of organisation?', in A. Brown and R. Parry (eds), *The Scottish Government Yearbook 1990*, Edinburgh: Edinburgh University Press, 86.

2. R. Davidson (2018), *Yes She Can: Why Women Own the Future*, London: Hodder & Stoughton, 11–13.
3. Davidson had spent a year running Annabel Goldie's office at Holyrood prior to the 2011 elections. There were also controversial moves to ensure Davidson was top of the Glasgow regional list. See A. Convery (2014), 'The 2011 Scottish Conservative Party leadership election: Dilemmas for statewide parties in regional contexts', *Parliamentary Affairs* 67:2, 306–27.
4. *Guardian*, 5 September 2011.
5. Names under consideration included the 'Scottish Unionists', as it was 'consistent' with the party's pre-1965 history, and the 'Progressive Conservatives', which also drew on its local government heritage (*Scotland on Sunday*, 2 October 2011).
6. D. Torrance (2012), 'Centenary blues: 100 Years of Scottish Conservatism', in D. Torrance (ed.), *Whatever Happened to Tory Scotland?*, Edinburgh: Edinburgh University Press, 8–9.
7. A. Convery (2014), 319.
8. *Scotsman*, 24 November 2012.
9. D. Torrance (2020), '"Ruth Davidson's Conservatives", 2011–19', in D. Torrance (ed.), *Ruth Davidson's Conservatives: The Scottish Tory Party, 2011–19*, Edinburgh: Edinburgh University Press, 3.
10. *Herald*, 10 November 2012.
11. A. Cochrane (2014), *The Cochrane Diaries – Alex Salmond: My Part in His Downfall*, London: Biteback, 85.
12. *Scotland on Sunday*, 2 June 2013.
13. See J. Mitchell and A. Convery (2012), 'Conservative Unionism: Prisoned in marble', in D. Torrance (ed.), *Whatever Happened to Tory Scotland?*, Edinburgh: Edinburgh University Press, 170–84.
14. A. Seldon and P. Snowdon (2015), *Cameron at 10: The Inside Story 2010–2015*, London: William Collins, 126–7.
15. 'Sir John Major dresses in tartan for devolution argument', BBC News online, 9 July 2011.
16. A. Seldon and P. Snowdon (2015), 126–7.
17. D. Cameron (2019), *For the Record*, London: William Collins, 315–17.
18. J. Pike (2015), *Project Fear: How an Unlikely Alliance Left a Kingdom United but a Country Divided*, London: Biteback, 16.
19. See D. Torrance (2013), 'The Scottish Conservatives and the 2014 Independence Referendum', in K. Adamson and P. Lynch (eds), *Scottish Political Parties and the 2014 Independence Referendum*, Cardiff: Welsh Academic Press.
20. This campaign also allowed the Scottish Conservatives to acquire the contact details of around 70,000 pro-Union supporters, a

database that would prove crucial at the 2016 Holyrood election. See A. Liddle (2018), *Ruth Davidson and the Resurgence of the Scottish Tories*, London: Biteback, 9.

21. *Scotsman*, 17 February 2012.
22. See A. Convery (2014), 'Devolution and the limits of Tory statecraft: The Conservative Party in coalition and Scotland and Wales', *Parliamentary Affairs* 67:1.
23. D. Torrance (2020), '*Standing Up for Scotland*': *Nationalist Unionism and Scottish Party Politics, 1884–2014*, Edinburgh: Edinburgh University Press, 93.
24. U. Cameron (2019), 316.
25. D. Torrance (2020), 93.
26. D. Torrance (2020), 93.
27. D. Torrance (2020), 93.
28. Lord Strathclyde, now Leader of the Lords, had also chaired a 1997 commission on Scottish Conservative organisational reform.
29. *Scotsman*, 27 May 2013.
30. A. Liddle (2018), 148.
31. Scottish Parliament Official Report, 20 November 2013.
32. See J. Thomson (2020), '"A lesbian with family values": Gender and sexuality in Ruth Davidson's leadership of the contemporary Scottish Conservative Party', in D. Torrance (ed.), *Ruth Davidson's Conservatives: The Scottish Tory Party, 2011–19*, Edinburgh: Edinburgh University Press, 105.
33. D. Torrance (2020), 5–6.
34. *Herald*, 17 March 2014.
35. A. Convery (ed.) (2016), *Light Blue: Policy Adventures for Scottish Conservatives*, Edinburgh: Edinburgh University Press, 4.
36. D. Torrance (2020), 6.
37. A. Convery (2014), 'A new direction for the Conservatives on devolution?', University of Edinburgh blog, 3 June.
38. SCUP (2014), *Commission on the Future Governance of Scotland*, Edinburgh: Scottish Conservative and Unionist Party, 3–4.
39. *Scotland on Sunday*, 1 June 2014.
40. See D. Patrick (2020), 'Riding the Unionist wave: Ruth Davidson, the media and the re-emergence of the Scottish Conservatives', in D. Torrance (ed.), *Ruth Davidson's Conservatives: The Scottish Tory Party, 2011–19*, Edinburgh: Edinburgh University Press, 107–25.
41. The former Scottish Conservative MSP Nick Johnston said he would vote 'Yes', while the Independent Conservative councillor Peter de Vink and historian Michael Fry (who had left the party

in 2007) formed a centre-right, pro-independence group called 'Wealthy Nation'.

42. A. Liddle (2018), 175–6.
43. D. Law (2016), *Coalition: The Inside Story of the Conservative–Liberal Democrat Coalition Government*, London: Biteback, 512–13.
44. J. Pike (2015), 215.
45. J. Pike (2015), 197.
46. S. Mcintyre, J. Mitchell and G. Roy (2022), 'Careful what you wish for? Risk and reward with Scottish tax devolution', *Political Quarterly* 93:3.
47. D. Torrance (2020), 3–4.
48. *Scottish Daily Mail*, 1 October 2014.
49. A. Liddle (2018), 166.
50. *Scottish Daily Express*, 26 April 2015.
51. See T. Bale (2010), *The Conservative Party: From Thatcher to Cameron*, Cambridge: Polity.
52. *Scottish Daily Mail*, 9 April 2015.
53. T. Shipman (2017), *Fall Out: A Year of Political Mayhem*, London: William Collins, 384.
54. T. Shipman (2017), 385.
55. J. Mitchell (2015), 'Sea change in Scotland', in A. Geddes and J. Tonge (eds), *Britain Votes 2015*, Oxford: Oxford University Press, 100.
56. *Sunday Herald*, 10 May 2015.
57. D. Torrance (2020), 9.
58. *Daily Record*, 7 December 2015.
59. D. Torrance (2020), 9.
60. D. Torrance (2020), 9.
61. ICCFTS (2016), *A Dynamic Scotland*, Edinburgh: Independent Commission for Competitive and Fair Taxation in Scotland.
62. J. Pike (2015), 287.
63. See A. Gray and A. Tomkins (2005), *How We Should Rule Ourselves*, Edinburgh: Canongate.
64. *Financial Times*, 6 March 2016.
65. BBC News online, 6 May 2016.
66. *Daily Record*, 6 May 2016.
67. *Telegraph*, 7 May 2016.
68. M. Diffley (2020), 'Tory revival in Scotland? Recent evidence, future prospects', in D. Torrance (ed.), *Ruth Davidson's Conservatives: The Scottish Tory Party, 2011–19*, Edinburgh: Edinburgh University Press, 33.
69. *Telegraph*, 20 June 2016.
70. OpenDemocracy website, 19 May 2017.

71. D. Torrance (2020), 11.
72. A. Liddle (2018), 247.
73. A. Convery (2020), 'The Scottish Conservative Party', in M. Keating (ed.), *The Oxford Handbook of Scottish Politics*, Oxford: Oxford University Press, 251.
74. *Telegraph*, 5 October 2016.
75. R. Hayton (2020), 'The Conservative "Territorial Code" under strain', in D. Torrance (ed.), *Ruth Davidson's Conservatives: The Scottish Tory Party, 2011–19*, Edinburgh: Edinburgh University Press, 132.
76. *Telegraph*, 5 October 2016.
77. *Independent*, 23 June 2016.
78. *Independent*, 13 July 2016.
79. MailOnline, 15 September 2016.
80. A. Convery (ed.) (2016), 4.
81. J. Mitchell (2016), 'Tories smiling but challenges ahead', Centre on Constitutional Change blog, 10 May 2016.
82. D. Torrance (2020), 12.
83. *Financial Times*, 4 March 2017.
84. *Guardian*, 12 June 2015.
85. G. Hassan (2018), 'Still differently, only slightly less so: Scotland', in P. Cowley and D. Kavanagh (eds), *The British General Election of 2017*, London: Palgrave Macmillan, 141.
86. D. Torrance (2020), 13.
87. A. Henderson and J. Mitchell (2018), 'Referendums as critical junctures? Scottish voting in British elections', in J. Tonge et al. (eds), *Britain Votes 2017*, Oxford: Oxford University Press, 117.
88. *Observer*, 29 April 2017.
89. See M. Diffley (2020), 35.
90. MailOnline, 23 April 2017.
91. *Scotsman*, 2 May 2017.
92. *Daily Record*, 24 April 2017.
93. D. Torrance (2020), 15.
94. T. Shipman (2017), 385.
95. G. Hassan (2018), 139.
96. J. Tonge, C. Leston-Bandeira and S. Wilks-Heeg (eds) (2018), *Britain Votes 2017*, Oxford: Oxford University Press, 2.
97. D. Torrance (2020), 15.
98. T. Ross and T. McTague (2017), *Betting the House: The Inside Story of the 2017 Election*, London: Biteback, 334.
99. A. Henderson and J. Mitchell (2018), 120 & 123.
100. One source told the journalist Tim Shipman that the Scottish Conservatives might actually have done better had the UK cam-

paign been more of a success: 'it cost the Scottish Tories five seats (T. Shipman, 2017, 422–3).

101. *Scottish Mail on Sunday*, 11 June 2017.
102. BuzzFeed, 10 June 2017.
103. See P. Gourtsoyannis (2020), '"Standing up for Scotland" at Westminster?', in D. Torrance (ed.), *Ruth Davidson's Conservatives: The Scottish Tory Party, 2011–19*, Edinburgh: Edinburgh University Press, 60.
104. A. Henderson and J. Mitchell (2018), 120.
105. D. Torrance (2020), 16.
106. *Guardian*, 3 May 2019.
107. *Spectator*, 13 December 2017.
108. *Sunday Herald*, 4 February 2018.
109. D. Torrance (2020), 18.
110. J. Mitchell and A. Henderson (2020), 'Tribes and turbulence: The 2019 UK General Election in Scotland', in J. Tonge, S. Wilks-Heeg and L. Thompson (eds), *Britain Votes: The 2019 General Election*, Oxford: Oxford University Press, 149.
111. HC Deb 4 Dec 2017 Vol. 632 c733.
112. P. Gourtsoyannis (2020), 61.
113. *Mirror*, 19 March 2018.
114. Since 2016, David Mundell's son Oliver had been a Member of the Scottish Parliament.
115. P. Gourtsoyannis (2020), 62–6.
116. *Sunday Times*, 16 September 2018.
117. *Sunday Express*, 23 September 2018.
118. *Telegraph*, 1 October 2018.
119. *The Times*, 23 March 2019.
120. *Holyrood*, 22 February 2019.
121. D. Torrance (2020), 23.
122. Davidson responded in kind: 'I have never had a problem standing up to the alpha males in my party. I wonder whether the First Minister has always been able to say the same' (Scottish Parliament Official Report, 22 May 2019).
123. *Scotsman*, 29 July 2018.
124. *Financial Times*, 29 August 2019.
125. *Guardian*, 2 October 2018.
126. *Telegraph*, 23 June 2019.
127. *Daily Record*, 11 June 2019.
128. BBC News online, 18 June 2019.
129. BBC Radio 4, 28 July 2019.
130. A. Henderson (2021), 'The devolved nations: Scotland', in R. Ford, T. Bale, W. Jennings and P. Surridge (eds), *The British General Election of 2019*, London: Palgrave Macmillan, 423.

131. L. Graham (2019), 'The modern Briton', in G. Freeman (ed.),
     Britain Beyond Brexit, London: Centre for Policy Studies, 34.
132. *Scotsman*, 24 July 2019.
133. For a more recent attempt to articulate the New Unionism, see
     A. Bowie MP (2021), *Strength in Union: The Case for the United
     Kingdom*, London: Centre for Policy Studies.
134. *Scotland on Sunday*, 28 July 2019.
135. M. Kenny and J. Sheldon (2019), 'What was Boris up to in
     Scotland?', Centre on Constitutional Change blog, 9 September
     2019.
136. A. Convery (2020), 'The Scottish Conservative Party and
     the three Unionisms', in D. Torrance (ed.), *Ruth Davidson's
     Conservatives: The Scottish Tory Party, 2011–19*, Edinburgh:
     Edinburgh University Press, 139.
137. P. Gourtsoyannis (2020), 72.
138. *Sunday Times*, 28 July 2019.
139. *Scottish Mail on Sunday*, 28 July 2019.
140. See J. Evershed (2020), 'Scottish Conservatism and Northern
     Ireland: Mapping an ambivalent relationship', in D. Torrance
     (ed.), *Ruth Davidson's Conservatives: The Scottish Tory Party,
     2011–19*, Edinburgh: Edinburgh University Press, 162–3.
141. *Scottish Mail on Sunday*, 1 September 2019.
142. *Evening Standard*, 23 October 2019.
143. *Sunday Times*, 1 September 2019.
144. BBC News online, 29 August 2019.
145. *Scotsman*, 3 September 2019.
146. *The Times*, 6 December 2019.
147. A. Henderson (2021), 430.
148. BBC News online, 30 September 2019.
149. *Telegraph*, 30 September 2019.
150. *The Times*, 9 December 2019.
151. Anonymous interview, 26 October 2022.
152. *Guardian*, 14 February 2020.
153. Anonymous interview, 26 October 2022.
154. M. Sandford (2023), '"Muscular unionism": The British political
     tradition strikes back?', *Political Studies* 71:2.
155. Anonymous interview, 26 October 2022.
156. Anonymous interview, 26 October 2022.
157. The SNP criticised this arrangement even though it mirrored
     closely what had happened when Alex Salmond was re-elected
     leader of his party in 2004 and Nicola Sturgeon led the party at
     Holyrood until his return as an MSP in 2007.
158. See 'Scottish Conservatives U-turn on university tuition fees',
     Holyrood, 6 October 2020.

159. *The National*, 20 February 2020.
160. SCUP (2021), *Rebuild Scotland: The Scottish Conservative and Unionist Party Manifesto 2021*, Edinburgh: Scottish Conservative and Unionist Party.
161. Anonymous interview, 26 October 2022. At the 2019 general election, the unsuccessful Conservative candidate in Lanark and Hamilton East confidently declared it a 'solid unionist royalist Rangers supporting heartland' (*The Times*, 9 December 2019).
162. *Herald*, 7 May 2017.
163. *Scotsman*, 10 May 2021.
164. Politico, 6 August 2021.
165. 'Jacob Rees-Mogg calls Scottish Tory leader a "lightweight"', BBC News online, 13 January 2022.
166. *Daily Record*, 21 July 2014.
167. *Herald*, 5 October 2022.
168. *Scotland on Sunday*, 30 October 2022.
169. *Financial Times*, 2 April 2020. A spokesman for the then Chancellor said he could not recollect such remarks.
170. I. McLean (2022), 'Can muscular unionism save the Union?', Constitution Unit blog, 3 November 2022.
171. 'Attitudes to the UK Government's blocking of the Gender Recognition bill', Ipsos Scotland, 7 February 2023.
172. *Spectator*, 18 February 2023.
173. *Daily Record*, 20 April 2023.

Conclusion

The striking thing to have emerged from this history of the Scottish Conservative and Unionist parties is the persistence of certain themes. The view of Conservatism as somehow 'alien' or an English imposition, for example, was as much a feature of late 19th-century Scottish political discourse as it was in the closing decades of the 20th. As a consequence, the expression 'Conservative' or 'Tory' came to be seen as a pejorative term, although again this was nothing new, the label having been dropped in 1912 on that basis. Even jokes regarding the party's weakness have a certain familiarity. During the 19th century it was humorously posited that all Scotland's Conservatives could fit inside a single train carriage; in the early 21st century it was said that there were more pandas in Edinburgh Zoo. There is rarely anything new, it might be said, under the political sun.

The other half of the party's identity – 'Unionist' – speaks to another persistent theme: an appeal beyond ideology to a concept of 'nation', which in the United Kingdom's case has long been multiple. There was usually more than one Union at play, respectively regal, Anglo-Scottish, British-Irish, Imperial and, during the 20th century, the idea of what might be called a 'social union' between the different classes which inhabited all those broader constructs. A major preoccupation for Scottish Conservative and Unionists, therefore, was how to navigate (and balance) nation, nationality and nationalism. Sometimes they succeeded, at other points they badly misjudged public opinion in Scotland.

PLAYING THE 'SCOTTISH' CARD

Between the late 1960s and the early 2010s, a perception of the Scottish Conservative and Unionist Party as essentially 'English' in leadership and character became axiomatic. Even its own managers worried that it had become little more than a 'branch office' or 'satellite' of the London-based party. Yet until 1965 the Scottish Unionist Party, as it was between 1912 and 1965, was perhaps the most autonomous of the three main 'unionist' parties contesting elections in Scotland (the others being Labour and the Liberals in their various guises).

Not only was it autonomous, but the party made a point of asserting its 'independence' from London, believing this – and particularly the party's distinct Scottish identity and name – to be a necessary feature of electoral success. This instinct was not purely organisational, for its championing of Scotland's distinctiveness within the United Kingdom and a promotion of greater autonomy spans the party's existence. In the 1850s it was the Earl of Eglinton's cultural nationalism and in the mid-1880s the championing of what became known as 'administrative devolution', the demand for a specific department and minister for Scotland to safeguard its interests at Westminster.

This 'nationalist unionism' was also articulated in 1914, during the early 1930s and after the Second World War, all with a view to extending that administrative autonomy. And while the party's red line was usually any diminishment of parliamentary sovereignty, Scottish Conservatives were not dogmatic. There was a surprising willingness to contemplate legislative devolution after the First World War (though preferably as part of 'Home Rule all Round'), while in the late 1960s Edward Heath took the party's long-standing commitment to administrative devolution to its logical conclusion in his 'Declaration of Perth'. In the latter case, the policy suffered not only as a result of significant opposition within the Scottish party, but because of a tendency 'to revert to a policy of inaction as soon as the immediate external pressure prompting the adoption of a devolutionary perspective died away'.[1]

It is too simplistic, however, to draw a consistent line between Scottish Conservative support for constitutional reform and electoral success. Playing the Scottish card, it might be said, was necessary but not sufficient. Lord Salisbury's attempt to 'redress the wounded dignities of the Scotch people' in 1884–5 made little difference to the party's then weakness north of the border, while Scottish Unionism peaked in 1924 without much of a distinctly Scottish agenda or policy. But when the party's nationalist unionism aligned with other factors, there is clear evidence of a beneficial effect, particularly in the period between the late 1930s and mid-1950s, when the Scottish Unionists were perceived by voters as credible 'vehicles' for (and protectors of) Scottish distinctiveness within the Union. Advocating 'Scottish Control of Scottish Affairs' paid particular dividends at the general elections of 1950, 1951 and 1955.

Yet when the stars were not aligned, playing the Scottish card made little difference. Elections in the early 1970s, for example, suggested Heath's commitment to a Scottish Assembly had failed to boost his party's fortunes north of the border. Indeed, the experience of the 1979 and 1992 elections even suggested there was support to be gained from *opposing* devolution. By 1997, however, the Overton Window had shifted, leaving the Scottish Conservatives stranded on the periphery.[2] This suggested the party had to get ahead of the constitutional curve, something it finally managed prior to the independence referendum of 2014. Once the party learned to stop worrying and love devolution – and more of it – the basis of an electoral recovery was laid. In this respect, Welsh Conservatives had pointed the way a decade earlier.

Unionism has long been a multi-faceted ideology. Indeed, it was the Conservatives who had promoted what Graeme Morton called 'Unionist Nationalism' in mid-19th-century civic Scotland. From then until the 1960s, Unionism represented a tradition that combined respect for Scottish heritage and distinctiveness – voters were repeatedly assured that their 'Scottishness' could find its truest and fullest expression within the Union. This changed in the 1970s, when the UK party leadership (chiefly but not exclusively Margaret Thatcher) cooled on the idea of devolution and found itself increasingly detached from a Scottish polity in which the constitutional question assumed an ever-increasing salience during the 1980s and 1990s.

Even after a Scottish Parliament was established in 1999, the Scottish party (unlike the Welsh) appeared grudging participants. They were reminded constantly of their opposition to devolution, just as resistance to franchise reform in 1832 had hindered the 19th-century party's recovery for several decades.

Conservatives would do well to remember that Scottish voters have long memories. Only between 2012 and 2014 did Scottish Conservatism begin to move beyond rather 'banal unionism' and proactively articulate a defence of the increasingly embattled Anglo-Scottish Union; to develop, in other words, what Convery has called a 'philosophy of devolution'. This was accompanied by an intriguing shift in the discourse. Until 1999 a political 'unionist' was anyone opposed to a Scottish Parliament; after 2011 it had come to mean anyone opposed to independence. Each definition had embraced a different mix of parties – the only constant was the Scottish Conservative and Unionist Party.

Ironically, therefore, the independence referendum of 2014 allowed Scottish Conservatives, hitherto 'imprisoned in marble', to carve out a new path – one with a deep provenance – which combined a strong defence of Scotland's place in the Union with an advocacy of greater fiscal autonomy. The political 'sweet spot' came in effectively combining Conservative fiscal policy with a forward-looking constitutional agenda. An intriguing 'what if' thus presents itself: what if Mrs Thatcher had championed rather than rejected legislative devolution after 1979, harnessing it as a vehicle for an individualist self-help policy agenda to which Scottish voters were not necessarily opposed? Instead, the party (and particularly the Scottish Office) had contrived to 'stand up for Scotland' against its own party leaders and, of course, the Prime Minister herself.

There were, of course, contradictions in all of this. Conservatives never quite managed to explain why administrative devolution was acceptable but the legislative variety was not, a tension highlighted by the existence of an Ulster Unionist-dominated Stormont parliament between 1921 and 1972. Playing the Scottish card could also produce hostages to fortune. In the late 1940s, Winston Churchill suggested that a future 'socialist' government would have no right to impose its will on Scotland despite commanding the confidence of the House of Commons, a 'no mandate' argument that would be brutally turned against Conservatives after 1970. And having done so much to frame 'Scotland' as a separate political and economic unit within the UK, Conservatives were inevitably held responsible for its neglect. Labour would come to recognise the same dilemma after it too weaponised nationalist rhetoric in opposition to Thatcher and Thatcherism during the 1980s.

ANGLO-SCOTTISH RELATIONS

As well as having to navigate the 'union state', Scottish Conservatives have had to manage relationships within their own party, something which often mirrored broader constitutional considerations. The Scottish Unionist Party was born as the British-Irish Union appeared close to fracture in 1912 and was reorganised when the Anglo-Scottish Union came under strain in the mid-1960s. Colin Kidd has described the inflections of the party between 1912 and 1965 as 'neither English nor metropolitan, but rather those of an embattled presbyterian provincialism somewhat distrustful of the motives of the English core of the United Kingdom'.[3]

Doubtless conscious of this, London-based party managers essentially left the Scottish party to its own devices, that is until they felt compelled to intervene in the mid-1960s. As Stevens has noted, organisation 'can help win elections and it can help lose them. But it cannot in itself win elections. Organization can help sell a message; but only if someone wants to buy it.'[4] Indeed, the formation of the National Union of Conservative Associations for Scotland in 1882 did not lead to immediate electoral success, and nor did the 1965 reforms. Rather, reorganisation was usually a response to electoral weakness rather than its cause. And all too often Scottish Conservatives hid behind further reorganisation (see 1977, 1987, 1992, 1997 and 2010) rather than tackle deeper – and therefore less soluble – aspects of their political unpopularity.

It was often clear that Scottish Unionists were electorally successful in spite, rather than because, of organisation. Even in the 1920s and 1950s, periods during which the party was at its most popular, the success of Unionist candidates often took local associations by surprise. It could win seats where the party was poorly organised, and lose them where it had built a highly efficient party machine. This also lulled the party into a false sense of security. Relative Scottish Unionist success at the general election of 1945, for example, meant the party ducked a process of post-war modernisation embarked upon by the Conservatives in England. The 1955 election result consolidated a complacent belief that all was well, yet even as Scottish Unionists (and their allies) celebrated capturing a majority of Scottish seats and votes, it was clear to many that the party was not in good shape. Intra-association squabbling was rife, while the Glasgow- and Edinburgh-based Western and Eastern Divisional Councils could often view each other with the same distrustful provincialism that characterised Edinburgh–London relations.

By 1960, this tendency to blame malfunctioning organisation rather than message and messenger for poor election results proved the last straw for party leaders in London. Lord Hailsham thought the state of the Scottish Unionists 'horrible'; Harold Macmillan believed it 'old-fashioned and semi-feudal'. To Lord Aldington it looked 'ghastly' from London and got worse the closer one got to Edinburgh and Glasgow. Even the influential Scottish Unionist Members Committee, a sort of party within a party at Westminster, was inclined to view the Scottish Unionist Association as 'feudalistic', even using the press to brief against it.

Yet London's belief that closer integration between the English and Scottish parties would cure all northern ills also proved misguided. By the 1970s, Douglas Hurd was lamenting a party which concealed its political weakness behind 'portentous titles and procedures', while in turn Scottish party officials grumbled about English Tories appearing 'ignorant, insensitive and colonial in their attitude to Scotland'. Even the impeccably Anglo-Scottish George Younger complained of a 'very anti-Scottish attitude' from his party and its leader (Mrs Thatcher) when it came to agreeing Scotland-specific policy such as the dispersal of civil service jobs from Whitehall.

Matters did not improve in the 1980s. A Thatcher aide despatched to Edinburgh called London's relations with the Scottish party 'a mess', while in the 1990s John Major's aides were shocked by the degree to which politics was kept away from the Bute House breakfast table. Two decades later, Cameroons like George Bridges still viewed the Scottish organisation as 'completely ramshackle'. Finances were also a constant worry, with Scottish Conservatives reliant on individual donors or Central Office in London to sustain themselves through good electoral times as well as bad. Throwing money at the party only worked, however, when its stance resonated beyond its core vote and when that stance was articulated by a 'leader of stature' (and unequivocal Scottishness), the best example of which was Ruth Davidson in 2016–17.

Successful Scottish Conservatism and Unionism also required empathy from the party's UK leadership. Indeed, the most successful British Conservatives cast themselves as Anglo-Scottish: Stanley Baldwin, Winston Churchill and Harold Macmillan. Some even *were* Scottish: Arthur Balfour, Andrew Bonar Law and Sir Alec Douglas-Home. Others worked hard to get the tone right: Edward Heath understood the importance of nationalism in Scotland even if his response did not land as expected, while Sir John Major and David Cameron tried to articulate a less banal Unionism (although the latter quickly lost interest after 2014). Mrs Thatcher, meanwhile, found it almost impossible to wrap herself in tartan, instead attempting to reframe the 'devolution of power' around individuals rather than institutions.

At the same time, the impact of Thatcher (and Thatcherism) on the fortunes of the Scottish Conservative Party have often been overstated. The party in Scotland enjoyed a modest revival under her leadership in 1979 and held up remarkably well in 1983, given high unemployment and industrial decline. Similarly, against all the odds, John Major managed to avert doomsday in 1992 and even improved the party's showing despite the apparently calamitous 'Poll Tax'. Arguably more culpable was Heath in the 1970s, yet his support for legislative devolution has likely masked this in subsequent assessments.

It must also be noted that as a sub-state party operating within a multi-national union, the Scottish Conservative Party has never been the complete master of its own fate. Indeed, at crucial points in its history it found itself trapped between a rock and a hard place, vociferous opposition on the periphery and a leader or Prime Minister having adopted an unpopular stance at the centre. Sir Robert Peel's approach to the Church patronage question in the 1840s proved unhelpful for Scottish Conservatives, as did Harold Macmillan's economic boosterism in the late 1950s and Mrs Thatcher's perceived antipathy to the Scottish dimension in the second half of the 1980s.

By the mid-1960s, meanwhile, the party's 'grouse moor' image had become a liability, epitomised by Macmillan and Douglas-Home and reinforced by the media. Its MPs were indeed disproportionately drawn from English public schools, Oxbridge and titled families. Even in the 1980s scions of the Scones, Lothians and Hamiltons could be found on the green and red benches at Westminster, while in the 'new politics' apparently embodied by the Scottish Parliament there remained baronets or the sons of baronets: Sir Alex Fergusson, Sir Jamie McGrigor, Sir Edward Mountain and Donald Cameron (of Lochiel). No matter how hard the party tried to inject new and less aristocratic blood – for example, at the 2016 Holyrood election – certain representatives of the party tended to justify certain caricatures of Scottish Toryism.

Relations between the Scottish and English Conservative parties improved with electoral success – Ruth Davidson, for example, was lauded by the London political-media elite – while this did not mean all was harmonious within Scotland itself. After 1999 there was perennial tension between Scottish Central Office and the MSP group, each regarding the other as hopeless and out of touch. It did not help that until 2011–12 leadership was blurred between a party-elected leader in the Scottish Parliament and a Scottish chairman appointed, as in the 1950s, by the UK leader.

Beyond endless internal reorganisations, the Scottish party tried everything from new logos to clever marketing campaigns to arrest its decline between 1959 and 2011. A persistent suggestion in the 1990s and 2000s was the restoration of its pre-1965 nomenclature, although the UK leadership cheerfully admitted that no matter how hard they tried the party would still be viewed by many voters as the 'effing Tories'. Taking a hard-headed view of this seemingly irreversible toxicity was Murdo Fraser, who in his bid for the leadership in 2011 finally embraced the nuclear option and proposed scrapping the party and starting afresh. Although Ruth Davidson rejected such radicalism, she later embraced much of the Fraser agenda and echoed the approach spearheaded by the Welsh Conservatives after 2007.

IDEOLOGY

When it came to Conservative ideology, there was another persistent theme connecting the 19th and 20th centuries. Just as 'Toryism' came to be 'identified with certain historical contentions incompatible with the Scottish creed of independence' after 1832,[5] the same was true of Thatcherism in the 1980s, even though that 'ism' had a solid provenance in Enlightenment economics and the lecture theatres of St Andrews University.

Like all political parties, the Scottish Conservative Party embraced a range of views, although for most of the party's existence charges of right-wing dogmatism were misplaced. More often than not, the Scottish Conservative and Unionist parties were more progressive than their English counterparts. In the 1890s this was due to an infusion of 'Liberal' Unionism from the West of Scotland, something that had such an impact on the Scottish party that even by the early 1960s it remained a coalition embracing various manifestations of Liberalism dating back to the coalitions and 'national' governments of the 1920s and 1930s. Not only were Scottish Unionist MPs less enthusiastic attendees at the famous Carlton Club meeting in October 1922 but the subsequent Conservative government even included a Liberal Secretary for Scotland. Four decades later, Scottish Secretary John Maclay would remind officials that he was not a 'Tory' despite serving in a Conservative Cabinet.

What united this 'coalition' was opposition to 'socialism' (otherwise known as the Labour Party in Scotland, itself usually quite moderate). Until the 1970s, the Scottish Conservative Party was ostentatiously centrist, preaching moderation at every turn in order to attract the broadest possible range of small 'c' conservative and (often ex) Liberal voters. Although not exactly non-ideological, post-war 'Butskellism' came easily to the majority of Scottish Unionists beyond a few isolated 'die-hards'. In opposition and in office they preached a 'Middle Way' between untrammelled capitalism and full state control, emblematic of which was a long-standing policy of promoting publicly owned (as well as private) housing. Successive Unionist Scottish Secretaries did much between the 1930s and 1960s, meanwhile, to encourage the idea that 'Scotland' was a separate unit of economic management, to some degree a fiction but a construct which supported the contention that Scottish problems required distinctly Scottish solutions or, as contemporary campaigning had it, 'Scottish Control of Scottish Affairs'. Acutely conscious that Scotland's economy was in trouble, particularly between the wars and after the Second, Conservatives wholeheartedly embraced industrial intervention, New Towns and the 'dispersal' of civil servants beyond London. Although it often proved a hard sell politically, Scottish Conservatism was usually vindicated in its efforts to diversify and modernise the Scottish economy. As Thatcher herself concluded, an audit of her premiership in a Scottish context was economically positive but politically negative.

Pragmatism, that most Conservative of values, was key to Scottish success in the first half of the 20th century, while a growing inability to adapt the party to shifting socio-economic circumstances in the 1960s caused it harm, although not for want of trying. Of the various declinist theories that have been applied to Scottish Conservatism, the most convincing is ideological, a fragmenting of the party's 'individualist' appeal between the Conservatives, Liberals and Scottish National Party from the late 1960s. Even before that ideological moment, it remains underappreciated that the SNP, founded in 1934, emerged in part from a split in Scottish Unionism. This included a reactionary, sectarian element which opponents of both parties attempted to depict as concerted and mainstream.

But as David Seawright's work has made clear, orthodox explanations of Scottish Conservative decline between 1959 and 2015 – class differences north and south of the border and the Protestant 'Orange' vote – are flawed or at least considerably overstated. More important was the interplay between the party's Scottish credentials (which did not necessarily entail support for legislative devolution) and shifts in Scotland's left–right spectrum. The great irony was that despite many Scottish voters having limited aversion to home ownership, consumerism and greater choice, the messenger left them cold. After 1990, this hardened into what Gerry Hassan called the 'first cardinal rule' of Scottish politics, 'that is namely to vilify, degrade and denounce Thatcher and Thatcherism with every word in your vocabulary, while being influenced, shaped and following in her footsteps'. Much as opponents have tried, it is difficult to argue that Scotland rejected the central ideological tenets of Thatcherism. If it had, then why did most of them remain undisturbed more than three decades after the Iron Lady's resignation?

That Scottish Conservatism's dislocation from mainstream Scottish society – most dramatically in 1997 – was fuelled by mythology highlights the importance of storytelling when it comes to selling political ideas. With its public housing, militant trade unions and ailing heavy industries, parts of Scotland in the 1980s resembled northern England and southern Wales, only more so. Nevertheless, the 'Scottish political system' with all its nuances and contradictions made it more resistant to the politics if not the policies of Thatcherism. This Mrs Thatcher (and indeed Sir Robert Peel before her) found baffling. How could it be that the freedom of markets, once the cornerstone of Scottish economic thinking, had come to be seen as an anti-Scottish aberration?

One ideological tenet that *was* rejected by Scots (and by the English too) was the Poll Tax. This may have been a 'Scottish' idea but it was embraced by the party in Scotland for practical and (misplaced) strategic reasons as well as ideological. And far from being 'tested' on Scotland like the guinea pig of political lore, it was actually demand-led, an ostentatious attempt to put the Scottish Conservative Party in the driving seat of its own policy agenda ahead of the 1987 general election. Another feature of Thatcherism, the 'Right to Buy', also owed something to the idea of a 'property-owning democracy' promoted by the Scottish Unionist MP Noel Skelton in the mid-1920s.

A striking factionalism took hold of Scottish Conservatism during the mid- to late 1980s, an exaggerated form of long-standing but generally benign tensions between right and centre-right which were most likely exacerbated by Mrs Thatcher's neo-liberal agenda. In response to the 'New Right' led by Michael Forsyth, the Scottish Tory Reform Group emerged with its own agenda, although genuine policy differences often got lost in personality politics. This clash at least produced pamphlets and policies. By the devolved era, the Scottish party had come to lack original thinkers; there was no one to rival David Melding, the Welsh party's philosopher-king. Although this was true of other political parties and formed part of a general weakening of policymaking in Scotland after 1999, Scottish Conservatives did little to arrest it.

There was one notable contribution, the idea of greater 'fiscal autonomy' for the Scottish Parliament, something that also found favour among Scottish Nationalists and Liberal Democrats and was introduced via the *Scotland Acts* of 2012 and 2016. In a further irony, these new powers were used by devolved Scottish Governments to increase rather than cut taxes, just as Michael Forsyth had warned they would in the 1990s. Otherwise the Scottish Conservative Party of the devolved era played it safe, embracing the vaguely 'social democratic' consensus as readily as it had Butskellism in the 1950s. While Scottish Unionists had confronted nationalism from a position of strength after the Second World War (even sponsoring a nationalist candidate at the 1948 Paisley by-election), the same was not true of the 2007–11 Scottish Parliament, when Scottish Conservative MSPs supported SNP Budgets in return for policy concessions. It did the party little good at election time, but demonstrated that its pragmatism had not completely disappeared.

WHITHER SCOTTISH CONSERVATISM?

During the wilderness years of 1997 to 2016, Scottish political columnists regularly resorted to asking, rhetorically, whither Scottish Conservatism? Following the party's revival between 2016 and 2021, this question came to be asked less often, even though the party remained some distance from forming a devolved Scottish Government, however secure its position as the principal 'unionist' opposition at Holyrood. Indeed, the 2021 Scottish Parliament election demonstrated that even in the absence of Ruth Davidson (and in the midst of turbulent events at Westminster), the party was still able to muster a formidable coalition of anti-independence voters.

Just as opposition to Irish Home Rule had enabled the Scottish Conservatives to attract new voters in the late 19th century, and opposition to (or rather fear of) 'socialism' had again in the 1920s, opposition to a second Scottish independence referendum won the party often unlikely new supporters after 2016, finally negating at least some of the toxicity previously associated with Scottish Conservatism. This pattern highlighted both the party's inherent weakness *and* strength: in and of itself Toryism, however moderate, was rarely sufficient to attract mainstream support (its weakness), but when the Scottish Conservative and Unionist Party proved itself nimble enough to latch on to an appeal, usually national, *beyond* ideology, it performed relatively well (its strength).

As has been demonstrated, this nimbleness proved central to the revival of the Scottish Conservative Party after the independence referendum of 2014. Having already acquired an authentically 'Scottish' leader who defied stereotypes (Ruth Davidson), the party finally adopted a constitutional narrative (greater fiscal autonomy) which sat easily with both party members and prospective voters. Both of these were necessary yet insufficient. Only two years *after* the referendum were the Scottish Conservatives reconstituted as the most energetic and, crucially, credible 'unionist' party. At that point, particularly with the SNP still dominant, the political stars aligned.

Yet there remained weaknesses. Conservative ideology was not resuscitated or refashioned, and relations between the Scottish and English parties deteriorated once the 'devo-pragmatism' of David Cameron and Theresa May gave way to the 'muscular unionism' of Boris Johnson and Liz Truss. This illustrated that no degree of organisational and policymaking autonomy could fully separate Scottish Conservatives from a UK party to which they were irredeemably associated through branding and (ultimate) leadership. A *unionist* party leader in Scotland could only put so much distance between them and someone who either is, or aspires to become, a Conservative Prime Minister of the United Kingdom.

That said, the Scottish Conservatives performance at the 2021 Holyrood election matched that of 2016 in spite of Brexit and all the considerable internal party ructions which followed that divisive 'constitutional moment'. It made little difference to unionist (if not Conservative) voters that Douglas Ross, the Scottish party leader, had felt compelled to adopt a range of policy and personnel stances which reflected the shifting sands of Westminster politics. If anything, the 2021 result confirmed that an independence referendum was mutually beneficial for both the SNP and the Scottish Conservatives. But with the immediate prospect of a second plebiscite removed by the Supreme Court judgement of November 2022, would that dynamic remain? Looking further into the future, what would happen if the long-standing and ever-changing 'Scottish Question' was once again put to voters in some form? The history of the Scottish Conservative and Unionist Party, here given what James Kellas called a 'general account' for the first time, points to a number of possibilities, either pragmatic accommodation with new constitutional realities or another prolonged period in the wilderness. Only to a degree can Scottish Conservatives make their own political luck. They will also be required nimbly to respond to what Harold Macmillan characterised as 'events, dear boy, events'.

NOTES

1. P. Lynch (1999), *The Politics of Nationhood: Sovereignty, Britishness and Conservative Politics*, London: Macmillan, 171.
2. As conceived by Joseph Overton, the Overton Window is the range of policies politically acceptable to mainstream voters at a given time.
3. C. Kidd (2008), *Union and Unionisms: Political Thought in Scotland, 1500–2000*, Cambridge: Cambridge University Press, 14.
4. C. Stevens (1990), 'Scottish Conservatives – A failure of organization?', in A. Brown and R. Parry (eds), *The Scottish Government Yearbook 1990*, Edinburgh: Edinburgh University Press, 77.
5. D. W. Urwin (1965), 'The development of Conservative Party organisation in Scotland until 1912', *Scottish Historical Review* 44(2):138, 91.

Appendix 1 – Party Leaders

PRESIDENTS

Scottish National Constitutional Association
Earl of Dalkeith (1867–82)[1]

National Union of Conservative Associations for Scotland
Sir James Campbell MP (1882–3)
9th Earl of Kintore (1884–5)
9th Marquess of Lothian (1886)
6th Lord Balfour of Burleigh (1887–8)
John Scott (1889)
Sir Charles Dalrymple, Bt, MP (1890)
Sir William Hozier, Bt (1891)
Donald Cameron of Lochiel (1892)
5th Duke of Montrose (1893)
Charles Balfour MP (1894)
Sir William Laird (1895–6)
7th Earl of Hopetoun (1897)
7th Earl of Glasgow (1898)
3rd Marquess of Ailsa (1899)
Sir Mark MacTaggart-Stewart, Bt, MP (1900–1)
6th Earl of Mansfield (1902)
James Baird Thorneycroft (1903)
Sir George Younger, Bt (1904)
John George Alexander Baird MP (1905)
Sir Herbert Eustace Maxwell, Bt (1906)

2nd Lord Newlands (1907–8)
Charles Scott Dickson (1909)
William Whitelaw (1910)
Henry Brock (1911)
Charles Scott Dickson (1912)

Scottish Unionist Association

Charles Scott Dickson (1913)
Sir Matthew Arthur, Bt (1914–19)
Sir George Baxter, Bt (1920)
Sir John MacLeod, Bt, MP (1921)
Col. Sir John Hope, Bt, MP (1922)
Sir Peter Mackie, Bt (1923)
8th Duke of Atholl (1924)
Sir William Russell (1925)
Sir Robert Gordon-Gilmour, Bt (1926)
Sir Robert Horne MP (1927)
Lady Findlay of Aberlour (1928)
Sir Henry Mechan (1929)
Sir Patrick Ford, Bt, MP (1930)
Sir John Gilmour, Bt, MP (1931)
Sir Robert Spencer Nairn (1932)
Sir David Allan Hay (1933)
Sir Harry Hope, Bt (1934)
Prof. Sir John Graham Kerr (1935)
Sir William Maxwell (1936)
Sir Alexander Taylor (1937)
Maj. Sir Samuel Strang Steel, Bt (1938)
A. J. Barber-Fleming (1939–44)
Maj. Sir Jackson Millar (1944)
Sir Charles Connell (1945)
Sir Robert S. Stewart (1946)
Lord Dunglass (1947)
Bailie Sir William Bennett (1948)
Capt. Sir John McEwen, Bt (1949)
Prof. Sir John Craik Henderson (1950)
Sir George Williamson (1951)
Mrs R. Stirling Brown (1952)
Mrs David Crichton (1953)
Sir Charles McFarlane (1954)

Brig. Sir Alick Buchanan-Smith (1955)
Sir William Sinclair (1956)
Gen. Sir Philip Christison, Bt (1957)
Sir Norman Cadzow (1958)
Sir William McNair Sadden, Bt (1959)
Sir Gilmour Menzies Anderson (1960)
A. R. Mathewson (1961)
Iain Barber-Fleming (1962)
Neil Pattullo (1963)
William H. Hunter (1964)

Scottish Conservative and Unionist Association

Sir Russell Fairgrieve (1965)
J. Vera Finlay (1966)
John A. Cameron (1967)
Ronald S. McNeill (1968)
Alan Anderson (1969)
Walter Scott (1970)
Maurice Mitchell (1971)
Councillor A. F. Mutch (1972)
Mary Pinkerton (1973)
Col. A. Forbes Hendry (1974)
Ronald B. Anderson (1975)
Councillor T. H. N. Young (1976)
Sir Russell Sanderson (1977–8)
Dr Alistair Smith (1979–80)
David Mitchell (1981–3)
Donald Maclean (1983–5)
Iain A. McCrone (1985–7)
James B. Highgate (1987–9)
Ross Harper (1989)
Michael Hirst (1989–92)
Adrian Shinwell (1992–4)
David McLetchie (1994–8)
Sir Malcolm Rifkind (1998)

CHAIRS

Scottish Unionist Association

James Stuart (1st Viscount Stuart of Findhorn) (1950–62)
Michael Noble (1962–3)
Sir John George MP (1963–5)

Scottish Conservative and Unionist Association

Sir John Gilmour, Bt, MP (1965–7)
Sir Gilmour Menzies Anderson (1967–71)
Sir William McEwan Younger, Bt (1971–4)
George Younger MP (1974–5)
Sir Russell Fairgrieve MP (1975–80)
Michael Ancram MP (1980–3)
Lord (James) Goold (1983–9)
Michael Forsyth MP (1989–90)
Lord Sanderson (1990–3)
Sir Michael Hirst (1993–7)
Raymond Robertson (1997–8)

Scottish Conservative and Unionist Party

Raymond Robertson (1998–2001)
David Mitchell (2001–4)
Peter Duncan (2004–7)
David Mundell MP (2007–8)
Andrew Fulton (2008–14)
David Mundell MP (2011–14)
Lord Keen of Elie (2014–15)
Rab Forman (2015–22)
Craig Hoy MSP (2022–)

LEADERS

Scottish Conservative and Unionist Party

David McLetchie (1999–2005)
Annabel Goldie (2005–11)
Ruth Davidson (2011–19)

Jackson Carlaw (2019–20)
Douglas Ross (2020–)

Source for personnel until 1980, J. T. Ward (1982), *The First Century: A History of Scottish Tory Organisation 1882–1982*, Edinburgh: SCUA. Also G. Warner (1988), *The Scottish Tory Party: A History*, London: Weidenfeld & Nicolson.

NOTE

1. Dalkeith, later the 6th Duke of Buccleuch, was President of the SNCA until it was absorbed into its successor body.

Appendix 2 – Election Results

WESTMINSTER ELECTION RESULTS, 1832–2019

Election year	Vote share %	Number of MPs	Seats contested	Total no. of seats
1832	21	10		53
1835	37.2	15		53
1837	46	20		53
1841	38.3	22		53
1847	18.3	19		53
1852	27.4	20		53
1857	15.2	15		53
1859	33.6	15		53
1865	14.6	12		53
1868	17.5	8		60 (2 uni seats)
1874	31.6	20		60
1880	29.9	7		60
1885	34.3	10		72
1886	46.4	12 C; 17 Lib Un		72
1892	44.4	10 C; 12 Lib Un		72
1895	47.4	19 C; 14 Lib Un		72
1900	49	21 C; 17 Lib Un		72
1906	38.2	8 C; 4 Lib Un		72
1910 (Jan)	39.6	8 C; 3 Lib Un		72
1910 (Dec)	42.6	7 C; 4 Lib Un		72
1918	30.8	32 Coalition Un		74 (3 uni seats)
1922	25.1	15 Un; 12 LN		74
1923	31.6	16		74
1924	40.7	38		74
1929	35.9	22		74

Election year	Vote share %	Number of MPs	Seats contested	Total no. of seats
1931	54.4	50 Un; 8 LN		74
1935	35	37 Un; 8 LN		74
1945	40.3	26 Un; 3 LN	68	74
1950	44.8	26 Un; 5 LN	68	71 (uni seats abolished)
1951	48.6	29 Un; 5 LN	70	71
1955	50.1	30 Un; 6 LN	71	71
1959	47.2	25 Un; 6 LN	70	71
1964	40.6	24	71	71
1966	37.6	20	71	71
1970	38	23	70	71
1974 (Feb)	32.9	21	71	71
1974 (Oct)	24.7	16	71	71
1979	31.4	22	71	71
1983	28.4	21	72	72
1987	24	10	72	72
1992	25.6	11	72	72
1997	17.5	0	72	72
2001	15.6	1	71	72
2005	15.8	1	58	59
2010	16.7	1	59	59
2015	14.9	1	59	59
2017	28.6	13	59	59
2019	25.1	6	59	59

Sources: For number of MPs between 1832 and 1979, J. T. Ward (1982), *The First Century: A History of Scottish Tory Organisation 1882–1982*, Edinburgh: SCUA, 45.

SCOTTISH PARLIAMENT ELECTION RESULTS, 1999–2021

Election year	Constituency vote	Regional vote	Number of MSPs	Total no. of seats
1999	15.6	15.4	18	129
2003	16.6	15.5	18	129
2007	16.6	13.9	17	129
2011	13.9	12.4	15	129
2016	22	22.9	31	129
2021	21.9	23.5	31	129

Sources: House of Commons Library.

Bibliography

PRIMARY SOURCES

Bonar Law Papers, London: The Parliamentary Archives
Churchill Papers, Cambridge: Churchill Archives Centre
Conservative Party Archive, Oxford: Bodleian
George Younger Papers, Edinburgh: National Library of Scotland
Gilmour Papers, Edinburgh: National Archives of Scotland
Goodwood MSS, Chichester: West Sussex Record Office
PREM files, London: The National Archives
Scottish Conservative & Unionist Association papers, Edinburgh: National Library of Scotland
Tweedsmuir Papers, Edinburgh: National Library of Scotland
Walter Elliot Papers, Edinburgh: National Library of Scotland
Walter Long Papers, London: British Library

SECONDARY SOURCES

Adamson, K. & P. Lynch (eds), *Scottish Political Parties and the 2014 Independence Referendum*, Cardiff: Welsh Academic Press.
Ascherson, N. (2002), *Stone Voices: The Search for Scotland*, London: Granta.
ASI (1984), *Omega Report: Scottish Policy*, London: Adam Smith Institute.
Atholl, Duke of (ed.) (1932), *A Scotsman's Heritage*, London: Alexander Maclehose & Co.
Atholl, K. (1958), *Working Partnership*, London: Arthur Barker.
Bale, T. (2010), *The Conservative Party: From Thatcher to Cameron*, Cambridge: Polity.

Balfour, A. J. (1913), *Nationality and Home Rule*, London: Longmans, Green & Co.

Balfour, Lord (1954), *Royal Commission on Scottish Affairs 1952–1954*, Cmnd 9212, Edinburgh: HMSO.

Ball, S. (2013), *Portrait of a Party: The Conservative Party in Britain 1918–1945*, Oxford: Oxford University Press.

Ball, S. & I. Holliday (eds) (2002), *Mass Conservatism: The Conservatives and the Public since the 1880s*, London: Frank Cass.

Bennie, L., J. Brand & J. Mitchell (1997), *How Scotland Votes: Scottish Parties and Elections*, Manchester: Manchester University Press.

Biffen, J. (1976), *A Nation in Doubt*, London: Conservative Political Centre.

Blake, R. (1966), *Disraeli*, London: Eyre & Spottiswoode.

—— (1997), *The Conservative Party from Peel to Major*, London: Heinemann.

Bochel, J., D. Denver & A. Macartney (eds) (1981), *The Referendum Experience: Scotland 1979*, Aberdeen: Aberdeen University Press.

Boothby, B. (1962), *My Yesterday, Your Tomorrow*, London: Hutchinson.

Bowd, G. (2013), *Fascist Scotland: Caledonia and the Far Right*, Edinburgh: Birlinn.

Bowie, A. MP (2021), *Strength in Union: The Case for the United Kingdom*, London: Centre for Policy Studies.

Brown, A., D. McCrone & L. Paterson (1998), *Politics and Society in Scotland* (Second Edition), London: Macmillan.

Brown, A., D. McCrone, L. Paterson & P. Surridge (1998), *The Scottish Electorate: The 1997 General Election and Beyond*, Basingstoke: Palgrave Macmillan.

Budge, I. & D. W. Urwin (1966), *Scottish Political Behaviour: A Case Study in British Homogeneity*, London: Longmans.

Burness, C. (2003), *'Strange Associations': The Irish Question and the Making of Scottish Unionism, 1886–1918*, East Linton: Tuckwell Press.

Butler, D. & D. Kavanagh (1974), *The British General Election of February 1974*, London: Macmillan.

Butler, R. (1960), *A Message to Scotland: Conserve–Unite–Construct*, Glasgow: Conservative Political Centre.

Butt, J. & J. T. Ward (eds) (1976), *Scottish Themes, Essays in Honour of Professor S. G. E. Lythe*, Edinburgh: Edinburgh University Press.

Bryant, A. (1929), *The Spirit of Conservatism*, London: Methuen.

Cameron, D. (2019), *For the Record*, London: William Collins.

Cameron, E. A. (2010), *Impaled Upon a Thistle: Scotland since 1880*, Edinburgh: Edinburgh University Press.

Campbell, J. (2000), *Margaret Thatcher Volume One: The Grocer's Daughter*, London: Jonathan Cape.

—— (2013), *Edward Heath: A Biography*, London: Pimlico.

Carman, C., R. Johns & J. Mitchell (2014), *More Scottish than British: The 2011 Scottish Parliament Election*, Basingstoke: Palgrave Macmillan.

Catterall, P. (ed.) (2011), *The Macmillan Diaries Vol. II: Prime Minister and After 1957–1966*, London: Macmillan.

Cawood, I. (2012), *The Liberal Unionist Party: A History*, London: I. B. Tauris.

Chamberlain, Sir A. (1936), *Politics from the Inside: An Epistolary Chronicle 1906–1914*, London: Cassell.

Checkland, S. & O. (1984), *Industry and Ethos: Scotland, 1832–1914*, London: Edward Arnold.

Chrimes, S. B. (ed.) (1950), *The General Election in Glasgow: February, 1950*, Glasgow: Jackson, Son & Company.

Cochrane, A. (2014), *The Cochrane Diaries – Alex Salmond: My Part in His Downfall*, London: Biteback.

Convery, A. (ed.) (2016), *Light Blue: Policy Adventures for Scottish Conservatives*, Edinburgh: Edinburgh University.

—— (2016), *The Territorial Conservative Party: Devolution and Party Change in Scotland and Wales*, Manchester: Manchester University Press.

Cook, C. (1975), *The Age of Alignment*, London: Macmillan.

Cooper, C. A. (1896), *An Editor's Retrospect: Fifty Years of Newspaper Work*, London: Macmillan.

Coote, C. (1965), *A Companion of Honour: The Story of Walter Elliot in Scotland and in Westminster*, London: Collins.

CPC (1975), *The Scottish Conservatives: A Past and a Future*, London: Conservative Political Centre.

CPS (1946), *Notes on Conservative Policy*, London: Conservative Parliamentary Secretariat.

Cowley, P. & D. Kavanagh (eds) (2018), *The British General Election of 2017*, London: Palgrave Macmillan.

CRD (1989), *The Campaign Guide 1989*, London: Conservative and Unionist Central Office.

CUCO (1949), *The Days Ahead*, London: Conservative and Unionist Central Office.

—— (1955), *United for Peace and Progress*, London: Conservative and Unionist Party.

CUP (1949), *The Right Road for Britain: The Conservative Party's Statement of Policy*, London: Conservative and Unionist Party.

—— (1951), *Britain Strong and Free*, London: Conservative and Unionist Party.

—— (1964), *The Campaign Guide, 1964: The Unique Political Reference Book*, London: Conservative and Unionist Party.

Darling, Sir W. (1952), *So It Looks To Me*, London: Odhams Press.

Davidson, R. (2018), *Yes She Can: Why Women Own the Future*, London: Hodder & Stoughton.

Denver, D., J. Mitchell, C. Pattie & H. Bochel (2000), *Scotland Decides: The Devolution Issue and the 1997 Referendum*, London: Routledge.

Devine, T. M. & R. Finlay (eds) (1996), *Scotland in the 20th Century*, Edinburgh: Edinburgh University Press.

Devine, T. M. (1999), *The Scottish Nation 1700–2000*, London: Allen Lane.

—— (ed.) (2008), *Scotland and the Union 1707–2007*, Edinburgh: Edinburgh University Press.

Dickson, A. & J. H. Treble (eds) (1992), *People and Scotland in Society Volume III 1914–1990*, Edinburgh: John Donald.

Douglas, F. (1945), *The Scottish Tories: A Political Exposure*, Glasgow: Scottish Committee of the Communist Party.

Douglas-Hamilton, J. (2009), *After You, Prime Minister*, London: Stacey International.

Douglas-Home, A. (1976), *The Way the Wind Blows: An Autobiography*, London: Collins.

Dutton, D. (2008), *Liberals in Schism: A History of the National Liberal Party*, London: I. B. Tauris.

Dyer, M. (1996), *Capable Citizens and Improvident Democrats: The Scottish Electoral System 1884–1929*, Aberdeen: Scottish Cultural Press.

—— (1996), *Men of Property and Intelligence: The Scottish Electoral System prior to 1884*, Aberdeen: Scottish Cultural Press.

ECA (1987), *Apostles Not Apologists: The Eastwood View*, Paisley: Eastwood Conservative Association.

EDC (1950), *The East of Scotland Year Book 1950*, Edinburgh: Eastern Divisional Council.

—— (1951), *The East of Scotland Year Book 1951*, Edinburgh: Eastern Divisional Council.

Elliot, W. (1927), *Toryism and the Twentieth Century*, London: Philip Allan.

Fairbairn, N. (1987), *A Life is Too Short: Autobiography: Volume One*, London: Quartet.

FCS (1984), *A Conservative Manifesto for Scotland*, Edinburgh: Federation of Conservative Students.

Ferguson, W. (1968), *Scotland: 1689 to the Present*, London: Oliver & Boyd.

Fergusson, Bt, Sir J. (1960), *The Sixteen Peers of Scotland: An Account of the Elections of the Representative Peers of Scotland 1707–1959*, Oxford: Clarendon Press.

Finlay, R. (1997), *A Partnership for Good? Scottish Politics and the Union since 1880*, Edinburgh: John Donald.

Ford, R., T. Bale, W. Jennings & P. Surridge (eds) (2021), *The British General Election of 2019*, London: Palgrave Macmillan.

Forsyth, M. & D. McLetchie (1975), *The Scottish Conservative Party: A New Model for a New Dimension*, Edinburgh: SCUA.

Forsyth, M. (1985), *The Case for a Poll Tax*, London: Conservative Political Centre.

Fox, L., M. Mayall & A. B. Cooke (1988), *Making Unionism Positive*, London: Centre for Policy Studies.

Francis, M. and I. Zweiniger-Bargielowska (eds) (1996), *The Conservatives and British Society 1880–1990*, Cardiff: University of Wales Press.

Freeman, G. (ed.) (2019), *Britain Beyond Brexit*, London: Centre for Policy Studies.

Fry, M. (1997), *Patronage and Principle: A Political History of Modern Scotland*, Aberdeen: Aberdeen University Press.

—— (2002), *The Scottish Empire*, Edinburgh: Birlinn.

—— (2004), *The Dundas Despotism*, Edinburgh: John Donald.

—— (2013), *A New Race of Men: Scotland 1815–1914*, Edinburgh: Birlinn.

Garnett, M. & P. Lynch (eds) (2003), *The Conservatives in Crisis: The Tories after 1997*, Manchester: Manchester University Press.

Geddes, A. & J. Tonge (eds) (2015), *Britain Votes 2015*, Oxford: Oxford University Press.

Gilmour, I. (1993), *Dancing With Dogma: Britain Under Thatcherism*, London: Pocket Books.

Gray, A. & A. Tomkins (2005), *How We Should Rule Ourselves*, Edinburgh: Canongate.

Green, E. H. H. (1995), *The Crisis of Conservatism: The Politics,*

Economics and Ideology of the British Conservative Party, 1880–1914, London: Routledge.

—— (2002), *Ideologies of Conservatism: Conservative Political Ideas in the Twentieth Century*, Oxford: Oxford University Press.

Gregory, J. & D. J. R. Grey (eds) (2017), *Union and Disunion in the Nineteenth Century*, London: Routledge.

Hanham, H. J. (1959), *Elections and Party Management: Politics in the Time of Disraeli and Gladstone*, Brighton: Harvester Press.

—— (1969), *Scottish Nationalism*, London: Faber & Faber.

Harper, J. R. (1988), *Devolution: A Short Background Paper for Scottish Conservatives*, Glasgow: Society of Scottish Conservative Lawyers.

Harper, R. (2016), *Beyond Reasonable Doubt: A Memoir*, Edinburgh: Black & White.

Harris, R. (2011), *The Conservatives: A History*, London: Bantam Press.

Heath, E. (1998), *The Course of My Life: My Autobiography*, London: Hodder & Stoughton.

Hetherington, S. J. (1989), *Katharine Atholl 1874–1960: Against the Tide*, Aberdeen: Aberdeen University Press.

Hogg, S. & J. Hill (1996), *Too Close to Call: Power and Politics – John Major in No. 10*, London: Warner.

Howard, A. & R. West (1965), *The Making of the Prime Minister*, London: Jonathan Cape.

Hurd, D. (2003), *Memoirs*, London: Little, Brown.

—— (2007), *Robert Peel: A Biography*, London: Weidenfeld & Nicolson.

Hutchison, I. G. C. (1986), *A Political History of Scotland, 1832–1924: Parties, Elections and Issues*, Edinburgh: John Donald.

—— (2001), *Scottish Politics in the Twentieth Century*, Basingstoke: Palgrave.

—— (2020), *Industry, Reform and Empire: Scotland, 1790–1880*, Edinburgh: Edinburgh University Press.

ICCFTS (2016), *A Dynamic Scotland*, Edinburgh: Independent Commission for Competitive and Fair Taxation in Scotland.

Jackson, A. (2011), *The Two Unions: Ireland, Scotland, and the Survival of the United Kingdom, 1707–2007*, Oxford: Oxford University Press.

Johns, R., D. Denver, J. Mitchell & C. Pattie (2010), *Voting for a Scottish Government: The Scottish Parliament Election of 2007*, Manchester: Manchester University Press.

Keating, M. (2009), *The Independence of Scotland: Self-government and the Shifting Politics of Union*, Oxford: Oxford University Press.
—— (ed.) (2020), *The Oxford Handbook of Scottish Politics*, Oxford: Oxford University Press.
Kellas, J. G. (1968), *Modern Scotland: The Nation since 1870*, London: Pall Mall Press.
—— (1980), *Modern Scotland* (Revised Edition), London: George Allen & Unwin.
Kemp, A. (1993), *The Hollow Drum: Scotland since the War*, Edinburgh: Mainstream.
Kidd, C. (2008), *Union and Unionisms: Political Thought in Scotland, 1500–2000*, Cambridge: Cambridge University Press.
Lang, I. (2002), *Blue Remembered Years: A Political Memoir*, London: Politico's.
Law, D. (2016), *Coalition: The Inside Story of the Conservative–Liberal Democrat Coalition Government*, London: Biteback.
Layton-Henry, Z. (ed.) (1980), *Conservative Party Politics*, London: Macmillan.
—— (ed.) (1982), *Conservative Politics in Western Europe*, London: Palgrave Macmillan.
Levitt, I. (1992), *The Scottish Office: Depression and Reconstruction 1919–1959*, Edinburgh: Scottish History Society.
Liddle, A. (2018), *Ruth Davidson and the Resurgence of the Scottish Tories*, London: Biteback.
Linklater, M. & R. Denniston (eds) (1992), *Anatomy of Scotland: How Scotland Works*, Edinburgh: Chambers.
Lownie, A. (2002), *John Buchan: The Presbyterian Cavalier*, London: Pimlico.
Lynch, M. (1991), *Scotland: A New History*, London: Pimlico.
Lynch, P. (1999), *The Politics of Nationhood: Sovereignty, Britishness and Conservative Politics*, London: Macmillan.
McConnell, A. (2004), *Scottish Local Government*, Edinburgh: Edinburgh University Press.
MacCormick, J. M. (1955), *A Flag in the Wind: The Story of the National Movement in Scotland*, London: Victor Gollancz.
MacCormick, N. (ed.) (1970), *The Scottish Debate: Essays on Scottish Nationalism*, Oxford: Oxford University Press.
McCrone, D. (1991), *Understanding Scotland: The Sociology of a Stateless Nation*, Edinburgh: Edinburgh University Press.
Macdonald, C. M. M. (ed.) (1998), *Unionist Scotland 1800–1997*, Edinburgh: John Donald.

Macdonell, H. (2009), *Uncharted Territory: The Story of Scottish Devolution 1999–2009*, London: Politico's.

McFarland, E. (2014), *'A Slashing Man of Action': The Life of Lieutenant-General Sir Aylmer Hunter-Weston MP*, Oxford: Peter Lang.

McKechnie, G. (2013), *George Malcolm Thomson: The Best-Hated Man – Intellectuals and the Condition of Scotland Between the Wars*, Glendaruel: Argyll.

MacKenzie, M. L. (1988), *Scottish Toryism, Identity and Consciousness*, London: Tory Reform Group.

McLean, I. & A. McMillan (2005), *State of the Union: Unionism and the Alternatives in the United Kingdom since 1707*, Oxford: Oxford University Press.

McLynn, F. (1992), *Fitzroy Maclean*, London: John Murray.

McMillan, J. (1969), *Anatomy of Scotland*, London: Leslie Frewin.

Macmillan, Lord (1952), *A Man of Law's Tale: The Reminiscences of Lord Macmillan*, London.

McQuarrie, Sir A. (2013), *A Lifetime of Memories*, Durham: Memoir Club.

McTavish, D. (ed.) (2016), *Politics in Scotland*, London: Routledge.

Major, J. (1992), *Scotland in the United Kingdom*, London: Conservative Political Centre.

—— (1999), *John Major: The Autobiography*, London: HarperCollins.

Malcolm Thomson, G. (c. 1930), *The Kingdom of Scotland Restored*, Humphrey Toulmin.

Marr, A. (1992), *The Battle for Scotland*, London: Penguin.

Midwinter, A., M. Keating & J. Mitchell (1991), *Politics and Public Policy in Scotland*, Basingstoke: Palgrave Macmillan.

Miller, W. L. (1981), *The End of British Politics? Scots and English Political Behaviour in the Seventies*, Oxford: Clarendon Press.

Mitchell, J. (1990), *Conservatives and the Union: A Study of Conservative Party Attitudes to Scotland*, Edinburgh: Edinburgh University Press.

—— (2003), *Governing Scotland: The Invention of Administrative Devolution*, Basingstoke: Palgrave Macmillan.

—— (2014), *The Scottish Question*, Oxford: Oxford University Press.

Montrose, Duke of (1952), *My Ditty Box*, London: Jonathan Cape.

Moore, C. (2013), *Margaret Thatcher: The Authorized Biography – Volume One: Not For Turning*, London: Allen Lane.

—— (2019), *Margaret Thatcher: The Authorized Biography – Volume Three: Herself Alone*, London: Allen Lane.

Morton, G. (1999), *Unionist Nationalism: Governing Urban Scotland, 1830–1860*, East Linton: Tuckwell Press.

Murdoch, A. (ed.) (2007), *The Scottish Nation: Identity and History – Essays in Honour of William Ferguson*, Edinburgh: John Donald.

Murray, C. de B. (1938), *How Scotland is Governed*, Edinburgh: Moray Press.

Peel, M. (2013), *The Patriotic Duke: The Life of the 14th Duke of Hamilton*, London: Thistle.

Petrie, M. (2018), *Popular Politics and Political Culture: Urban Scotland, 1918–1939*, Edinburgh: Edinburgh University Press.

—— (2022), *Politics and the People: Scotland, 1945–1979*, Edinburgh: Edinburgh University Press.

Phillips, J. (2008), *The Industrial Politics of Devolution: Scotland in the 1960s and 1970s*, Manchester: Manchester University Press.

Pike, J. (2015), *Project Fear: How an Unlikely Alliance Left a Kingdom United but a Country Divided*, London: Biteback.

Porteous, J. A. A. (1935), *The New Unionism*, London: George Allen & Unwin.

Pym, F. & L. Brittan (1978), *The Conservative Party and Devolution: Four Viable Options*, Edinburgh: SCUA.

Rait, Sir R. (1914), *History of Scotland*, London: Thornton Butterworth.

Ramsden, J. (1978), *The Age of Balfour and Baldwin 1902–1940*, London: Longman.

—— (1995), *A History of the Conservative Party: The Age of Churchill and Eden, 1940–1957*, London: Longman.

—— (1996), *A History of the Conservative Party: The Winds of Change: Macmillan to Heath, 1957–1975*, London: Longman.

—— (1998), *An Appetite for Power: The History of the Conservative Party*, London: HarperCollins.

Rhodes James, R. (ed.) (1974), *Winston S. Churchill: His Complete Speeches, 1897–1963: Volume 8, 1950–63*, New York: Chelsea House.

—— (1991), *Bob Boothby: A Portrait*, London: Hodder & Stoughton.

Rifkind, M. (1976), 'Scottish Conservative Party Devolution Committee Proposals', Rowntree Devolution Conference.

—— (1986), *Leading Scotland*, Edinburgh: Scottish Conservative Party.

—— (1998), *Scotland's Future: The Report of the Scottish Conservative Policy Commission*, Edinburgh: Scottish Conservative and Unionist Party.

—— (2016), *Power and Pragmatism: The Memoirs of Malcolm Rifkind*, London: Biteback.

Ritchie, M. (2000), *Scotland Reclaimed: The Inside Story of Scotland's First Democratic Parliamentary Election*, Edinburgh: Saltire Society.

Ross, T. & T. McTague (2017), *Betting the House: The Inside Story of the 2017 Election*, London: Biteback.

Roy, K. (1989), *Conversations in a Small Country: Scottish Conversations*, Ayr: Carrick.

Sanderson, Lord (2010), *Building for Scotland: Strengthening the Scottish Conservatives*, Edinburgh: Scottish Conservative and Unionist Party.

Saunders, R. (2018), *Yes to Europe! The 1975 Referendum and Seventies Britain*, Cambridge: Cambridge University Press.

SCCO (1970), *Tomorrow Scotland: Better with the Conservatives*, Edinburgh: Scottish Conservative Central Office.

—— (1971), *Scotland and Europe: Seven Viewpoints*, Edinburgh: Scottish Conservative Central Office.

Scottish Office (1993), *Scotland in the Union: A Partnership for Good*, Cmnd 2225, Edinburgh: HMSO.

SCP (1978), *Onward to Victory: A Statement of the Conservative Approach for Scotland*, Edinburgh: Scottish Conservative Party.

SCUA (1966), *The Year Book for Scotland 1966*, Edinburgh: Scottish Conservative and Unionist Association.

—— (1974), *Freedom for All the People – A Charter for Scotland*, Edinburgh: Scottish Conservative and Unionist Association.

—— (1983), *Conference '83 Perth Thursday 12th–Saturday 14th May, 1983*, Edinburgh: Scottish Conservative and Unionist Association.

—— (1992), *Shaping Up For The Future: Interim Recommendations of the Review Committee*, Edinburgh: Scottish Conservative and Unionist Association.

—— (1998), Strathclyde Commission, *Made in Scotland – The Final Report*, Edinburgh: Scottish Conservative and Unionist Association.

SCUCO (1967), *The Year Book for Scotland*, Edinburgh: Scottish Conservative and Unionist Central Office.

SCUP (1999), *The Hampden Declaration*, Edinburgh: Scottish Conservative and Unionist Party.

—— (2014), *Commission on the Future Governance of Scotland*, Edinburgh: Scottish Conservative and Unionist Party.

—— (2021), *Rebuild Scotland: The Scottish Conservative and Unionist Party Manifesto 2021*, Edinburgh: Scottish Conservative and Unionist Party.

Seawright, D. (1999), *An Important Matter of Principle: The Decline of the Scottish Conservative and Unionist Party*, Aldershot: Ashgate.

—— (2010), *The British Conservative Party and One Nation Politics*, London: Continuum.

Seldon, A. (1981), *Churchill's Indian Summer: The Conservative Government, 1951–55*, London: Hodder & Stoughton.

Seldon, A. & S. Ball (eds) (1994), *Conservative Century: The Conservative Party since 1900*, Oxford: Oxford University Press.

Seldon, A. & P. Snowdon (2015), *Cameron at 10: The Inside Story 2010–2015*, London: William Collins.

Shipman, T. (2017), *Fall Out: A Year of Political Mayhem*, London: William Collins.

Smith, A. (2011), *Devolution and the Scottish Conservatives*, Manchester: Manchester University Press.

Snowdon, P. (2010), *Back from the Brink*, London: Harper Press.

Somerville, P. (2013), *Through the Maelstrom: A History of the Scottish National Party, 1945–1967*, Stirling: Scots Independent.

State Visit to Scotland: Her Majesty the Queen and His Royal Highness The Duke of Edinburgh, June 1953, Edinburgh: Pillans & Wilson.

Stewart, A. (1996), *The Long March of the Market Men*, Glendaruel: Argyll.

Stewart, D. (2009), *The Path to Devolution and Change: A Political History of Scotland Under Margaret Thatcher*, London: I. B. Tauris.

Stuart, J. (1967), *Within the Fringe: An Autobiography*, London: Bodley Head.

SUA (1914), *Campaign Guide* (Thirteenth Edition), Edinburgh: Scottish Unionist Association.

—— (1949), *Scottish Control of Scottish Affairs: Unionist Policy*, Edinburgh: Scottish Unionist Association.

—— (1954), *Scotland Under the Unionist Government*, Edinburgh: Scottish Unionist Association.

—— (1955), *The Year Book for Scotland 1955*, Edinburgh and Glasgow: Scottish Unionist Association.

—— (1957), *The Year Book for Scotland 1957*, Edinburgh and Glasgow: Scottish Unionist Association.

—— (1958), *The Year Book for Scotland 1958*, Edinburgh and Glasgow: Scottish Unionist Association.

—— (1964), *The Year Book for Scotland 1964*, Edinburgh and Glasgow: Scottish Unionist Association.

Sunter, R. M. (1986), *Patronage and Politics in Scotland, 1707–1832*, Edinburgh: John Donald.

Sutherland, C. (2016), *The Decline of the Scottish Conservative Party*, Kibworth: Book Guild Publishing.
SUWO (1932), *Scottish Nationalism*, Edinburgh: Scottish Unionist Whips Office.
Tanner, D. et al. (eds) (2006), *Debating Nationhood and Governance in Britain, 1885–1945*, Manchester: Manchester University Press.
Taylor, B. (2002), *Scotland's Parliament: Triumph and Disaster*, Edinburgh: Edinburgh University Press.
Taylor, E. M. (2008), *Teddy Boy Blue*, Glasgow: Kennedy & Boyd.
Taylor, T. (1968), *Hearts of Stone*, London: Johnson.
Thatcher, M. (1993), *The Downing Street Years*, London: HarperCollins.
—— (1995), *The Path to Power*, London: HarperCollins.
Thistle Group (1967), *T. G. P. Number 1*, Edinburgh.
—— (1968), *T. G. P. Number 2*, Edinburgh.
Thornton-Kemsley, C. (1974), *Through Winds and Tides*, London: Standard Press.
Thorpe, D. R. (1996), *Alec Douglas-Home*, London: Sinclair-Stevenson.
Tonge, J., C. Leston-Bandeira & S. Wilks-Heeg (eds) (2018), *Britain Votes 2017*, Oxford: Oxford University Press.
Tonge, J., S. Wilks-Heeg & L. Thompson (eds) (2020), *Britain Votes: The 2019 General Election*, Oxford: Oxford University Press.
Torrance, D. (2006), *The Scottish Secretaries*, Edinburgh: Birlinn.
—— (2008), *George Younger: A Life Well Lived*, Edinburgh: Birlinn.
—— (2009), *'We in Scotland': Thatcherism in a Cold Climate*, Edinburgh: Birlinn.
—— (2011), *Noel Skelton and the Property-Owning Democracy*, London: Biteback.
—— (ed.) (2012), *Whatever Happened to Tory Scotland?*, Edinburgh: Edinburgh University Press.
—— (2019), *Lord Clyde: The Orkney Judge*, Edinburgh: Birlinn.
—— (ed.) (2020), *Ruth Davidson's Conservatives: The Scottish Tory Party, 2011–19*, Edinburgh: Edinburgh University Press.
—— (2020), *'Standing Up for Scotland': Nationalist Unionism and Scottish Party Politics, 1884–2014*, Edinburgh: Edinburgh University Press.
—— (2022), *A History of the Scottish Liberals and Liberal Democrats*, Edinburgh: Edinburgh University Press.
Tosh, M. (1992), *Keep Right On. The Story of the Conservative Party in Ayr Burghs and Ayr Constituencies*, Ayr: Ayr Constituency Conservative Association.

Vincent, J. (ed.) (1986), *The Crawford Papers: The Journal of David Lindsay, 27th Earl of Crawford and 10th Earl of Balcarres, 1871–1940*, Manchester: Manchester University Press.

Wales, J. (2021), *Scottish Unionist Ideology 1886–1965: Political Thought, Ecclesiology and Historiography*, Baden-Baden: Nomos.

Ward, J. T. (1982), *The First Century: A History of Scottish Tory Organisation 1882–1982*, Edinburgh: SCUA.

Ward, P. (2005), *Unionism in the United Kingdom, 1918–1974*, Basingstoke: Palgrave Macmillan.

Warner, G. (1988), *The Scottish Tory Party: A History*, London: Weidenfeld & Nicolson.

Weir, Viscount, D. MacKay & A. Stewart (1990), *Scottish Assembly: We're Better Off Without It*, Edinburgh: Scottish Conservative Political Centre.

Williams, C. & A. Edwards (eds) (2015), *The Art of the Possible: Politics and Governance in British History, 1885–1997: Essays in Memory of Duncan Tanner*, Manchester: Manchester University Press.

Young, H. (1991), *One of Us: A Biography of Margaret Thatcher*, London: Macmillan.

Young, J. H. (1993), *A History of Cathcart Conservative and Unionist Association 1918 to 1993*, Glasgow: Cathcart Conservatives.

JOURNAL ARTICLES

Ball, S. (1990), 'The politics of appeasement: The fall of the Duchess of Atholl and the Kinross and West Perth by-election, December 1938', *Scottish Historical Review* 69, 49–83.

Convery, A. (2014), 'Devolution and the limits of Tory statecraft: The Conservative Party in coalition and Scotland and Wales', *Parliamentary Affairs* 67:1, 25–44.

—— (2014), 'The 2011 Scottish Conservative Party leadership election: Dilemmas for statewide parties in regional contexts', *Parliamentary Affairs* 67:2, 306–27.

Crapster, B. L. (1957), 'Scotland and the Conservative Party in 1876', *Journal of Modern History* 29:4, 355–60.

Denver, D. & H. Bochel (1995), 'Catastrophe for the Conservatives: The council elections of 1995', *Scottish Affairs* 13, 27–41.

—— (2007), 'A quiet revolution: STV and the Scottish council elections of 2007', *Scottish Affairs* 61, 1–17.

Dickson, A. D. R. (1988), 'The peculiarities of the Scottish: National culture and political action', *Political Quarterly* 59:3, 358–68.

Dixon, K. (2010), 'The Free Economy and the White State: Conservative student radicalism in St Andrews in the Sixties and Early Seventies', *Scottish Affairs* 71, 1–15.

Dyer, M. (2001), 'The evolution of the Centre-Right and the state of Scottish Conservatism', *Political Studies* 49:1, 30–50.

—— (2003), '"A Nationalist in the Churchillian Sense": John MacCormick, the Paisley By-election of 18 February 1948, Home Rule and the crisis in Scottish Liberalism', *Parliamentary History* 22:3, 285–307.

Gash, N. (1948), 'F. R. Bonham: Conservative "political Secretary", 1832–47', *English Historical Review* 63:249, 502–22.

Hanham, H. J. (1965), 'The creation of the Scottish Office 1881–87', *Juridical Review* 10, 205–44.

Hutchison, G. D. (2019), '"Party Principles" in Scottish political culture: Roxburghshire, 1832–1847', *Scottish Historical Review* XCVIII:248, 390–409.

—— (2020) '"A distant and Whiggish country": The Conservative Party and Scottish elections, 1832–1847', *Historical Research* 93:260, 333–52.

Jones, P. (1999), 'The 1999 Scottish Parliament elections: From anti-Tory to anti-Nationalist politics', *Scottish Affairs* 28, 1–9.

Keating, M. (2010), 'The strange death of Unionist Scotland', *Government and Opposition* 45:3, 365–85.

Kendrick, S. & D. McCrone (1989), 'Political studies in a cold climate: The Conservative decline in Scotland', *Political Studies* 37:4, 589–603.

McConnell, A. & R. Pyper (1994), 'A committee again: The first year of the revived Select Committee on Scottish Affairs', *Scottish Affairs* 7, 15–31.

McCrone, D., L. Paterson & A. Brown (1993), 'Reforming local government in Scotland', *Local Government Studies* 19:1, 9–15.

Mcintyre, S., J. Mitchell & G. Roy (2022), 'Careful what you wish for? Risk and reward with Scottish tax devolution', *Political Quarterly* 93:3.

Macwhirter, I. (1992), 'The disaster that never was: The failure of Scottish opposition after the 1992 general election', *Scottish Affairs* 1, 3–8.

—— (1995), 'Doomsday two: The return of Forsyth', *Scottish Affairs* 13, 15–26.

Millar, G. F. (2001), 'The Conservative split in the Scottish counties, 1846–1857', *Scottish Historical Review* 80(2), 221–50.

Miller, W., J. Brand & G. Jordan (1981), 'Government without a mandate: The Conservative Party in Scotland', *Political Quarterly* 52:2, 203–13.

Pentland, G. (2015), 'Edward Heath, the Declaration of Perth and the Scottish Conservative and Unionist Party, 1966–70', *Twentieth Century British History* 26:2, 249–73.

Petrie, M. (2018), 'Anti-Socialism, Liberalism and Individualism: Rethinking the realignment of Scottish politics, 1945–1970', *Transactions of the Royal Historical Society* 28, 197–217.

Saleh, T. (2017), 'The decline of the Scottish Conservatives in North-East Scotland, 1965–79: A regional perspective', *Parliamentary History* 36:2, 218–42.

Sandford, M. (2023), '"Muscular unionism": The British political tradition strikes back?', *Political Studies* 71:2.

Seawright, D. (1996), 'The Scottish Unionist Party: What's in a name?', *Scottish Affairs* 14, 90–102.

—— (1998), 'Scottish Unionism: An East–West divide?', *Scottish Affairs* 23, 54–72.

Seawright, D. & J. Curtice (1995), 'The decline of the Scottish Conservative and Unionist Party 1950–92: Religion, ideology or economics?', *Contemporary British History* 9:2, 319–42.

Smyth, J. J. (2003), 'Resisting Labour: Unionists, Liberals, and Moderates in Glasgow between the wars', *Historical Journal* 46:2, 375–401.

Stevens, C. (1990), 'Scottish Conservatives – A failure of organization?', in A. Brown and R. Parry (eds), *The Scottish Government Yearbook 1990*, Edinburgh: Edinburgh University Press, 76–89.

Tyrell, A. (2010), 'The Earl of Eglinton, Scottish Conservatism, and the National Association for the Vindication of Scottish Rights', *The Historical Journal* 53:1, 87–107.

Urwin, D. W. (1965), 'The development of Conservative Party organisation in Scotland until 1912', *Scottish Historical Review* 44(2):138, 89–111.

—— (1966), 'Scottish Conservatism: A party organization in transition', *Political Studies* 14:2, 145–62.

Ward-Smith, G. (2001), 'Baldwin and Scotland: More than Englishness', *Contemporary British History* 15, 61–82.

Ward, J. T. (1970), 'Tory-socialist: A preliminary note on Michael Maltman Barry, 1842–1909', *Scottish Labour History Society Journal* 2, 25–37.

—— (1986), 'The origins of Scottish Toryism', *Contemporary Review* 249:1446, 35–40.

UNPUBLISHED PHD THESES

Arnott, M. (1993), 'Thatcherism in Scotland: An Exploration of Education Policy in the Secondary Sector', University of Strathclyde.

Burness, C. (1983), 'Conservatism and Liberal Unionism in Glasgow, 1874–1912', University of Dundee.

Hutchison, G. D. (2017), 'The Origins of the Scottish Conservative Party, 1832–1868', University of Edinburgh.

Keating, M. (1975), 'The Role of the Scottish MP in the Scottish Political System, in the UK Political System and in the Relationship Between the Two', Glasgow College of Technology.

INTERVIEWS

Derek Brownlee, 1 December 2011
Jackson Carlaw MSP, 3 April 2018
Lord Forsyth, 22 April 2008
Murdo Fraser MSP, 20 May 2008
Michael Gove MP, 28 July 2008
David McLetchie MSP, 6 October 2008
Allan Stewart, 2 September 2008
Rae Stewart, 6 August 2008
Lord Turnbull, 3 June 2008

Index

EU representative:
Easy Access System Europe
Mustamäe tee 50, 10621 Tallinn, Estonia
Gpsr.requests@easproject.com

www.ingramcontent.com/pod-product-compliance
Lightning Source LLC
Chambersburg PA
CBHW071733270326
41928CB00013B/2659

* 9 7 8 1 3 9 9 5 0 6 4 3 4 *